International Political Theory

Series Editor

Gary Browning, Oxford Brookes University, Oxford, UK

The Palgrave International Political Theory Series provides students and scholars with cutting-edge scholarship that explores the ways in which we theorise the international. Political theory has by tradition implicitly accepted the bounds of the state, and this series of intellectually rigorous and innovative monographs and edited volumes takes the discipline forward, reflecting both the burgeoning of IR as a discipline and the concurrent internationalisation of traditional political theory issues and concepts. Offering a wide-ranging examination of how International Politics is to be interpreted, the titles in the series thus bridge the IR-political theory divide. The aim of the series is to explore international issues in analytic, historical and radical ways that complement and extend common forms of conceiving international relations such as realism, liberalism and constructivism. This series is indexed by Scopus.

Lars Erik L. Gjerde

Nordic Leviathans

A Weberian-Foucauldian Study of the Politics of COVID-19 in Norway and Sweden

palgrave
macmillan

Lars Erik L. Gjerde
Department of Social Sciences
University of Tromsø
Tromsø, Norway

ISSN 2662-6039 ISSN 2662-6047 (electronic)
International Political Theory
ISBN 978-3-032-00688-2 ISBN 978-3-032-00689-9 (eBook)
https://doi.org/10.1007/978-3-032-00689-9

This Palgrave Macmillan imprint is published by the registered company Springer Nature Switzerland AG
The registered company address is: Gewerbestrasse 11, 6330 Cham, Switzerland

Acknowledgements

This book is the product of several years of work. It is a revised version of my doctoral dissertation, written at the European University Institute between 2020–2024. While much of this has roots in a lonely office, it is also partly the result of discussions and feedback from a multitude of other scholars. I am grateful for all the intellectual stimuli obtained in this way, and to all who bothered to offer their opinions.

First and foremost, I want to thank my supervisor, Jeffrey T. Checkel, for his excellent and insightful recommendations and feedback. As this book is based on my dissertation, so it owes much to my supervisor's insights. The diverse and heterogenous interests of Jeff, and our theoretical, methodological and disciplinary differences, have aided me along the way. Jeff has assisted me in thinking beyond my own lenses, and he has helped me tremendously on my way towards the final destination. The many comments and reflections he shared with me, and our many discussions about the theoretical, methodological and analytical parts of the book have all helped me get to where I am now. The book would not be the same without you. Thank you for your professionalism, compassion and friendliness, Jeff!

I would also like to thank the rest of the IR theory working group. The group is a theoretically and disciplinarily diverse bunch. We discuss all manner of theoretical and empirical questions. The group has helped me tremendously along the way. For the many interesting discussions about my book and other relevant topics, and the general conversations and intellectual stimuli, I thank you all.

I must also thank the members of the thesis jury, Professor Stefano Guzzini, Associate Professor Julie Hassing Nielsen, and Research Professor Ole Jacob Sending, for their excellent feedback. Their comments were instrumental for the final polishing of this manuscript, both in their written comments prior to the thesis' defence, and in the aftermath, as some of their recommendations have motivated me to make some final changes in the conclusions of the empirical chapters and the final conclusion.

Last, I want to thank the European University Institute, this beautiful institution, and the many lovely people who work or have worked here. For accepting me to the programme, for the many learning possibilities offered within this university, of an academic, social and cultural nature, as well as the great memories and emotions associated with the Badia, Fiesole and Firenze.

Last, I must thank my family, friends and loved ones for their kind support during the lovely last years of hard work.

I have obtained informed consent from individual participants on their participation, and the publication of material based on their participation.

Lars Erik L. Gjerde (1992) is a Norwegian political scientist and sociologist. He has a Ph.D. in Political and Social Sciences from the European University Institute. Currently, he studies issues in the empirical fields of political antiracism and digital media, as well as the politics of COVID-19. Theoretically, his research revolves around questions of power, ideology and governmentality. His theoretical and empirical research is especially inspired by the scholarship of Michel Foucault, Michael Mann, Max Weber and Carl Schmitt. He has previously written a book on left-wing identity politics. This is his second book.

Contents

CHAPTER 1

Who Today Can Escape the Question of State Power?

1.1 Introduction

The measures implemented by states to deal with COVID-19, affecting citizens' daily lives from funerals to births, show the importance of a question posed by Poulantzas (1978: 11) decades ago; 'who today can escape the question of the State and power?' The state implemented and enforced strict rules, restricting civil liberties, from the right to work for those employed in professions considered non-essential without possibilities for home working, to the right to assemble, while closing borders and schools, and confining huge parts of the population to their homes or nearby areas. The same phenomenon can be observed, to different degrees, in countries as diverse as China (He et al. 2020), Nigeria (Onuh, 2021), Norway (Gjerde, 2021a, 2021b), Italy (Capano, 2020) and Israel (Bar-Siman-Tov, 2020). This issue is the object of interest of this book—as I study the politics of COVID-19 in Norway and Sweden.

Most states adopted a coercive approach to deal with the novel virus. The lockdown was the archetype of state coercion during the pandemic. Curfews were enforced, with governments obtaining executive powers at the expense of legislative branches, which allowed them to push through emergency measures of various kinds without voting in parliament. Social and democratic rights were suspended, including the right to assemble, or the freedom to work for those 'non-essential workers' for whom home working was not feasible; and borders were closed, all of which reveal the

L. E. L. Gjerde, *Nordic Leviathans*, International Political Theory,
https://doi.org/10.1007/978-3-032-00689-9_1

continued endorsement of state coercion. The threat of violence underpinned these measures (see Cheibub et al., 2020; Colombo, 2020; Green, 2021; Sotiris, 2020; Wagner et al., 2021).

The state has the power to ban people from receiving visitors, or prohibit them from leaving their private homes. The state can deny friends the possibility of attending a funeral or prevent a father from witnessing the birth of his child. These were exceptional measures when compared with 'normal' politics around the world. How could this occur—and furthermore—how could this occur through individuals inviting the state into their lives (see Buchanan, 2022; Green, 2021; Malm, 2020; Toscano, 2020)? Harsh measures towards pandemics have usually been highly controversial, also when they were of a much more dangerous calibre, such as actual plagues (Snowden, 2020). The ideological power of the state, as well as its autonomy, enabled restrictions to be enforced and compliance to be demanded with *relatively* little controversy during the recent pandemic.

While much has been written about the pandemic in the last couple of years, this book is an empirical exploration of the politics of COVID-19 in Norway and Sweden. The book and the empirical studies related to it (i.e. Gjerde, 2021a, 2021b, 2022, 2023) have also spawned theoretical objectives (cf Gjerde, 2024a, 2024b). Thus, this book is both an empirical study of the politics of COVID-19 in Norway and Sweden, and a theoretical interrogation of what the politics of COVID-19 teaches us about the issue of *state power*. Empirically, there are several gaps in the literature on the two countries, which we shall cover in detail in the next chapter. Theoretically, this revolves around synthesizing Weberian insights on the state and sources of power with Foucauldian insights on the mechanisms of power, so as to make the approaches compatible, so that we can bring forth theoretical lessons from the pandemic. Thus, this book engages in theory-building in order to hopefully support the collective work towards a deeper understanding of what state power is and how it works, especially within the crisis context where the state relegates non-state actors to the backseat. However, the possibility of such exceptional politics unveils, as Carl Schmitt (1996) would argue, the true nature or at least potential of the state and state power.

Note that, as a Foucauldian, the 'theorizing is typically not for its own sake but in response to the demands of a specific historical or critical project', making the theories 'temporary scaffoldings, erected for a specific purpose' (Gutting, 2006: 16). The purpose is a theory which 'opens insights in certain situations' (Gutting, 2006: 20), based on 'conceptual needs' (Foucault, 1994a: 327; see also Dean, 1994; Dreyfus & Rabinow, 1986; Driver, 1985).

The management of pandemics is useful for such a task. Historically, pandemics reveal the limits of legitimate state interventions (Porter, 1999). COVID-19 shows that the contemporary state's *legitimate* reach is great (Malm, 2020; Moisio, 2020). Politics is, among other things, a struggle to determine the legitimate boundaries between state and non-state spheres (Migdal, 1988; Mitchell, 1991). Pandemics allow states to transgress and cross the lines of previously non-state spheres (Porter, 1999), as seen during COVID-19 (Glitsos, 2021). Historically, measures such as quarantines have been implemented to protect public health, while also legitimizing illiberal politics (Ackerknecht, 2009). The political responses to COVID-19 are in this regard useful as they reveal the *potential* of our contemporary state to act, and consequentially, to refrain from acting. This is proven by more than the impressive capacities of states to interfere in the private lives of citizens. It is perhaps proven, most of all, by how legitimate the measures were (see Buchanan, 2022; Green, 2021; Malm, 2020; Toscano, 2020).

I cannot properly justify my theoretical choices in the introduction, as they are pragmatic, based on years of studies and the author's interpretation of thousands of pages of data, as well as the massive amount of literature on the issue of the politics of COVID-19 in general, and of the Norwegian and Swedish cases in particular. Beyond the utility for studying these cases, the Weberian and Weberian literatures have a certain symmetry. They complement one another, and that this allows us to explore the politics of COVID-19 in a nuanced, compelling manner, taking insights from both approaches. Theoretically, the objective is to open a new pathway, to invite Foucauldian scholars towards a state-centric approach, not to 'replace' the popular manner of studying 'power beyond the state' (i.e. Miller & Rose, 2008), but as an alternative agenda which may be prudent in state-centred contexts—something other Foucauldians also have recommended (cf. Jessen & von Eggers, 2020; J. Kim, 2021; Lessenich, 2011; Pera & Bianchi, 2022). As the Foucauldians Mitchell Dean and Kaspar Villadsen (2012: 30) problematize, governmentality scholars *tend* to bracket the state to study local practices and mechanisms of power, but why not study both?

Exploring the active state during the politics of COVID-19, I believe that Foucauldians have much to gain from engaging with a Weberian understanding of the state as an actor in general, and especially, as the state and state power are conceptualized in the work of Michael Mann. A core motivation for my theoretical objective is the diversity of the two cases. The Norwegian state is seen as close to the 'norm', while the Swedish state is found to stand out with a liberal approach largely avoiding state interventions (Cheibub et al., 2020; Habib, 2020; Giritli Nygren & Olofsson, 2020; Pierre, 2020). Scholars have also investigated Sweden vis-à-vis its neighbours, namely Denmark, Finland and Norway, discussing how and why it chose a different and more liberal strategy (see Askim & Bergström, 2021; Nielsen & Lindvall, 2021; Saunes et al. 2022). However, why would two such institutionally, culturally and politically similar countries (see Hilson, 2008; Lekvall et al. 2014) choose different approaches? To understand this enigma, political agency and state autonomy seem to be the natural point of departure. My analysis brought me to the theorizing on state autonomy—and thus a non-Foucauldian approach to the state. As Eric Nordlinger (1981) notes, states' actions are based on the subjective preferences of states, within a context the room to act is constrained by structural characteristics. As the structural, institutional and cultural characteristics of these two states are so similar, and yet the states chose different pathways, thus we must look elsewhere for an explanation of the differences. Indeed, we can largely bracket these characteristics from the analysis of the reasons behind the political choices, and focus exclusively on how the states' actions are based on preferences, preferences we can map by examining how the state actors represent the situation and rationalize their responses. Indeed, the similarities allow us to simplify, focusing exclusively on state agency.

However, as I will point out further below, the differences are relative. While the Swedish state is indeed somewhat of an 'outlier', the Norwegian and Swedish approaches are more similar than the literature implies. For instance, both states closed their borders and restricted the right to assemble. Similarly, voluntary measures are important also in the countries relying upon restrictions, such as Norway. Their communication campaigns are also highly similar, as the literature review and the empirical analysis will demonstrate. Hence, an important question to be addressed in the analysis is whether the differences are qualitative or quantitative. Does the Swedish state follow a unique strategy? Are the differences in degree or form? While most research indicates that the Swedish case is of a different form, as an 'exception' or 'experiment', my research somewhat nuances this picture. The Norwegian and Swedish states employ different means but they share common ends, and they seek to restructure society in similar ways, but with different levels of formalized measures, and different levels of applied coercion, as I shall examine further on.

My book will be guided by two overarching research questions, which my analysis and theory-building are structured around:

First, *how did the Norwegian and Swedish states govern their citizens and territories?* This question will be examined in Chapters 4 and 5—the case study chapters.

Second, *how did the Norwegian and Swedish states render reality governable?* This question guides Chapter 6, and it can be separated into two sub-questions, (a) what kinds of problems are identified? and (b) what solutions are identified? This question is based on Foucault's (1985) assertion that reality becomes governable based on governing actors' vision of reality, meaning that analysing discourse enables us to explore how reality itself becomes governable through how reality itself is represented and interpreted.

I have empirical and theoretical ambitions for answering these questions. The first question revolves around addressing empirical gaps and exploring what these cases tell us about the issue of (state) power, thereby enabling me to formalize the Weberian-Foucauldian marriage. The second question, also filling gaps with regard to the reasoning of the two states, explores why such 'sibling' states acted differently within a shared context, pointing out how these two states 'see' the situation (cf Scott, 1998). I shall elaborate on these empirical and theoretical objectives in the next chapter.

Before discussing the structure of the book, a brief point must be made regarding the terminology of this text. I am well-aware that terms such as 'violence' or 'coercion' have normative connotations, conveying something sinister, perhaps even 'evil'. However, as Carl Schmitt (1996: 30) pointed out long ago, 'all political concepts, images and terms have polemical meaning'. This is also the case with a core concept of my analysis power—which is essentially contested and always carries at least some political meaning (Guzzini 2013: 219–220). While political terms carry normative connotation, political science, sociology, international relations and other disciplines become void, failing to describe the empirical patterns before us, without them. Hence, scholars are forced to utilize terms which produce normative and affective connotation beyond our intentions. Yet, and this is important, I am uninterested in the terms' *normative* value. I use them in a descriptive manner. They define features of a political practice, without the *intention* to delegitimize or legitimize. It is up to the reader to read it 'objectively' or make judgements as he or she pleases. I will in either case seek to refrain from utilizing normative terms, *when* possible, and this study has no political objective related to the issue of *political* critique. I will, however, rather use 'normative' terms than obscure the analysis, and the exceptionality of the politics of COVID-19 vis-à-vis the liberal governance characterizing the pre-pandemic period (see Foucault, 2008; Green, 2021; Miller & Rose, 2008; Rose, 1999).

In this regard we should note that the politics of COVID-19 was the politics of life and death. States imposed restrictions, or refrained from doing so, based on their perceptions of the usefulness and dangers of these measures. People died regardless of what the states did. The states acting and the states refraining from acting were both likely to cause deaths due to their choices. To save some, others were sacrificed. To protect some values, others were discarded. Complex decisions were based on the information available to politicians and bureaucrats, as well as the political rationalities allowing them to interpret this information. This is a thankless job. There is no solution, as Thomas Sowell (1980) would put it. There are only trade-offs. It is not my task to consider, from my armchair, which trade-offs are 'right' and which are 'wrong', in the absence of any personal or professional responsibility for the hardships and suffering that some would, inevitably, face, as a direct consequence of any choice. That is the task of the people's representatives and the people they represent.

Therefore, my study will refrain from evaluating the strategies, or the decision-makers' performances or choices with regard to their impact on COVID-19, individual well-being, civil rights or other questions of relevance. Reflections will only be based on the relative performances of measures as forms of power. The objective is not to evaluate the merits of the Norwegian or Swedish approaches with regard to infection control. Rather, I am interested in the question of power, and thus the control of the population. Whether the lockdowns and other measures were 'right' or 'wrong' are questions left outside of this study.

The book utilizes various methods within my case study design. To collect data, I did both online archive work and interviews, which gave me data for Chapters 4 and 5. I refer to 21 informants for my Norwegian case, and 17 for the Swedish case. The document data consists of 2581 pages for the Norwegian case, and 1633 pages for the Swedish case. I also conduct a discourse analysis in Chapter 6, which analyses public data obtained from the online archive work. The online archive work will be the basis of my study, as I gathered data to answer all of my research questions with this method. The interviews supplement this data, giving me more detailed thick descriptions and deeper insights into the local contexts. I will offer some brief methodological reflections when introducing the empirical chapters, and interested readers can explore my online appendix (see Gjerde, 2025).

1.1.1 A Road-Map

The book is structured as follows. Chapter 2 is a literature review, covering the politics of past plagues and the politics of COVID-19. I contextualize the politics of COVID-19 within its historical trajectory, offering some insights on the politics of COVID-19 as a global phenomenon. Thereafter, I cover two literatures on the pandemic, both of the utmost importance to the book: first, the literature on politics of COVID-19 in Norway and Sweden, to identify any gaps in the literature which our project will seek to fill. Second, I explore the Foucauldian literature on the politics of COVID-19, what it teaches us, and how this literature would appear to invite a Weberian approach to the state, implicitly through the backdoor. This allows me to also introduce Weberian work—especially that of scholars influenced by Michael Mann—into the discussion—so as to show how these two literatures complement one another. This steers us towards the theory-building of Chapter 3.

Chapter 3 takes up the challenge presented in Chapter 2—how can we make the Foucauldian approach to the question of power and rule compatible with the Weberian approach? For this purpose, I discuss how we can combine the two analytical frameworks by compatibility and careful handling of the key concepts of the two approaches. Moreover, I discuss the manner in which a Weberian theory of the state can be used within a Foucauldian analytical framework, and why I believe the Foucauldian theory of the state faces shortcomings in this empirical context, due to its explicit denial of potential state autonomy and agency. We end this chapter by operationalizing the theory, preparing for the coming analysis.

Chapters 4 and 5 revolve around the two case studies. The two cases—Norway and Sweden—are analysed on the basis of the empirical and theoretical objectives clarified in Chapter 2. I seek to fill empirical gaps and operationalize the Weberian-Foucauldian theory of the state in the process. The different political measures of the two states are explored, with some superficial reflections on differences and similarities between the two states. Here, the effects of the measures on the virus or normative discussions on the appropriateness of measures are ignored. As stated above, the attention centres on the effects the measures have upon the objects of governance, i.e. the populations in question.

Chapter 6 builds upon the case study chapters, seeking to explain the different policy outcomes by examining the political rationalities of the two states. How did the Norwegian and Swedish states see the pandemic, and how does this relate to their responses? This chapter starts with a brief exploration of the (dis)similarities between the two states' approaches, so to better clarify what we must explain. Thereafter, we seek to make sense of the political reasoning which enabled the two states to act as they did.

Chapter 7 concludes my book. This brief chapter will entail theoretical reflections about the insights of my study, including theoretical lessons, shortcomings and the way forward for studies on the pandemic and beyond.

References

Ackerknecht, E. H. (2009). Anticontagionism between 1821 and 1867: The Fielding H Garrison lecture. *International Journal of Epidemiology, 38*(1), 7–21.

Askim, J., & Bergström, T. (2021). Between lockdown and calm down. Comparing the COVID-19 responses of Norway and Sweden. *Local Government Studies*, 1–21.

Bar-Siman-Tov, I. (2020). COVID-19 meets politics: The novel coronavirus as a novel challenge for legislatures. *The Theory and Practice of Legislation, 8*(1–2), 11–48. https://doi.org/10.1080/20508840.2020.1800250

Buchanan, I. (2022). Biopolitics, Discipline and Governmentality. In: Das, S. S., and Pratihar, A. R. (Eds.), *Technology, Urban Space and the Networked Community*, 1–28. Palgrave Macmillan.

Capano, G. (2020). Policy design and state capacity in the COVID-19 emergency in Italy: If you are not prepared for the (un)expected, you can be only what you already are. *Policy and Society, 39*(3), 326–344. https://doi.org/10.1080/14494035.2020.1783790

Cheibub, J. A., Hong, J. Y. J., & Przeworski, A. (2020). Rights and deaths: Government reactions to the pandemic. Working paper. https://doi.org/10.2139/ssrn.3645410

Colombo, E. (2020). Human rights-inspired governmentality: COVID-19 through a human dignity perspective. *Critical Sociology*. https://doi.org/10.1177/0896920520971846

Dean, M. (1994). *Critical and effective histories. Foucault's methods and historical sociology*. London: Routledge.

Dean, M. and Villadsen, K., (2012). *Statsfobi og Civilsamfund. Foucault og hans arvingers blik på staten*. Fredriksberg: Nyt fra Samfundsvidernskaberne.

Dreyfus, H. L., & Rabinow, P. (1986). What is maturity? Habermas and Foucault on 'what is enlightenment?'. In D. C. Hoy (Ed.), *Foucault: A critical reader*. Basil Blackwell.

Driver, F. (1985). Power, space, and the body: A critical assessment of Foucault's discipline and punish. *Environment and Planning D: Society and Space, 3*(4), 425–446.

Foucault, M. (1985). Discourse and Truth: The Problematization of Parrhesia, Evanston, IL: Northwestern University Press.

Foucault, M. (1994a). Subject and power. In F. D. Faubion (Ed.), *Michel Foucault. Power. Essential works of Foucault 1954–1984 Volume 3* (pp. 326–349). The New Press.

Foucault, M. (2008). *The birth of biopolitics - Lectures at the Collège de France, 1978–1979*. Palgrave Macmillan.

Gjerde, L. E. L. (2021). From liberalism to biopolitics: Investigating the Norwegian government's two responses to COVID-19. *European Societies, 23*(sup1), S262–S274. https://doi.org/10.1080/14616696.2020.1824003

Gjerde, L. E. L. (2021). Governing humans and 'things': Power and rule in Norway during the Covid-19 pandemic. *Journal of Political Power, 14*(3), 472–492. https://doi.org/10.1080/2158379X.2020.1870264

Gjerde, L. E. L. (2022). Den norske regjeringens diskursive muliggjøring av koronapolitikken: Et Foucauldiansk perspektiv. *Norsk Sosiologisk Tidsskrift,* (3), 29–45. https://doi.org/10.18261/nost.6.3.3

Gjerde, L. E. L. (2023). Biopolitical and juridical creations of the quarantine hotel: A discourse analysis of the Norwegian case. *Acta Sociologica, 66*(4), 357–371. https://doi.org/10.1177/00016993221136038

Gjerde, L. E. L. (2024a). Marrying the sources and mechanisms of power? Understanding the Quarantine Hotel through Michel Foucault and Michael Mann. *Journal of Political Power*. https://doi.org/10.1080/2158379X.2024.2337617

Gjerde, L. E. L. (2024b). Biopolitical Leviathan: Understanding state power in the era of COVID-19 through the Weberian-Foucauldian theory of the state. Theoria: *A Journal of Social and Political Theory, 71*(1), 48–74. https://doi.org/10.3167/th.2024.7117803

Gjerde, L. E. L. (2025). Methodology: Digital appendix. *Research Gate*. https://www.researchgate.net/publication/387958773_Methodology_Digital_Appendix

Glitsos, L. (2021). COVID-19 and the 'perfectly governed city.' *Journal for Cultural Research*. https://doi.org/10.1080/14797585.2021.194381

Gutting, G. (2006). Introduction: Michel Foucault: A user's manual. In G. Cutting (Ed.), *The Cambridge companion to Foucault. 2nd edition* (pp. 1–28). Cambridge University Press.

Guzzini, S. (2013). *Power, realism and constructivism*. London: Routledge.

Green, T. (2021). *The Covid consensus: The new politics of global inequality*. London: Hurst.

Habib, H. (2020). Has Sweden's controversial covid-19 strategy been successful? *BMJ*, 369.

He, A. J., Shi, Y., & Liu, H. (2020). Crisis governance, Chinese style: distinctive features of China's response to the COVID-19 pandemic. *Policy Design and Practice*, 1–17.

Hilson, M. (2008). *The Nordic model: Scandinavia since 1945*. Reaktion Books.

Jessen, M. H., & von Eggers, N. (2020). Governmentality and statification: Towards a Foucauldian theory of the state. *Theory, Culture & Society, 37*(1), 53–72.

Kim, J. (2021). Rethinking public administration and the state: A Foucauldian governmentality perspective. *International Review of Public Administration, 26*(2), 175–191. https://doi.org/10.1080/12294659.2021.1889102

Lekvall, P., Gilson, R. J., Hansen, J. L., Lønfeldt, C., Airaksinen, M., Berglund, T., ... & Sjöman, E. (2014). The Nordic corporate governance model. *The Nordic Corporate Governance Model, Per Lekvall, ed., SNS Förlag, Stockholm*, 14–12.

Lessenich, S. (2011). Constructing the socialized self. Mobilization and control in the "active society". In Bröckling, S. Krasmann, & T. Lemke (Eds.), *Governmentality: current issues and future challenges* (pp. 304–319). Routledge.

Malm, A. (2020). *Corona, climate, chronic emergency: War communism in the twenty-first century*. London: Verso.

Migdal, J S. (1988). *Strong Societies and Weak States: State-society relations and state capabilities in the Third World*. Princeton University Press.

Miller, P., & Rose, N. (2008). *Governing the present: Administering economic, social and political life*. Polity Press.

Mitchell, T. (1991). The limits of the state: Beyond statist approaches and their critics. *The American Political Science Review, 85*(1), 77–96.

Moisio, S. (2020). State power and the COVID-19 pandemic: The case of Finland. *Eurasian Geography and Economics*, 1–8.

Nordlinger, E. (1981). *The autonomy of the democratic state*. Harvard: Harvard University Press.

Nielsen, J. H., & Lindvall, J. (2021). Trust in government in Sweden and Denmark during the COVID-19 epidemic. *West European Politics, 44*(5–6), 1180–1204.

Giritli Nygren, K. & Olofsson, A. (2020). Managing the COVID-19 pandemic through individual responsibility: the consequences of a world risk society and enhanced ethopolitics, *Journal of Risk Research*.

Pera, M., & Bianchi, I. (2022). Governmentality, the local state, and the commons: An analysis of civic management facilities in Barcelona. *Social Inclusion, 10*(1), 115–125.

Pierre, J. (2020). Nudges against pandemics: Sweden's COVID-19 containment strategy in perspective. *Policy and Society, 39*(3), 478–493.

Poulantzas, N. (1978). *State, power, socialism*. New Left Books.

Porter, D. (1999). *Health, civilization, and the state: A history of public health from ancient to modern times*. Routledge.

Rose, N. (1999). Powers of freedom: Reframing political thought. Cambridge University Press.

Onuh, P. A. (2021). Nigeria's response to COVID-19: Lockdown policy and human rights violations. *African Security, 14*(4), 439–459.

Saunes, I. S., Vrangbæk, K., Byrkjeflot, H., Jervelund, S. S., Birk, H. O., Tynkkynen, L. K., …, & Karanikolos, M. (2022). Nordic responses to Covid-19: Governance and policy measures in the early phases of the pandemic. *Health Policy, 126*(5), 418–426.

Schmitt, C. (1996). *The concept of the political*. Chicago: University of Chicago Press.

Scott, J. C. (1998). *Seeing like a state: How certain schemes to improve the human condition have failed*. Yale University Press.

Snowden, F. M. (2020). *Epidemics and society: From the black death to the present*. Yale University Press.

Sotiris, P. (2020). Thinking beyond the lockdown: On the possibility of a democratic biopolitics. *Historical Materialism, 28*(3), 3–38.

Sowell, T. (1980). *Knowledge and decisions*. Basic Books.

Toscano, A. (2020). The state of the pandemic. *Historical Materialism, 28*(4), 3–23.

Wagner, A., Matulewska, A., & Marusek, S. (2021). Pandemica panoptica: Biopolitical management of viral spread in the age of covid-19. *International Journal for the Semiotics of Law-Revue internationale de Sémiotique juridique*, 1–37.

CHAPTER 2

The Politics of Pandemics

2.1 Introduction

While the politics of COVID-19 may appear novel, the political measures experienced during the pandemic tend to be ancient in origins. Indeed, the pandemic itself is an ancient social context (Scott, 2017; Snowden, 2020). As the state long has embraced the task of protecting society—its formal *raison d'être* (Hobbes, 1996)—so pandemics are one of several events where the state is likely to be compelled to act. Indeed, the limits of the state can be explored by analysing how the state acts, and is allowed to act, during a pandemic (Porter, 1999). In the past, the politics of pandemics led to much resistance (Snowden, 2020). However, as further discussed below, the politics of COVID-19 was largely accepted, showing the enhanced legitimacy and ideological powers of the state. The state's legitimacy and its legitimate reach increase.

First, I start this chapter by discussing the 'plague state'—offering a historical account of the different ways in which states have combatted 'plagues' (i.e. pandemics which may or may not relate to the *actual* plague and the bacteria causing it, *Yersinia pestis*). I account for the history of the 'plague state' to allow us to better understand the role of the state with regard to the recent pandemic.

Second, I engage with the literature on the politics of COVID-19 more generally. This is done to contextualize the case. I seek to delineate how the politics of the pandemic was a global phenomenon based on

L. E. L. Gjerde, *Nordic Leviathans*, International Political Theory,
https://doi.org/10.1007/978-3-032-00689-9_2

seemingly unprecedented political measures which, in the final instance, revolve largely around old techniques, but with new instruments available as the state has increased its capacities over the centuries.

Third, I explore the politics of COVID-19 in Norway and Sweden. I examine the literature on the politics of COVID-19 in our two cases, in order to better contextualize my coming analyses. This section has two objectives. First, I seek to further elucidate my cases by discussing how the politics of COVID-19 was enacted in the two contexts. Second, I seek to contextualize the empirical contributions. What is missing, and what am I adding? Unlike the case of Norway (i.e. Gjerde, 2021a), the political reasoning of the Swedish state has not been empirically studied. Moreover, the Norwegian and Swedish cases share several gaps. First, the border control regimes have not been handled adequately as series of mechanisms of power. The closed borders have been discussed, but the border control regimes are more complex than border closure. Second, in both contexts the mobilization of society has been addressed only in its moral, and not its formal, form. As we shall see, the two states mobilize the entire society. This, and the mechanisms of power working through the mobilization of society, has not been studied. Third, I allude to the theoretical issues of state power, which have been touched upon, but not developed, as the lessons of the massive exercise of state power in these two countries have not been theoretically elaborated.

Fourth, I engage with the Foucauldian literature on the politics of COVID-19, as well as the Weberian work based on Michael Mann's work on state power. This is a more theoretically informed literature review compared to the previous three parts, rooted in empirical and theoretical insights from my past years of study (i.e. Gjerde, 2021a, 2021b, 2022, 2023). The study started out with a more orthodox Foucauldian position, but analytical and tactical needs made it necessary to look beyond the Foucauldian approach to better handle the active state which the study focuses upon. Thus, I found it necessary to move beyond my own Foucauldian position. Based on this, I also identified an implicit consensus among Foucauldians regarding the need to deal with the state as an actor when exploring the politics of COVID-19. Nevertheless, such implicit solutions—operating with a non-Foucauldian approach to the state with a Foucauldian lens—have weaknesses. It should be made explicit for the purpose of theoretical development, especially as the agency of the state is a black box, a major question mark, when it is not developed. This invited me to theory-building, as the Foucauldian scholarship on the pandemic indicates that there may be a use of a Weberian-Foucauldian theory of the state, at the very least for state-centric contexts such as the politics of COVID, but also similar cases such as revolutions, war, environmental disasters, etc. In the fourth part of this literature review, I will start making my case for such a marriage.

2.2 The Plague State

Pandemics have haunted humanity for millennia. Indeed, pathogens have become increasingly dangerous with the spread of permanent settlements. Huge populations living in close quarters, living off monotonous diets based on agriculture rather than the diverse diets of hunter-gatherers, make humans easy prey for pathogens (Scott, 2017; Snowden, 2020). This has also spawned a specific form of politics—the politics of pandemics—which revolves around protecting populations from disease.

This is a topic Foucault (1990, 2008a) wrote much about—biopolitics. While Foucault (1990) discusses how biopolitics emerged as a prominent political problem space during the early-modern era, with the politics of public health becoming a core issue during the eighteenth century as the state sought to foster the vitality of its population and protect it from diseases (Foucault, 1994a, 1994b), the state (and other political authorities) retained biopolitical or at least proto-biopolitical responsibilities, prior to the biological knowledge underpinning modern biopolitics. Biopolitics has at the least medieval roots, for instance in contemporary Italy, where most measures we know today first emerged. Political measures were developed as states combatted diseases (Foucault, 1991a). Therefore, the state appropriating the medical apparatus—creating state medicine—is an important part of the centralization and growth of state power (Foucault, 1994a, 1994b). Moreover, states increased their legitimacy and scope by successful interventions in the social body to limit pandemic spread (Porter, 1999: 16). While the existence of pathogens as microorganisms was unknown to premodern minds, the idea of contagion and origins beyond the will of God was not. Scholars and laymen thought that illnesses' origins could be traced to unhealthy air, filth, etc., which dispersed the sickness (Henderson, 2018). Moreover, it was known that illnesses proliferated. The existence of human-to-human contagion was identified, despite the concrete mechanisms of pathogenic contagion receiving near-hegemonic acceptance within medical and political circles only in the late 1800s (Ackerknecht, 2009).

The premodern state, while smaller in size and scope, had many of the characteristics of the modern state, and should thus be understood as a state (Mann, 1986; Scott, 2017; Tilly, 1992). However, though they were also compulsory political organizations based on mastery over territories, premodern states did not possess a monopoly over the legitimate means of violence, and the territorial basis of the premodern state was more flexible and fluid. Thus, prior to states obtaining a monopoly over the means of violence and, before power was so clearly concentrated within the state apparatus, biopolitical responsibilities fell upon a multitude of actors. Kings, lords and local notables became responsible.

The politics of plagues was constitutive of the growth of state power (Foucault, 1991a; Jensen, 2020; Porter, 1999). However, the premodern state initially lacked both the legitimacy and the institutional means to intervene effectively in society. The infamous Black Death of the mid-thirteenth century helped change this. The plague, leading to a death toll likely far above 100 million globally, killed up to 50% of the population of Europe within the timespan of a few years, leaving entire cities and areas void of inhabitants (Snowden, 2020). Scholars in the thirteenth century understood that the plague was contagious—despite their lack of knowledge about the exact mechanisms of infection. This led premodern states to police urban environments to ensure that filth and germ-ridden air were kept out of cities and towns (Rawcliffe & Weeda, 2019).

In practice, this entailed monitoring the poor and their social environments, which were particularly filthy during the economically poor times of the medieval period. In fact, authorities were obliged to burn down the dirtiest of houses, as filth and unsanitary conditions were seen as major threats to public health on the basis of the medical knowledge then available (Henderson, 2018). While such measures break with contemporary forms of pandemic politics, several methods of infection control have recently been popularized again.

For instance, Italian decision-makers in various city states and smaller fiefdoms implemented quarantines on travellers—an Italian invention in the plague world, as well as armed patrols at its borders during times of outbreaks. The concepts 'quarantine' and 'isolation' are in fact both Italian terms, based on the words '*quaranta*' (forty) (the original quarantine lasted for forty days), and '*isola*' (island) (isolation usually occurred on islands) (Jensen, 2020). Moreover, the authorities did not exclusively govern through coercion. Italian authorities also promulgated information to citizens on how to avoid the plague in order to socialize them as infection control agents, while implementing various sanitary regimes (Rawcliffe & Weeda, 2019).

Hence, the rise of pandemics also led to a rise in governing techniques, as political actors acquired new responsibilities for handling the bodies and spaces of individuals. Similarly, the curfew—a measure we have come to know well in the post-COVID period—was transformed from a general means of controlling the population by denying individuals the freedom to walk outside after dusk (see Conner, 2017)—to the more totalizing curfew we know today (see Foucault, 1991a). Individuals were confined to their homes, with guards patrolling towns and cities to ensure that nobody left their homes, with severe punishments meted out for wrongdoers, with the potential eyes of the premodern state always upon the transgressor, as anyone could function as a state agent from their windows. A disciplinary gaze turned the spatial spaces of towns and cities into instruments of power to divide, and segregated households emerged (Foucault, 1991a).

However, premodern states and other political authorities faced many challenges when implementing biopolitical restrictions. For instance, hordes of people would seek to flee the cities, not to escape the plague, but to escape curfews (Snowden, 2020). In fact, in early-modern Britain, measures such as quarantine were highly controversial. They were considered barbaric, which prompted political debates and eventually such measures ceased to be adopted during the modern era (Ackerknecht, 2009)—until 2020. Thus, while the politics of pandemics revolves around old techniques, in the past, such techniques were illegitimate, because the state lacked the symbolic resources needed to interfere in such a totalizing manner. The premodern and early-modern state was not illegitimate as such, insofar as it stayed out of private lives. Nevertheless, its legitimate reach was low by modern standards. Therefore, what we call the lockdown could be more terrifying to individuals than even the most dangerous of plagues (Snowden, 2020). The old states may have used similar measures to the contemporary state, but its lack of legitimacy made such measures hated, despite the horrors of past pandemics.

More recent examples show the extent of state power, and help us understand the corporate agency and various means of control used by the state to handle the plague. The Ottoman and Habsburg empires provide useful cases of early-modern states engaged in the politics of pandemics. Starting with the Habsburg Empire, I refer to the study of Bronza (2019) on Habsburgian border control. As Bronza (2019) notes, the plague was largely eradicated from Western and Central Europe by the 1700s, but it remained a threat in much of the world. As it remained a threat in the Ottoman Empire, so Habsburgian authorities crafted an impressive anti-plague border regime. The Habsburg Empire created quarantine locales along its border to the east. 4,000 border guards lived at these *cordons sanitaires* during 'normal' times. They patrolled the border on horseback, enforcing strict quarantine rules upon all travellers seeking to cross over. If Habsburg spies found the nearby Ottoman territories to be haunted by plague, then this number increased to 11,000. This strengthened the empire's territorial control and knowledge about its borders and those crossing it, as the state's capacities to regulate the border and guard the border regions increased.

This is impressive when considering how the US, with a much vaster territory and larger population, as well as strict migration policies in play, employed approximately 20,000 border guards as of 2020—but in 1992, the number was equivalent to the total number of the Habsburg Empire during normal times (cbp.gov, 2020). Habsburgian authorities made an institution of border control for ensuring that the bacteria stayed outside of its borders, granting the empire immense control over its borders, especially by the standards of the period. The state acted to solidify its borders, for the purpose of controlling pandemics, meaning that the (perceived) presence of the plague in the Ottoman Empire effectively aided the Habsburg Empire in greatly enhancing its reach, as it increased its institutional capacities.

Something similar occurred in the Ottoman Empire, as covered by Ottomanist scholars (see Balmus, 2012; Bolaños, 2019; Varlik, 2015). The Ottoman Empire was initially fatalistic with regard to pandemics. Life was in the hands of God, a notion also shared by many Christians during the same period, even if there was some variety and exceptions to this philosophy, as God's will could and was questioned by many Ottomans (White, 2010). Nevertheless, politically dealing with the plague was seen as morally dubious and therefore too politically controversial by Ottoman authorities. While fatalism did not allow anyone to leave the sick to their fate, it was not the task of the state to 'play God', altering His designs by actively safeguarding the population from plagues. However, biopolitical considerations became increasingly important in the Ottoman Empire, as it changed its stance on plague outbreaks during the 1700s and 1800s, and the increased mobility of people made pandemics increasingly relevant, prompting political changes (Bolaños 2019). It started regulating dead and living bodies to degrees unheard of in the Islamic world prior to the emergence of biopolitics.

With this change, efforts were made to regulate the hygiene, cleaning and planning of Istanbul and other large cities. Conservatives and modernists had two different solutions. Conservatives wanted to purge society of spiritual impurity, such as prostitution, as the pollution of the soul was seen as the cause of the plague. Modernists wanted to cleanse society of physical filth and unsanitary conditions, which were defined as a danger in a typical biopolitical and medical manner. The Ottoman state went for a combination. The Ottoman Empire started regulating air, water and morality, the three critical components of health politics in Ottoman discourse (Varlik, 2015: 276). The Ottoman state, quite lenient towards its subjects' day-to-day activities, became increasingly concerned with micro-managing daily lives when undertaking public health services. The state even expelled, i.e. excluded, individuals considered immoral, such as prostitutes and criminals, from Constantinople, present-day Istanbul, while regulating the sizes and locations of new buildings, also placing restrictions on where burial grounds, slaughterhouses and other 'impure' buildings could be located. Border control also meant that travellers and traders were likely to be quarantined, placed in islands along the coast, to protect the core of the empire from imported contagion. This represents a 'critical turning point in Ottoman history' as the Ottoman state, already a powerful military empire and the dominant power in the Near-East, emerged as a powerful, modern state with an administrative apparatus capable of regulating citizens' daily lives (Varlik, 2015: 245–250). While biopolitics was not the only factor in this development, it was an important piece of the puzzle. Another was, naturally, the Ottoman state's desire to better control its borders and limit the effects of free trade by imposing implicit sanctions on foreign traders (Varlik, 2015; Bolaños 2019).

There are few similar cases in recent times. The Spanish Influenza caused little political outcry (Snowden, 2020). Tuberculosis led to restrictions, but of a personal, rather than universal, nature. For instance, individuals with tuberculosis were prohibited from working with food in Norway in the early 1900s, and they could be forced to isolate (Grindheim, 2021). While causing outcries and calls for strong state interventions, and leading to heavy death tolls on an annual basis (Pandey & Galvani, 2019), the AIDS pandemic has not given rise to such measures. The AIDS pandemic is of a slower and more endemic nature, thereby having less symbolic impact than 'immediate' dangers, as mortality rates matter less than the cultural interpretations of diseases when it comes to political responses (Rosenberg, 1989).

While the Spanish Influenza filled the cultural *and* political criteria of a great pandemic, it failed to produce any significant political response. It occurred in a world ravaged by a brutal war, and a world less sensitive to death in general, and biopolitical concerns in particular, than our own. We can identify other reasons why states have not implemented the harsh measures seen in the Habsburgian and Ottoman empires on a national scale for more than a century. Some malevolent illnesses have been reduced in strength or even eradicated by the development of vaccines, such as smallpox; others have been benign, such as the avian and swine flu pandemics of recent decades; others have been contained in regions of the world receiving less attention, where the state is unable and/or unwilling to act in the harshest manner, even if we have seen some levels of impressive state capacity in certain African countries, like Liberia, in dealing with Ebola (Blair et al., 2017). Such political measures have however been mild compared to the case of COVID-19.

2.3 The COVID-19 State

The COVID-19 state can be considered the plague state of the twenty-first century. Obviously, there are major *pathological* differences between COVID-19 and *Yersinia pestis*, and they must be addressed to avoid overstating the pathological similarities. For instance, COVID-19 seems to have killed approximately 2 out of 700 million Europeans, or in other words, just under 0.3% of the population, from 2020 to 2023 (Statista, 2023), whereas the Black Death may, as mentioned earlier, have killed as much as *half* of the population of Europe between 1347 and 1351, while conservative estimates put the death toll at closer to 30% (Snowden, 2020). In a few years, even without modern means of spreading, the plague essentially altered the demographic landscape of the continent for centuries to come. These pathogens' *pathological* impact cannot be compared.

However, objective mortality rates matter less than cultural interpretations (Rosenberg, 1989). Therefore, the questions of interest are political, ideological and cultural, rather than pathological. After all, the Ottoman Empire refrained from intervening to deal with the plague for centuries, as the plague was not rendered governable. Rendering an object governable is only partially dependent upon the characteristics of the object (Dean, 1999; Foucault, 1985, 1991b, 2008a; Miller & Rose, 2008; Rose 1999). Whether a pandemic will be politically handled or not depends more upon how it is perceived than on its pathological characteristics. Therefore, the measures implemented to deal with COVID-19 are the same as those implemented against the plague, albeit at a global rather than local or national scale, and there are certain differences to how the measures are implemented. This makes the politics of COVID-19 a continuation of the politics of plagues. The main question is—why? While I will address some Foucauldian reflections on the biopolitical nature of the political reasoning behind the politics of COVID-19 in this chapter, this issue will be handled in depth in Chapter 6.

The coronavirus known as COVID-19 originated in China in late 2019, leading the Chinese state to confine the entire region of Wuhan and the tens of millions of citizens living there to their homes during the winter of 2020 (Cheibub et al., 2020). While initially slow to react, the Chinese state 'mobilised unprecedented governmental, economic, technological, scientific and human resources in order to get the viral outbreak under control' (Martinez, 2020: 311).

At first, the Chinese strategy was seen as incompatible with liberal democratic values and political culture (Green, 2021). This makes much sense from our Foucauldian perspective, as Foucauldian scholarship has spent decades exploring the manner which governance occurs in the present. Foucault (2008a) noted more than four decades ago that liberal rule through freedom overtook discipline as the major form of governance. Nikolas Rose (2009) has similarly covered how the issue of biopolitics—the politics of life itself—over the last decades has become increasingly voluntaristic and based on self-regulation. The individual is to be governed through self-regulation, as freedom becomes an instrument of governance. This is based on a political rationality—a manner of understanding how the world is and how it ought to be governed—which posits that the state should reduce its interventions in society, and that the most efficient and appropriate governance occurs through rather than against freedom (see Foucault, 1991b, 2008a; Lemke, 2019; Miller & Rose, 2008; Merlingen, 2011; Rose 1999). However, as referred to below, the liberal understanding of the pandemic—based on past plans and decades of liberal governance—was replaced within a matter of days when the pandemic arrived (Gjerde, 2021a).

This occurred as the Chinese approach was quickly appropriated by most countries, democratic as well as autocratic, albeit in most cases to a softer degree than that seen in China (Cheibub et al., 2020; Green, 2021). Countries as different as Norway (Gjerde, 2021a, 2021b; Sandset & Villadsen, 2023), Nigeria (Onuh, 2021), Italy (Capano, 2020) and Israel (Bar-Siman-Tov, 2020) to a greater or lesser extent, appropriated the Chinese approach in practice. Entire cities, like Wuhan or Milan, were isolated. Within these cities, entire populations were confined to their private homes. The curfew returned at a global level. Cities became spatial sites of control, where citizens could be confined to either their homes, or to specific sectors of the city. Essential workers could for instance be allowed to travel the road between their workplace and their home. States at every continent implemented social distancing measures, which revolved around reducing the number of people meeting, and increasing the physical distance between those still able to meet. The state restricted the movements and activities of the entire population through a combination of administrative regulation and the use of explicit state coercion through the police.

With this, 'states that issue orders make a strong comeback' (Jensen, 2020: 131; cf Anisin, 2022), with states regulating the entirety of society. Some, such as Slavoj Žižek (2020: 123–124), make counter-intuitive, and erroneous, claims that COVID-19 revealed the weakness and impotence of the state. Such conclusions are disconnected from the political context where entire countries were placed under lockdowns and curfews. The pandemic did not reveal state weakness, but rather, massive state capacities. Entire societies were strictly regulated and administered from above. This transgressed many state/non-state boundaries (Glitsos, 2021). The state transgresses these boundaries by banning numerous activities, suspending various liberties and rights, for private individuals as well as non-state associations like religious communities or businesses. Indeed, the state showed its great power over the market (Malm, 2020; Moisio 2020).

While one should beware of overstating the opposition between state and market, as there is a reciprocal relationship, something also alluded to by scholars on state-market relations during the pandemic (Van Apeldoorn & De Graaff 2022), the pandemic revealed the power of the state to intervene in and control the market. This is shown by states acting in a manner similar to the 'war communism' seen during the world wars and the Russian civil war, where the state appropriated goods and services while controlling vast parts of the market (Malm, 2020). For instance, the state enforces quotas upon private businesses, even appropriating them when needed. The US commanded private enterprises to provide essential goods, while Spain nationalized several private health facilities. This reveals the state's autonomy from economic elites, and how the state can embed itself within the market so as to govern and control it for its own security purposes (Malm, 2020).

While the liberal pre-COVID, and one can assume, post-COVID, state, has been governed based on the principle that one must govern neither too much nor too little (i.e. Foucault, 2008a; Rose 1999), the politics of COVID-19 worked based on interventionist principles where liberal concerns with balancing were discarded. During the pandemic, the state tended to become the COVID-19 state (cf Graver, 2020a, 2020b; Green, 2021). The COVID-19 state was a state granting COVID-19 and concerns related to the pathogen the central position during its decision-making process. This entailed suspending various legal, social and political norms, including rights and other laws, for the purpose of protecting society. The lockdown may have been the ultimate expression of the COVID-19 state, but other forms of rule, also when they were softer, are of the highest importance. This relates to the state's sovereign capabilities, in the Schmittian sense. Essentially, by defining a situation as exceptional, the state can, and does, implement rules and measures that contradict its own laws (Schmitt, 1996, 2008, 2014, 2020). Several scholars, covering different countries, discuss the politics of COVID-19 as a state of exception, analysing it from sociological and legal perspectives (see Graver, 2020a; Zinn, 2020). Importantly, as Philip Lipscy (2020) writes, the core of any crisis, including the pandemic, is 'threat, time-pressure and uncertainty', which allows decision-making processes to break with everyday politics. During the crisis, political choices, always relevant, become especially important (Weiss & Thurbon, 2022).

Some dispute such claims, claiming that it is more accurate to speak about a state of emergency than a state of exception—as only certain laws are suspended/cancelled—meaning that the legal order is not suspended per se, but rather, certain parts of it are (Greene, 2021). However, the juridical formalities are in this regard of little interest. The core object of interest is the state's capacities to suspend rights and laws when this is found to be necessary, and how this was a global phenomenon during the pandemic. States around the world show massive decision-making capacities, albeit with much variation in how effectively they can engage in controlling the population and thus infection in practice.

It should be noted that my analysis is very state-centric. However, non-state actors play an important role in this political game. They both spread information and legitimize specific forms of action. The WHO was chief among these non-state entities during the COVID-19 pandemic. The WHO justifies strict measures if it declares a situation to be a pandemic (Hanrieder & Kreuder-Sonnen, 2014). Similarly, the lack of an official sanction from the WHO makes it harder for states to legitimize interventions and expansions into society. The WHO has considerable symbolic resources. Through this role, the WHO was instrumental in promulgating the lockdown strategy, taking a pro-Chinese stance due to the Chinese state's efficacy in dealing with COVID-19. The WHO declared the Chinese response one of the most effective anti-pandemic strategies of all time in the aftermath of the Chinese 'conquest' of the virus (Green, 2021).

The WHO legitimizes the state's presence within the social body, because it calls for state action to protect society from diseases. This enabling of the state also restrains it. By legitimizing action, the WHO delegitimizes inaction. The state is invited to protect society, and thus, also compelled to act to protect its protection-obedience relations with society. While non-state actors are of importance, one should not overstate their significance. A state can withstand the normative pressure created by the WHO's recommendations and its ideological power, as the Swedish state shows. The state remains sovereign and thus keeps its rights to determine whether a situation is exceptional or not, and if it is, then the state determines the severity of measures. A state-centric view is therefore justified, both because the state keeps its sovereign right to decision-making, and because few spheres were allowed to remain private under the pandemic.

2.4 The Nordic COVID-19 State

While the COVID-19 state was a global occurrence, there remains numerous differences between different states. For instance, the Nordic cases are all relatively liberal, as seen by the lack of curfews (Cheibub et al., 2020). However, there is also much variation, as seen by the difference between Sweden and Iceland, on the one hand, and Norway, Denmark and Finland, on the other.

In mid-March 2020, the Norwegian state, like the Danish, Finnish and most other European states, closed down society. The lockdowns in the Nordic countries entailed closing down educational facilities and non-essential businesses, as well as most social and cultural events, without imposing curfews, (Bjørkdahl et al., 2021; Cheibub et al., 2020; Gjerde, 2021a, 2021b; Sandset & Villadsen, 2023; Triantafillou, 2022), whereas the Swedish and Icelandic states refrained from closing down (Girtli Nygren & Olofsson, 2020; Ólafsson, 2021).

Comparative studies have unsurprisingly found the Norwegian state to act in a stricter manner than the Swedish state (Conyon et al. 2020; Laage-Thomsen & Frandsen, 2022; Nanda et al. 2021). Indeed, it is found that the Swedish model of infection control during the pandemic was based around a model of network-governance, whereas the Norwegian, but also the Danish and Finnish models, were hierarchical (Christensen et al., 2023). However, there are also many similarities. For instance, the different states used similar rhetorical strategies (see Bjørkdahl et al., 2021), even if some find the Swedish approach to have been communicatively more 'informative' and the Norwegian approach more 'political' (see Almlund et al., 2023). In both Norway and Sweden, communitarian ethics are used to make compliance morally mandatory, everywhere and at all times (see Bjørkdahl et al., 2021; Girtli Nygren & Olofsson, 2020; Larsson, 2022; Sandset & Villadsen, 2023). Both Norway and Sweden, as well as Denmark, sought to steer the population through nudging through rhetorical techniques (Almlund et al., 2023). Moreover, the high levels of compliance and acceptance have been traced to the legitimacy of these states (see Baekkeskov et al., 2021; Christensen & Lægreid, 2020a, 2020b;), as well as to the high levels of trust Swedes and Norwegians have in one another and in the state (see Helsingen et al., 2020; Hedenigg, 2021; Nielsen & Lindvall, 2021; Gross, 2023).

To make these differences and similarities clearer, so to explore the empirical gaps my study addresses, I will first discuss the literature on Sweden, and thereafter, on Norway. The Swedish state is 'infamous' for having refused to close down society, breaking with the 'global norm', the 'COVID consensus' (see Green, 2021), even if some other states too did refuse to implement lockdowns. The Swedish state relied heavily on voluntarism and self-governance when dealing with COVID-19. This revolved around steering individuals to voluntarily engage in infection control measures by 'nudging' individuals into behaving in an appropriate manner (Girtli Aucante, 2022; Nygren & Olofsson, 2020; Petridou, 2020; Pierre, 2020; Winblad et al., 2022). The Swedish case is often cited as unique (Claeson & Hanson, 2021; Girtli Nygren & Olofsson, 2020, 2021; Holmström, 2021; Kamerlin & Kasson, 2020; Larsson, 2022; Lindström, 2021; Orlowski & Goldsmith 2020; Pierre, 2020). It has been described as 'the Swedish experiment' (see Aucante, 2022; Esaiasson et al., 2021). Moreover, numerous studies seek to explain the 'exceptionalism' of the Swedish COVID-19 response (see Andersson & Aylott, 2020; Claeson & Hanson, 2021; Giritli Nygren & Olofsson, 2021; Holmström, 2021; Jonung, 2020).

Notably, the Swedish state, while swearing to voluntarism as its primary instrument of governance, became less averse to coercion over time, combining voluntarism with 'soft law' (Winblad et al., 2022). This is seen in the ban of gatherings. While initially only targeting gatherings where more than 500 met, the limit was reduced to 50 by the end of March. This is quite modest compared to the Norwegian or other 'typical' bans on gathering. However, in November 2020, the ban was further tightened to 8—equating it with the Norwegian and similar bans (cf Aucante, 2022; Larsson, 2022). The differences between Sweden and the global norm related to the 'COVID consensus' are therefore relative. Moreover, the differences shrank throughout the pandemic, even if the Swedish state remained committed to its approach, and thus never locked down (Aucante, 2022; Winblad et al., 2022). For instance, the Swedish state only started lifting its restriction during the fall of the autumn of 2021, essentially lifting restrictions later than its stricter Western neighbour, Norway, even though this too is early in a global perspective (Aucante, 2022; Winblad et al., 2022). Thus, while not closing down, the Swedish state implemented a system of proscriptions and prescriptions within schools, hospitals, offices and other sites, where personnel had to impose the state's will in local contexts (Aucante, 2022; Larsson, 2022). This essentially entails mobilizing society—an issue which, as will be discussed below, was not adequately handled in either of the two countries.

However, *why* did Sweden act in a softer manner? The pandemic commander-in-chief Anders Tegnell himself has claimed that Swedish law hinders the state from implementing lockdowns (Paterlini 2020; Tegnell 2021). The Swedish Constitution only offers emergency powers of a sovereign nature during military crises (SOU, 2008). Scholars following this understanding have written that the Swedish government and parliament lack legal rights to 'overrule' decisions from the Public Health Agency (Larsson, 2022; Pashakhanlou, 2022; Winblad et al., 2022). Scholars have also posited that the Swedish approach is a result of its decentralized health system and the strong positions of experts (Bylund & Packard 2021; Laage-Thomsen & Frandsen, 2022; Larsson, 2022; Winblad et al., 2022).

Such studies partly illustrate how Sweden differs. While the Swedish path is 'coherent with Sweden's institutional framework and procedures designated for times of crisis and with the lack of specific legal instruments for peacetime emergencies' (Aucante, 2022: 7), this only gives us a hint of why the Swedish state refrained from enforcing stricter measures. As Yohann Aucante (2022: 47) notes, the Swedish state faced similar restrictions of a legal nature as did the Danish state, and Sweden did later alter the legal framework. The Danish state, while one of the first in Europe to close down, had to alter its legal framework for the lockdown of the private sphere to be legal, as it initially lacked the legal capacities to force private actors to close down (see Regeringen, 2020), unlike in Norway, where no such legal barriers existed. The Norwegian state too, however, had a more liberal plan for how the pandemic was to be handled, which also characterized the brief pre-lockdown phase (see Gjerde, 2021a).

Thus, as the governmentality literature posits, we must look towards the political rationalities of the Swedish state. As pointed out by Katarina Giritli Nygren and Anna Olofsson (2020), the Swedish approach revolves largely around a liberal rationality of the utility of responsibilization and voluntarism, combined with concerns about democratic erosion. Oscar Leonard Larsson (2022) also refers to Swedish political fears of creeping authoritarianism, through restrictive biopolitical measures. Similarly, Grothe-Hammer and Roth (2021) argue that the Swedish approach is based around a more holistic problematization of the dangers of the pandemic, which includes concerns beyond the strictly biopolitical fears of COVID-19 itself.

These arguments reveal the roots of the Swedish state's so-called exceptionalism. The Swedish state had a different vision. This relates partly to the fears of what state coercion and top-down governance can do to institutional and legal norms. However, it also relates to how the situation is perceived. The institutional and legal norms which the Swedish state upholds presuppose a norm, but in the absence of normality, such norms are suspended (Schmitt, 1996, 2020). However, there is a fear of what restrictions can do to society. Yet, as of now, this understanding or framework—the discourse underpinning the Swedish strategy—has not been explored. Therefore, this political rationalization has only been alluded to. To handle this issue, I must explore the political rationalizations of the state by exploring the manner in which COVID-19 became a problem in Sweden. Moreover, the literature on the Swedish approach seems to overplay its voluntaristic aspects. The Swedish state also used formal measures, and the state moved beyond the moral mobilization of society, which worked through imposing moral obligations upon citizens to act in accordance with communitarian responsibilities. The state also mobilized society formally. Similarly, the Swedish border control regime has only been alluded to, as referred to below. Moreover, the capacities of the Swedish state, which allow it to govern as such, have not been handled. These gaps will be discussed further below, as they also relate to the Norwegian case. Therefore, they should be addressed together.

The Norwegian state closed down on 12 March 2020. With this, a multitude of restrictions were imposed (Christensen & Lægreid, 2020a, 2020b). The lockdown is comparably soft vis-à-vis other countries, as the Norwegian state refrained from implementing curfews, and allowed certain businesses to remain open (Cheibub et al., 2020; Christensen & Lægreid, 2020a). While the Norwegian lockdown was not 'total', due to the lack of curfews, a multitude of restrictions were imposed. Physical distancing and restrictions on gatherings led to the closing down of schools and other educational facilities, numerous 'non-essential' businesses and cultural and religious activities, were combined with a closed border, which only residents and citizens were allowed to cross. A multitude of proscriptions and prescriptions were imposed upon the population. The ways they were implemented made Hans Petter Graver (2020a, 2020b) declare that the politics of COVID-19 in Norway *resembled* a state of exception in the *Schmittian* sense. While Norway was the strictest of the Scandinavian countries (Conyon et al. 2020; Nanda et al. 2021), the Norwegian response was moderate compared to the strictest countries at the global stage, such as China or Italy (Cheibub et al., 2020; Nanda et al. 2021).

Although the Norwegian strategy was based on both protecting individuals from the virus, protecting the economy and addressing social costs (Ursin et al. 2020), the former motivation had priority at the expense of other issues (Gjerde, 2021a, 2022). This became clear with the lockdown implemented on 12 March 2020 (Christensen & Lægreid,

2020a, 2020b; Sandset & Villadsen, 2023; Staupe-Delgado, 2021). It was decided that it was not enough to slow the propagation of the virus during this time—rather, the virus had to be eradicated from Norway (see Staupe-Delgado, 2021). As Christensen and Lægreid (2020a) note, the state varied between suppression and control strategies, with the former demanding the eradication of the virus, and the latter accepting a low reduction of the diffusion (cf Sandset & Villadsen, 2023).

The Norwegian analysis is re-examined with a Foucauldian lens. This also builds upon previous work of the author, which is rooted in the book, and written prior to the Weberian-Foucauldian merger we shall discuss in the next chapter (i.e. Gjerde, 2021a, 2021b, 2022), which motivates the empirical analyses at hand. This also builds upon the Foucauldian study of Kaspar Villadsen and Tony Sandset (2023). These Norwegian studies have two species of blind-spots which need to be filled, which also relate to the Swedish case. First, there are theoretical gaps, a point in common with the Swedish case. What is the link between these micro-physics of power and the macrophysics of power? How could the Swedish and Norwegian states exercise power in such extensive and intensive ways? While the aforementioned studies are grounded in the Foucauldian work on biopolitics and thus one of Foucault's (2003, 2008a, 2009) attempts to theorize the macrophysics of power, there still remain gaps. Thus, the macro–micro link is relatively neglected, even if Villadsen and Sandset's (2023) study is useful in developing insights on this issue, as they explore the biopolitics of predictive and calculative rule.

This is not to say that the sources of power which enabled the states to govern have been ignored. Of course, the legitimacy of the two states has been referred to. Legitimacy makes the communication campaigns trust-worthy, thereby making individuals more likely to comply (Almlund et al., 2023). Similarly, the administrative capacities of the Norwegian state have been addressed (Christensen & Lægreid, 2020a, 2020b), as has the tech-nocratic bureaucracy in Sweden (Andersson et al., 2022), as well as the expertise and scientific knowledge underpinning and enabling the two states' responses (i.e. Brusselaers et al., 2022; Christensen & Lægreid, 2022). While it has been noted that the Norwegian state's approach revolves around 'a high-trust society with a reliable and professional bureaucracy, a strong state, a good economic situation, a big welfare state, and low population density' (Christensen & Lægreid, 2020a: 774), there has been little theorizing on how this relates to the issue of *state power*—something which has been explored in other countries (i.e. Ali et al.,

2021; Harriss & Luong, 2022; Jiang & Ong, 2022; Lee & Chung, 2023; Weiss & Thurbon, 2022). Studies of a more holistic nature that bring the question of state power explicitly into the picture have not been pursued in Norway and Sweden, something I shall return to below, as I discuss the Foucauldian and Weberian literature inspired by Mann's work on the pandemic.

Moreover, there are numerous empirical gaps. Understandably, the Norwegian studies focus upon the lockdown, its powers and the period when it was in force (i.e. Christensen & Lægreid, 2020a, 2020b; Gjerde, 2021a, 2021b, 2022; Sandset & Villadsen, 2023). However, while the lockdown has been given much attention, how it worked from a Foucauldian perspective has not been thickly described—the Foucauldian work discussing the lockdown has not covered the mechanisms of power working through the lockdown at length. My past study (Gjerde, 2021b) was a more preliminary and descriptive analysis, whereas Sandset and Villadsen (2023) focus upon surveillance of the pathogen and the reproduction number. Hence, how the lockdown itself worked during the pandemic has still only been preliminarily studied.

Moreover, beyond the lockdown, the issue of the ***dugnad***, i.e. the informal mobilization of society, has been granted massive attention from numerous scholars (see Gjerde, 2021b, 2022; Gross, 2023; Moss & Sandbakken, 2021; Nilsen & Skarpnes 2020; Sandbakken & Moss, 2021; Sandset & Villadsen, 2023). A dugnad is a Norwegian communitarian effort deeply embedded within the Norwegian traditions of communitarianism and common efforts. In a dugnad, the individual subordinates narrow personal interests for the common good (Gross, 2023; Moss & Sandbakken, 2021; Nilsen & Skarpnes 2020; Sandbakken & Moss, 2021). The dugnad is a culturally significant Norwegian practice, and thus its relevance as a political and moral practice during the pandemic has for obvious reasons attracted numerous studies. The dugnad was the moral mobilization of society—but as emerges in the analysis, the state also *formally* mobilized society. In Sweden, the focus is upon the apparent exceptionalism of Sweden not closing down when other states do close-down (i.e. Girtli Nygren & Olofsson, 2020). Almlund et al. (2023) make similar notes, as they explore how the communication campaigns in Norway, Sweden and Denmark seek to govern individuals through self-regulation, as also covered in the aforementioned studies. However, while Swedish communitarian ethics and their use as political instruments have been discussed (i.e. Almlund et al., 2023), albeit less than in Norway, a more general study of the politics of COVID-19 in Sweden contextualizing the use of communitarian rhetoric and emotions as parts of a strategic whole, (as has been done in Norway in a *limited* manner, i.e. Gjerde, 2021b; Sandset & Villadsen, 2023) would be useful, as the communication is articulated within a context of numerous political measures. The communication campaign is not autonomous, but a piece in a greater political puzzle.

Through these studies, we see how the regulation of individuals manifests in the governance of mundane activities like washing hands, standing in line or hugging and hand greeting which are formalized and regulated in an infection control manner, as bodies are disciplined and regulated throughout spatial and social spaces, partly through their own voluntary compliance (Almund et al; Giritli Nygren & Olofsson, 2020; Sandset & Villadsen, 2023). These studies cover how private individuals are mobilized through the state's communication campaigns and focus upon voluntarism, albeit without shedding light on how this relates to the ideological power of the state, something I shall discuss more in depth below.

However, this is only part of the issue of mobilization. The mobilization of society is not merely voluntaristic, but also formal and infrastructural (cf Martinez, 2020; Weiss & Thurbon, 2022). Throughout the pandemic in Sweden, and in-between lockdowns in Norway, as in other countries, the state regulated all of social life. The Swedish state regulated more because it denied less—other states were more prone to denying activities from taking place through closing down social sites and events. This regulation is a productive form of power, in Foucauldian terminology. The state imposed infection control regulation criteria on all kinds of social activities by imposing prescriptions and proscriptions on social actors, mobilizing them for infection control purposes. The state acted to make social distancing a part of everyday life for all citizens. This would be the case insofar as citizens were not exclusively confined to their homes, and the more they were allowed to move around society, the more the state would seek to encourage the right behaviour by altering how partying, clubbing, education, etc., would take place. This formalized mobilization through the *conscription* of individuals as infection control agents has not been studied in these two countries.

Similarly, the issue of how the border control regimes of the two countries serve as mechanisms of power and how this was enabled has only been somewhat touched upon. From a Foucauldian perspective, the closed border in Norway has been briefly discussed as a negative assertion of power (i.e. Gjerde, 2021b; Sandset & Villadsen, 2023). Moreover, the border restrictions of all Nordic countries have been discussed (D. Gordon et al., 2021; Gustavsson, 2022; Heinikoski & Hyttinen, 2022). Similarly, past studies cover the experiences regarding border closure of would-be migrants and partners of Norwegian citizens and residents who were denied entry (see Bell et al., 2023), including how the quarantine hotel was discursively framed and experienced (Gjerald & Hande Eslen-Ziya, 2022; Gjerde, 2023). However, the way in which the border worked as an instrument of power to control access, and how the Norwegian and Swedish states in different ways used control over the border to regulate entries, has not been covered beyond blunt exclusions and the quarantine hotel, an important but nevertheless partial aspect of a greater political issue. The manner which quarantine and isolation worked has only been alluded to in Norway, with the manner in which these forms of power worked at the micro-level left relatively unexplored (i.e. Gjerde, 2021b; Sandset & Villadsen, 2023), even if I have conducted a study of state power through the quarantine hotel (Gjerde, 2024a). However, the border control regime, which is a much wider topic than the quarantine hotel, remains unexplored.

Moreover, the aforementioned Foucauldian studies (i.e. Girtli & Nygren 2020; Gjerde, 2021a, 2021b, 2022; Sandset & Villadsen, 2023) operate with abstract data—primarily documents. While useful—and I too operate with such data—I supplement these data with interviews, so to obtain insights from the subjects and objects of governance themselves—something not done with a Foucauldian lens by scholars interested in the issue of power and rule in these two countries. Similarly, I study how the two states define the situation and how it relates to their political strategies. Theoretically, this is a golden opportunity to test the explanatory powers of governmentality studies. This has already been done in a preliminary manner in Norway (i.e. Gjerde, 2021a)—and I build upon this work by digging deeper into the political rationalizations and problematizations while also adding a comparative component as I seek to explore similarities and dissimilarities between the Norwegian and Swedish states' perspectives on the situation. If these similar countries' differences correlate with discursive differences related to the rationalizations of the two states, then this will show how political rationalities have a major impact on political choices, regardless of the cultural, institutional and ideological similarities of the two cases.

Beyond testing the explanatory capacities of the governmentality approach, this also tests the state-centric approach my book builds upon, which posits that the state is autonomous, and that this autonomy can be measured in terms of to what extent the state is able to act according to its own interests (i.e. Mann, 1984, 1986, 1993, 2012; Nordlinger, 1981; Skocpol, 1979). If the two states' different approaches correlate with their rationalizations, then this indicates that state agency was exercised relatively independently of institutional and cultural factors, which the two states largely share. This will chiefly illustrate that state agency and thus state autonomy explain the different pathways chosen during the pandemic. This, as I will further discuss in Chapter 6, will reveal the potency of a governmentality lens, and of an agential approach to the state. Empirically, this allows us to better understand the political reasoning of the two states, and the nature of their choices, which has only been superficially addressed in an empirical manner, and only in Norway (i.e. Gjerde, 2021a).

2.4.1 *Foucault and Mann, a Meeting During the Pandemic?*

While I do aim to fill the aforementioned empirical gaps, I also have theoretical objectives, rooted in years of study. To make this clear, I will contextualize the study within the Foucauldian literature on the politics of COVID-19, focusing on the gaps in the literature which I aim to fill through theorizing in chapter 3 and the empirical analyses using this analytical framework. Note that much has been written on the politics of COVID-19 from a Foucauldian perspective—including by me (i.e. Gjerde, 2021a, 2021b, 2022, 2023).

On the one hand, the pandemic is a perfect case for Foucauldians. Many types of power flow throughout society. Kindergartens and schools, nursing homes and football fields, all serve as sites of power and rule. Overt and subtle forms of power interweave in formal and informal contexts. On the other hand, the picture is somewhat ambiguous for an orthodox Foucauldian, due to the state's active role. This relates to two issues. First, many Foucauldians prefer to study power 'beyond the state' (i.e. Rose 1999; Miller & Rose, 2008; Merlingen, 2011), even though Foucault (2003, 2008a, 2009) explicitly handles the state. However, studies of power 'beyond the state' are naturally less useful within such a state-centric context, where the state is seemingly ineluctable and thus all power relates, directly or indirectly, to the active use of state power.

Indeed, the claim that there are 'multiple' centres of power (i.e. Miller & Rose, 2008: 63) may be right, but the state is the most powerful centre of power, contrary to the reasoning behind prioritizing 'power beyond the state'. At the very least, such a conclusion appears reasonable for a scholar studying the politics of COVID-19, and such a conclusion is supported by Foucauldian work on the pandemic. Second, and perhaps more significantly for our purposes than the issue of prioritization, is what the politics of COVID-19 entails for Foucauldian theorizing about the state. Foucauldians generally deny that the state is an actor. The state is defined as 'a type of governmentality' (Foucault, 2009: 234) and a 'process of continual statification and… a prism' enabling governmental operations to occur and be legitimized (Jessen & Eggers, 2020: 56). Such a conception of the state does not invite scholars to analyse the state's interventions in society, and it has been bracketed by most Foucauldians studying the pandemic.

Before discussing the issue of how the state should be conceptualized in a context where the state is an active subject, I will cover various Foucauldian lessons on the pandemic. Naturally, the Foucauldian scholarship is in many ways well-suited for the context of COVID-19. Therefore, many Foucauldian insights are of an uncontroversial and orthodox nature. The politics of COVID-19 is largely a biopolitical event. After all, the politics of COVID-19 revolves around a political rationale where the objective is to protect public health, fostering and administrating the biological lives of populations (see Baldoli & Radaelli, 2022; Buchanan 2022; Gjerde, 2021a, 2021b, 2022, 2023; Horvath & Lovasz, 2020; Kelly, 2023; Y. Kim, 2021; Walby, 2020). The biopolitical reasoning of the state, which underpins political responses from the lockdown to communication campaigns, is made clear from a Foucauldian perspective. Therefore, it appears appropriate to define the state during the pandemic through the model of Leviathan. The model of Leviathan entails understanding the state as an agent made up of many agents. This model is 'the most powerful image' of the state, showing 'the unity of [the state as] a political entity' dedicated to pacification and ensuring the security of the population (Schmitt, 2008: 5). During the pandemic, the state took Thomas Hobbes' (1996) teachings of the state being the guarantor of security to heart within the context of biopolitics. The state becomes increasingly preoccupied with protecting life. This explains the political responses to the pandemic (Antoniol, 2023; Kapust, 2023). The more sacred life becomes, the more interventionist the state becomes in the face of diseases and the lower the threshold for state intervention. While Foucault (2008a, 2009) asks us to dismiss the model of Leviathan, the Hobbesian understanding of the state is gaining ground as a result of how the state corresponded with Hobbesian imperatives during the pandemic (Antoniol, 2023; Kapust, 2023). I too subscribe to this notion: the COVID-19 state appears to be *biopolitical Leviathan* (cf Gjerde, 2024b).

While the model of Leviathan is useful, it must be noted that Leviathans are not homogenous. Leviathan depends upon a social contract (Hobbes, 1996). Different states will be built on different social contracts, wherein a complex interplay between historic, cultural, political and social factors matter. For instance, democratic states are at times considered 'tamed' Leviathans (see Slater, 2008; Ingrao, 2018). Their structural conditions differ from authoritarian states, like the Chinese or Russian, which are untamed. While liberal states can achieve the same form as authoritarian states during a great crisis, as observed during the pandemic, liberal states 'tamed' nature means that they depend more upon legitimacy and trust to exercise power over their populations in such spectacular ways. However, once a liberal state is legitimate and trusted sufficiently by its citizens, it will hold the capabilities to grow, acting like the great Leviathan making decisions on matters of life and death, normality and abnormality. During the pandemic, Nordic Leviathans obtained their great power through rather than against democratic institutions. However, as I discuss further below, this is a question of social conditions and state-society relations, questions I do not explore in the coming empirical chapters.

Similarly, Foucauldians reveal how the pandemic was largely governed on the basis of the predictive and calculative methods of rule Foucault (1990, 2008a) identifies as the core of biopolitics. The state predicted and calculated infection rates, making interpretations about trends and future trajectories, which then allowed it to decide upon the severity of measures (Jayasinghe et al., 2022; Sandset & Villadsen, 2023). In this regard, surveillance is understood as an instrument granting the state a vision, allowing it to accumulate information which it can use to predict, calculate and thereafter, ground decisions in the abstract knowledge of experts. This knowledge also makes it possible to act in a more efficient manner as the populations and the tendencies within them can be mapped and understood. This is, like the biopolitical problematizations, part of the foundations of the politics of COVID-19. Indeed, knowledge enables power. Increased knowledge increases the potency of power (Foucault,

1980, 1991a), and the state during the pandemic channelled the expertise and knowledge of a multitude of experts and scientists (Couch et al., 2020; Jayasinghe et al., 2022; Sandset & Villadsen, 2023; Sarrazin & Aguirre 2023).

The measures enforced to control the spread of COVID-19 are usually handled by a Foucauldian lens exploring this as a complex web of different types of power. Juridical-sovereignty and discipline, self-regulation and biopolitical calculations and predictions, are typical Foucauldian concepts for studying different forms of power in practice. These various types of power converged at the global stage during the pandemic, as found in various Foucauldian studies discussing the pandemic at an international and theoretical level (Ayala-Colqui, 2020; Colombo, 2020; Hannah et al., 2020; Sotiris, 2020; Wallace et al., 2023). This is also found in studies of individual countries that scholars have examined with Foucauldian lenses. Examples include Sweden (Girtli Nygren & Olofsson, 2020), Estonia and Finland (Makarychev & Romashko, 2020), Norway (Gjerde, 2021a, 2021b; Sandset & Villadsen, 2023), Australia, (Glitsos 2021), China (Habich-Sobiegalla & Plümmer, 2023; Li, 2021; Sun & Wang, 2022), Zimbabwe (Mhazo & Maponga, 2022) and Denmark (Højme, 2022; Triantafillou, 2022). The issue of control, laid out by Gilles Deleuze (1992) based on his reading of Foucault, has also been discussed and analysed (i.e. Leclercq-Vandelannoitte & Aroles, 2020; Oppegaard 2021; Tony See, 2022), while Charles Bowen (2021) reflects upon how discipline and control worked together in complex ways during the pandemic.

Following these Foucauldian studies, one can explore the different ways states governed their territories and populations during the pandemic, as well as the rationalizations and problematizations motivating such government. These studies identify the techniques the respective states in question used to govern their population, for instance through self-regulation, discipline and juridical-sovereignty, usually in a manner where these types converged in complex webs of power, while also discussing issues related to surveillance and the predictive models these states used. As I also find in the case study chapters, the politics of COVID-19 entailed the convergence of various forms of power. This signals a break with the Foucauldian manner of understanding the state and state power, and the identification of this break is the original breeding grounds for the Weberian-Foucauldian theorizing which this book revolves around. For instance, Foucault (1980, 2008b, 2009) dismisses the possibility of exploring the microphysics of power through a state-centric lens, describing the state apparatus as too abstract for such purposes, while dismissing the idea that the state is a centre of power. However, the aforementioned Foucauldian studies, basing themselves explicitly on Foucault's work on power, implicitly contradict him. These studies on the politics of COVID-19 contradict Foucault's theorizing about the relationship between the state and the microphysics of power, as they study how the state itself enforces discipline and juridical-sovereign repression upon entire populations, micro-managing every single social context, including what occurs within private homes, potentially even confining entire populations to their homes, while using self-regulation in a subtler manner. This can be seen by looking towards these studies, which discuss the 'disciplinary and sovereign power exerted by the state' (Sandset & Villadsen, 2023: 623), 'the state's great potential for exercising power' (Gjerde, 2021a: 486), 'state interventions to protect the health of the population' (Mhazo & Maponga, 2022: 2), 'the state's handling of the pandemic' (Triantafillou, 2022: 662) and how 'the state must step in to guide the situation' (Kelly, 2023: 57). They all explicitly conceptualize the state in an agential fashion, analysing it as a political actor in its own right. These studies do not criticize the Foucauldian approach to the state, but simply introduce a non-Foucauldian state theory through the backdoor.

Indeed, even discipline, the prototype of decentralized, non-state (or extra-state) power in the Foucauldian mind, claimed to be capillary and to not emanate from any single centre (see Foucault, 1991a, 2008b; Lemke, 2019), is found to be a manifestation of state power, exercised and exerted by the state. Discipline is analysed as being imposed, coordinated and controlled by the state, acting over and through society. After all, Foucauldians studying this political context enter a political context where the state stood vertically above all others, where the state governed all of society, and where the state's actions manifested at the micro-level, at the level of bodies, thoughts, habits, relations, practices, etc.

Some seek to keep the Foucauldian theory of the state intact by referring to the politics of COVID-19 as diverse and dispersive, and thus not under the control of the single entity of the state (i.e. Bhowmick & Alam, 2023; Makarychev et al., 2020). These other studies all implicitly disregard the Foucauldian theory of the state, by a) analysing the state as an actor, and b) dealing with the state as a centre of power, which regulated, controlled and exercised numerous types of power in an impressive governmental operation. As the state performs actions, so it is necessary to conceptualize it as an actor (Neumann & Sending, 2021). The aforementioned studies, defining the state as an actor, seemingly implicitly work with a Weberian understanding of the state, as a political organization with agency (see Mann, 1984, 1986, 1993; Weber 1978). However, as the theory of the state is implicit, so a key question is left unanswered. How can the state act in such ways? These studies consist of an implicit synthesizing, as Foucauldians studying the pandemic leave the Foucauldian definition of the state, for an agential approach. This synthesis can be made explicit, through Weberian-Foucauldian theory-building. This way, I can also ask and answer the question of how states can govern as such. However, can I make the Weberian and Foucauldian approaches to the question of (state) power compatible, so to formalize these analytical choices, into a coherent theoretical framework? Before I illustrate how I believe this can be done—and thereby pave the way for the theory-building in the next chapter—I wish to show that there are benefits to be made for both parties through this 'bridge building' (Checkel, 2012).

To explore these issues, it is useful to start by looking at how the Weberian theory of the state has been applied by scholars leaning upon Michael Mann's theory of the *sources* of state power. This theory has been successfully applied in Bangladesh (Ali et al., 2021), China (Jiang & Ong, 2022), South Korea (Lee & Chung, 2023), Australia and the United Kingdom (Weiss & Thurbon, 2022), Argentina, Bolivia, Brazil, Chile, Colombia, Paraguay, Peru and Uruguay (González-Bustamante, 2021) as well as India, Pakistan, Vietnam and South Korea (J. Harris & Luong 2022). In these studies, the state has been analysed in a Weberian manner, as an actor with capacities based on sources of power caged within the state machinery. This is central, as Weiss and Thurbon (2022) reveal, similar states, with cultural, institutional and ideological similarities, both isolated as islands, i.e. the UK and Australia, performed and acted very differently. As they note: 'political choice takes on a special significance in a national emergency' (Weiss & Thurbon, 2022: 699). This calls for an agential lens—which takes political choices into account. This is also necessary to understand the issue of state power—as '[p]olitical choice can enable dormant capacities to be activated' (Weiss & Thurbon, 2022: 705). Without an agential perspective on the state, one can hardly study how similar states act differently, because the cultural and institutional factors can be bracketed or ignored by political agency. Lacking an agential theory of the state, the politics of COVID-19 becomes enigmatic, as shown especially in cases where culturally, ideologically and institutionally similar states act and perform differently—such as in the case of Australia and the UK for Weiss and Thurbon, or Norway and Sweden for us. The Weberian perspective based on Mann's work allows scholars to understand how power is activated in the manner in which the aforementioned Foucauldian studies show that it is activated—it invites us to explore the resources of the state and how they are used.

While the aforementioned studies focus on institutional capacities, some studies prioritize studying the coercive powers of the state. For instance, pandemic politics in the Philippines is found to be characterized by weak institutional capacities and strong coercive capacity, leading to the politics of COVID-19 assuming an iron-fisted approach based on repressive measures (Hutchcroft & Gera, 2022). Similarly, coercive power is found to be key in the Chinese politics of COVID-19, where the state, which as mentioned above uses massive infrastructural capacities, also employs severely stringent measures, such as checkpoints and strictly enforced quarantine and curfew rules (Fu, 2023). However, the focus upon state coercion is at least somewhat narrow, as the concept is most commonly employed in contexts where authors find the state to be especially coercive. But as I briefly touched upon above, coercion is part of the core of the politics of COVID-19 in general. This is not merely the case in cases like the Chinese, but also in democratic and liberal countries, such as Norway, and to a lesser extent, Sweden. I shall explore this issue in the analysis. Moreover, pandemic surveillance is explored as enabled by infrastructural power (see Cingolani, 2023; Tréguer, 2021), as is the vaccination campaign (see Tubi, 2022). These valuable contributions to the issue of state power have not been carried out in Scandinavia, even if this lens has been used to study how digital mass media serve as an infrastructural resource for the distribution of information (see Kristensen & Hartley, 2023). These studies complement the Foucauldian studies on biopolitics and the power of knowledge, surveillance and predictions (cf Jayasinghe et al., 2022; Sandset & Villadsen, 2023), but with a different lens.

Looking at said states, the scholars at hand ask how the massive regulation of society which these states engaged in was possible, exploring the infrastructural resources of both strong states, such as China, and weaker states, such as Bangladesh. The potency of the state bureaucracy, its relationship with society, as well as infrastructural aspects of society such as literacy rates, and the technological and material infrastructure of society more generally, affects how efficient the states can act, altering the manner in which they can implement their policies throughout society (see J. Harriss & Luong, 2022). These studies show us the power of the state, and they explain how lockdowns, communication campaigns and other measures are made possible by the sources of power 'caged' within the state (cf Mann, 1993). Moreover, they make clear that similar states' actions must be taken into account, as sources of power do not automatically translate into practice (Weiss & Thurbon, 2022). Taking these insights seriously, one can enrich the Foucauldian approach by exploring the state as an actor, taking into account how the state can act as it does by examining the resources it employs.

However, this is not a unilateral issue. The Weberian approach based on Mann's work also has gaps. Beyond potentially granting infrastructural power too much priority vis-à-vis coercive power, the analyses are highly abstract. For instance, administrative capacity and the manner in which civil services are organized and professionalized, including the capacity of the healthcare sector, is explored in South America (see González-Bustamante, 2021). This is useful for exploring state capacity, but it tells us little about how this capacity *manifests* in practice. What does administrative capacities do, and how do they work in social contexts, such as classrooms, private homes, and offices? How do they structure the lives of populations? Similarly, Weiss and Thurbon (2022) note that infrastructural power allows the state to mobilize society. This is interesting—and an issue which I must address in Norway and Sweden since it has not been explored, as already observed above. But how does the mobilization occur? What does it entail to mobilize society? Using a Foucauldian approach, Habich-Sobiegalla and Plümmer (2023) discuss how grid managers in charge of local communities in China were mobilized by the Chinese state: more than 4 million managers in charge of 650,000 communities across the country. These managers, local actors not formally employed by the state, but members of their local communities, were made responsible for numerous infection control objectives, such as: managing quarantine rules, dividing responsibilities among residents, defining hygiene standards and controlling entry and exit to the communities during curfews where individuals could not legally leave their neighbourhoods. This mobilization resulted in numerous mechanisms of disciplinary power combined with biopolitical, predictive models for ruling. Combining a Weberian and Foucauldian approach I can tease out the link between how mobilization manifested in practice through how power works, and how the mobilization was enabled by the state enacting the sources of power it contains.

Naturally, one cannot criticize the Weberian studies based on Mann's work for being too abstract. The studies do what they are meant to—they explore the sources of power, which enhances capacities, so to explore how the state governs during the crisis, based on said capacities. Similarly, we cannot criticize the Foucauldian studies for focusing upon the mechanisms of power. They show how power manifests at the level of bodies, thoughts, relations, etc. However, there is a clear symmetry between these approaches to state power during the pandemic. One approach covers the macro-level of what a Foucauldian could call the macrophysics of power. Another covers the microphysics of power. Seemingly, these two approaches complement one another—thereby allowing us to do some compatibility work for the purpose of 'bridge building' (Checkel, 2012). If we combine these two approaches, we may obtain a powerful analytical lens for exploring the state and state power during the pandemic, as well as similar crises, and, within the state-centric context of our lives, likely for studying social and political life in general. This combination of two theoretical traditions allows us to explore both the state as an actor, the resources enabling the state to act as such (i.e. infrastructural power; coercive power) and the mechanisms of power manifesting when the state acts as such (i.e. discipline; self-regulation).

This is not the first step in such a direction. Many steps have been taken through the aforementioned Foucauldian studies, including by me (i.e. Gjerde, 2021a, 2021b, 2022), by the *silent* and *implicit* appropriation of a Weberian lens when exploring the state as an implicit actor exercising power in a manner creating numerous mechanisms of power in practice. I believe that formally marrying these two approaches, thereby ending this hidden love affair, making it official, may enrich the Foucauldian literature, by granting it an explicit state-centric approach suitable for the many contexts where the state has a dominant or at least important role, as an actor. I believe that this can be done within the spirit of Foucauldian scholarship, and I believe this is necessary, as the agential lens of Foucauldians studying state power shapes the state's agency as a black box of sorts. The state acts, but how can it act? How can discipline be enacted by the state, when discipline is a mechanism beyond the state's control? Indeed, discipline is a network of forces existing in action within relations based on institutional arrangements. How can it be enacted? The theoretical 'marriage' will allow me to uncover this issue.

References

Ackerknecht, E. H. (2009). Anticontagionism between 1821 and 1867: The Fielding H Garrison Lecture. *International Journal of Epidemiology, 38*(1), 7–21.

Ali, T. O., Hassan, M., & Hossain, N. (2021). The moral and political economy of the pandemic in Bangladesh: Weak states and strong societies during Covid-19. *World Development, 137*, Article 105216.

Almlund, P., E Kjeldsen, J., & Mølster, R. (2023). Expressions of governance, risk, and responsibility: Public campaigns in the crisis and risk management of Covid-19 in Denmark, Norway, and Sweden. In B. Johansson, Ø. Ihlen, J. Lindholm, & M. Blach-Ørsten (Eds.), *Communicating a pandemic: Crisis management and Covid-19 in the Nordic countries* (pp. 121–149). University of Gothenburg.

Andersson, S., & Aylott, N. (2020). Sweden and coronavirus: Unexceptional exceptionalism. *Social Sciences, 9*(12), 232.

Andersson, S., Aylott, N., & Eriksson, J. (2022). Democracy and technocracy in Sweden's experience of the COVID-19 pandemic. *Frontiers in Political Science, 4*, Article 832518.

Anisin, A. (2022). Pandemic surveillance capitalism: Authoritarian liberalism or democratic backsliding? *Journal of Political Power, 15*(2), 262–278.

Antoniol, V. (2023). Metamorphosis of biopolitics. A Foucauldian ecological perspective and the challenge of the pandemic: A review essay of Ottavio Marzocca, biopolitics for beginners. Knowledge of life and government of people. *Foucault Studies* (No. 35), 229–239. https://doi.org/10.22439/fs.i35.7082

Aucante, Y. (2022). *The Swedish experiment. The COVID-19 response and its controversies.* Bristol University Press.

Ayala-Colqui, J. (2020). Viropolitics and capitalistic governmentality: On the management of the early 21st century pandemic. *Desde El Sur, 12*(2), 377–395.

Baekkeskov, E., Rubin, O., & Öberg, P. (2021). Monotonous or pluralistic public discourse? Reason-giving and dissent in Denmark's and Sweden's early 2020 COVID-19 responses. *Journal of European Public Policy, 28*(8), 1321–1343.

Baldoli, R., & Radaelli, C. M. (2022). Unity in fragility: Nonviolence and COVID-19. *Italian Political Science Review/rivista Italiana di Scienza Politica, 52*(3), 378–390.

Balmus, B. (2012). *Plague, quarantines and geopolitics in the Ottoman Empire.* Edinburgh University Press.

Bar-Siman-Tov, I. (2020). COVID-19 meets politics: The novel coronavirus as a novel challenge for legislatures. *The Theory and Practice of Legislation, 8*(1–2), 11–48. https://doi.org/10.1080/20508840.2020.1800250

Bell, J., Staver, A. B., & Tolgensbakk, I. (2023). '"I am torn to pieces" transnational citizenship and COVID-19'. In M. Takle, J. Solstad Vedeler, M. Schoyen, K. Klette-Bøhler & A. Falch-Eriksen (Eds.), *Citizenship and social exclusion at the margins of the welfare state* (pp 162–174). Routledge.

Bhowmick, S., & Alam, M. (2023). Foucault meets novel coronavirus: Biosociality, excesses of governmentality and the "will to live" of the pandemicariat. *Foucault Studies* (No. 35), 145–166. https://doi.org/10.22439/fs.i35.7088

Bjørkdahl, K., Kjeldsen, J. E., Villadsen, L., & Vigsø, O. (2021). Argumentum ad solidaritatem: Rhetorical leadership strategies in Scandinavia during COVID-19. Communicating COVID-19: *Interdisciplinary Perspectives*, 163–184.

Blair, R. A., Morse, B. S., & Tsai, L. L. (2017). Public health and public trust: Survey evidence from the Ebola Virus Disease epidemic in Liberia. *Social Science & Medicine, 172*, 89–97.

Bolaños, I. A. (2019). The Ottomans during the global crises of cholera and plague: the view from Iraq and the Gulf. *International Journal of Middle East Studies, 51*(4), 603–620.

Bowen, C. (2021). Discipline and control and Covid-19. *La Deleuziana, 13*, 164–175.

Bronza, B. (2019). Austrian measures for prevention and control of the plague epidemic along the border with the Ottoman Empire during the 18th century. *Scripta Medica, 50*(4), 177–184.

Brusselaers, N., Steadson, D., Bjorklund, K., Breland, S., Stilhoff Sörensen, J., Ewing, A., …, & Steineck, G. (2022). Evaluation of science advice during the COVID-19 pandemic in Sweden. *Humanities and Social Sciences Communications, 9*(1).

Buchanan, I. (2022). Biopolitics, Discipline and Governmentality. In: Das, S. S., and Pratihar, A. R. (eds.). *Technology, Urban Space and the Networked Community*. Cham: Palgrave Macmillan (1–28).

Bylund, P. L., & Packard, M. D. (2021). Separation of power and expertise: evidence of the tyranny of experts in Sweden's COVID-19 responses. *Southern Economic Journal, 87*(4), 1300–1319.

Capano, G. (2020). Policy design and state capacity in the COVID-19 emergency in Italy: If you are not prepared for the (un)expected, you can be only what you already are. *Policy and Society, 39*(3), 326–344. https://doi.org/10.1080/14494035.2020.1783790

cbp.gov. (2020). United States Border Patrol. https://www.cbp.gov/sites/default/files/assets/documents/2020-Jan/U.S.%20Border%20Patrol%20Fiscal%20Year%20Staffing%20Statistics%20%28FY%201992%20-%20FY%202019%29_0.pdf

Checkel, J. T. (2012). Theoretical pluralism IR: Possibilities and limits. In W. Carlsnaes, T. Risse, & B. A. Simmons (Eds.), *Handbook of international relations* (pp. 220–241). Sage.

Cheibub, J. A., Hong, J. Y. J., & Przeworski, A. (2020). Rights and deaths: Government reactions to the pandemic. Working paper. https://doi.org/10.2139/ssrn.3645410

Christensen, T., Jensen, M. D., Kluth, M., Kristinsson, G. H., Lynggaard, K., Lægreid, P., ..., & Adolf Skúlason, G. (2023). The Nordic governments' responses to the Covid-19 pandemic: A comparative study of variation in governance arrangements and regulatory instruments. *Regulation & Governance, 17*(3), 658–676.

Christensen, T., & Lægreid, P. (2020a). Balancing governance capacity and legitimacy: How the Norwegian Government handled the COVID−19 crisis as a high performer. *Public Administration Review, 80*(5), 774–779. https://doi.org/10.1111/puar.13241

Christensen, T., & Lægreid, P. (2020b). The coronavirus crisis—Crisis communication, meaning-making, and reputation management. *International Public Management Journal, 23*(5), 713–729.

Christensen, T., & Lægreid, P. (2022). Scientization under pressure—The problematic role of expert bodies during the handling of the COVID-19 pandemic. *Public Organization Review, 22*(2), 291–307.

Cingolani, L. (2023). Infrastructural state capacity in the digital age: What drives the performance of COVID-19 tracing apps? *Governance, 36*(1), 275–297.

Claeson, M., & Hanson, S. (2021). COVID-19 and the Swedish enigma. *The Lancet, 397*(10271), 259–261.

Colombo, E. (2020). Human rights-inspired Governmentality: COVID-19 through a Human Dignity Perspective. *Critical Sociology*. https://doi.org/10.1177/0896920520971846

Conner, S. P. (2017). The paradoxes and contradictions of prostitution in Paris. In M. R. García, L. H. van Voss, & E. van Nederveen Meerkerk (Eds.), *Selling sex in the city: A global history of prostitution, 1600s–2000s* (pp. 171–200). Brill. http://www.jstor.org/stable/10.1163/j.ctv2gjwwht.12

Conyon, M., He, L., & Thomsen, S. (2020). Lockdowns and COVID-19 deaths in Scandinavia. *Available at SSRN* 3616969.

Couch, D. L., Robinson, P., & Komesaroff, P. A. (2020). COVID-19—Extending surveillance and the panopticon. *Journal of Bioethical Inquiry, 17*, 809–814.

Dean, M. (1999). *Governmentality: Power and rule in modern society*. Sage.

Deleuze, G. (1992). *Postscript on the society of control*. October 59:3–8

Esaiasson, P., Sohlberg, J., Ghersetti, M., & Johansson, B. (2021). How the coronavirus crisis affects citizen trust in institutions and in unknown others: Evidence from 'the Swedish experiment.' *European Journal of Political Research, 60*(3), 748–760.

Foucault, M. (1990). The history of sexuality, volume 1. An introduction. London: Penguin Books

Foucault, M. (1991a). *Discipline and punish: The birth of the prison.* Penguin Books.

Foucault. (1991b). Governmentality. In G. Burchell, C. Gordon, & P. Miller (Eds.), *The Foucault effect: Studies in governmentality.* The University of Chicago Press.

Foucault, M. (1994a). *The birth of social medicine.* In F. D. Faubion, M. Foucault (Eds.), *Power. Essential works of Foucault 1954–1984 volume 3* (pp. 134–156). The New Press.

Foucault, M. (1994b). The politics of health in the eighteenth century. In F. D. Faubion (Ed.), *Michel Foucault. Power. Essential works of Foucault 1954–1984 Volume* 3 (pp. 90–105). The New Press.

Foucault, M. (1980). *Power/Knowledge.* Pantheon books.

Foucault, M. (1985). *Discourse and truth: The problematization of Parrhesia.* Northwestern University Press.

Foucault, M. (2003). *Society must be defended: Lectures at Collège De France,* 1975–1976. New York: Pidacor

Foucault, M. (2008a). *The birth of biopolitics - Lectures at the Collège de France, 1978–1979.* Palgrave Macmillan.

Foucault, M. (2008b). *Psychiatric power: Lectures at the College de France, 1973–1974.* Macmillan.

Foucault, M. (2009). *Security, territory, population: Lectures at Collège de France, 1977–1978.* Palgrave Macmillan.

Fu, H. (2023). Pandemic control in China's gated communities. In C. Loh (Ed.), *How COVID-19 took over the world: Lessons for the future with comparative perspectives from health, politics, and socio-economics* (pp. 167–192). Hong Kong University Press.

Giritli Nygren, K., & Olofsson, A. (2020). Managing the COVID-19 pandemic through individual responsibility: The consequences of a world risk society and enhanced ethopolitics, *Journal of Risk Research.*

Giritli Nygren, K., & Olofsson, A. (2021). Swedish exceptionalism, herd immunity and the welfare state: A media analysis of struggles over the nature and legitimacy of the COVID-19 pandemic strategy in Sweden. *Current Sociology, 69*(4), 529–546.

Gjerald, O., & Hande Eslen-Ziya, H. (2022). From discontent to action: #quarantinehotel as not just a hashtag. *Cogent Social Sciences, 8*(1), 2051806. https://doi.org/10.1080/23311886.2022.2051806

Gjerde, L. E. L. (2022). Den norske regjeringens diskursive muliggjøring av koronapolitikken: Et Foucauldiansk perspektiv. *Norsk Sosiologisk Tidsskrift*, (3), 29–45. https://doi.org/10.18261/nost.6.3.3

Gjerde, L. E. L. (2024a). Marrying the sources and mechanisms of power? Understanding the quarantine hotel through Michel Foucault and Michael Mann. *Journal of Political Power*. https://doi.org/10.1080/2158379X.2024.2337617

Gjerde, L. E. L. (2024b). Biopolitical Leviathan: Understanding state power in the era of COVID-19 through the Weberian-Foucauldian theory of the state. *Theoria: A Journal of Social and Political Theory, 71*(1), 48–74. https://doi.org/10.3167/th.2024.7117803

Gjerde, L. E. L. (2021a). From liberalism to biopolitics: Investigating the Norwegian government's two responses to COVID-19. *European Societies, 23*(sup1), S262–S274. https://doi.org/10.1080/14616696.2020.1824003

Gjerde, L. E. L. (2021b). Governing humans and 'things': Power and rule in Norway during the Covid-19 pandemic. *Journal of Political Power, 14*(3), 472–492. https://doi.org/10.1080/2158379X.2020.1870264

Gjerde, L. E. L. (2023). Biopolitical and juridical creations of the quarantine hotel: A discourse analysis of the Norwegian case. *Acta Sociologica, 66*(4), 357–371. https://doi.org/10.1177/00016993221136038

Glitsos, L. (2021). COVID-19 and the 'perfectly governed city.' *Journal for Cultural Research*. https://doi.org/10.1080/14797585.2021.194381

González-Bustamante, B. (2021). Evolution and early government responses to COVID-19 in South America. *World Development, 137*, Article 105180.

Gordon, D. V., Grafton, R. Q., & Steinshamn, S. I. (2021). Cross-country effects and policy responses to COVID-19 in 2020: The Nordic countries. *Economic Analysis and Policy, 71*, 198–210.

Graver, H. P. (2020b). *Pandemi og unntakstilstand. Hva covid-19 sier om den norske rettstaten*. Dreyers Forlag.

Graver, H. P. (2020a). COVID-19 regulation in Norway and state of exception. COVID-19 and constitutional law (pp. 167–175). Universidad Nacional Autónoma de México.

Green, T. (2021). *The Covid consensus: The new politics of global inequality*. Hurst.

Greene, A. (2021). *Emergency powers in a time of pandemic*. Bristol University Press.

Grindheim, J. E. (2021). Hva kan vi lære av kampen mot tuberkulosen i kampen mot covid-19?«Spytt ikkje på golvet! Host ikkje mot nokon!». *Tidsskrift for Velferdsforskning, 24*(2), 1–14.

Gross, L. (2023). "Not a major or complicated task": Activating Dugnad under COVID-19 and the imagination of equality in the Norwegian welfare state. *Anthropologica, 65*(1).

Grothe-Hammer, M., & Roth, S. (2021). Dying is normal, dying with the coronavirus is not: A sociological analysis of the implicit norms behind the criticism of Swedish 'exceptionalism.' *European Societies, 23*(sup1), S332–S347.

Habich-Sobiegalla, S., & Plümmer, F. (2023). Topologies of power in China's grid-style social management during the COVID-19 pandemic. *Security Dialogue, 54*(2), 192–210.

Hannah, M., Hutta, J. S., & Schemann, C. (2020). Thinking Corona measures with Foucault. *Zitierdatum, 14*, 20.

Hanrieder, T., & Kreuder-Sonnen, C. (2014). WHO decides on the exception? Securitization and emergency governance in global health. *Security Dialogue, 45*(4), 331–348.

Harriss, J., & Luong, H. V. (2022). Covid-19 in Asia: governance and the politics of the pandemic. *Pacific Affairs, 95*(4), 685–706.

Hedenigg, S. (2021). "In others we trust": Finland and Norway-high trust societies in the COVID-19 pandemic. *Interdisciplinary Journal of Partnership Studies, 8*(2), 3–3.

Heinikoski, S., & Hyttinen, T. (2022). The impact of Covid-19 on the free movement regime in the North: Analysis of border closures in Denmark, Finland, Norway and Sweden. *Nordic Journal of International Law, 91*(1), 80–100.

Helsingen, L. M., Refsum, E., Gjøstein, D. K., Løberg, M., Bretthauer, M., Kalager, M., & Emilsson, L. (2020). The COVID-19 pandemic in Norway and Sweden–threats, trust, and impact on daily life: A comparative survey. *BMC Public Health, 20*(1), 1–10.

Henderson, J. (2018). "Filth is the mother of corruption": Plague, the poor and the environment in early modern Florence. In L. Engelmann, J. Henderson, & C. Lynteris (Eds.), *Plague and the city. Body and the city* (pp. 69–90). Routledge.

Hobbes, T. (1996). *Leviathan*. Oxford University Press.

Højme, P. (2022). Biopolitics and the COVID-19 Pandemic: A Foucauldian interpretation of the Danish government's response to the pandemic. *Philosophies, 7*(2), 34.

Holmström, M. (2021). Sverige sämst i Norden: Långsam och otillräcklig krishantering ledde till högsta andelen döda i covid-19. *Statsvetenskaplig tidskrift, 123*(5).

Horvath, M., & Lovasz, A. (2020). Foucault in the age of COVID-19: Permitting contingency in biopolitics. *Identities: Journal for Politics, Gender and Culture* (1), 144–153.

Hutchcroft, P. D., & Gera, W. (2022). Strong-arming, weak steering: Central-local relations in the Philippines in the era of the pandemic. *Philippine Political Science Journal, 43*(2), 123–167.

Ingrao, B. (2018). The dream to tame the Leviathan: Authoritarian power and the market. In Mosca, M (Ed.), *Power in economic thought* (pp. 17–49). Palgrave Macmillan.

Jayasinghe, K., Jayasinghe, T., Wijethilake, C., & Adhikari, P. (2022). Biopolitics and calculative technologies in COVID-19 governance: Reflections from England. *International Journal of Health.*

Jensen, A. F. (2020). *Brave new normal. Learning from epidemics.* Philosophers.net.

Jessen, M. H., & von Eggers, N. (2020). Governmentality and statification: Towards a Foucauldian theory of the state. *Theory, Culture & Society, 37*(1), 53–72.

Jiang, G., & Ong, L. (2022). Strengthening the state through crisis management: Battles against the SARS and COVID-19 pandemics in China. *Issues & Studies, 58*(03), 2250002.

Jonung, L. (2020). Sweden's constitution decides its COVID-19 exceptionalism. *SSRN*. https://doi.org/10.2139/ssrn.3796848

Kamerlin, S. C., & Kasson, P. M. (2020). Managing coronavirus disease 2019 spread with voluntary public health measures: Sweden as a case study for pandemic control. *Clinical Infectious Diseases, 71*(12), 3174–3181.

Kapust, D. J. (2023). Plague and the Leviathan. *Hobbes Studies, 1*(aop), 1–13.

Kelly, M. G. E. (2023). Securing the pandemic: Biopolitics, capital, and COVID-19. *Foucault Studies*, (No. 35), 42–65. https://doi.org/10.22439/fs.i35.7072

Kim, Y. (2021). Bio or Zoe?: Dilemmas of biopolitics and data governmentality during COVID-19. *Cultural Studies, 35*(2–3), 370–381.

Kristensen, L. M., & Hartley, J. M. (2023). The Infrastructure of news: Negotiating infrastructural capture and autonomy in data-driven news distribution. *Media and Communication, 11*(2), 307–318.

Laage-Thomsen, J., & Frandsen, S. L. (2022). Pandemic preparedness systems and diverging COVID-19 responses within similar public health regimes: A comparative study of expert perceptions of pandemic response in Denmark, Norway, and Sweden. *Globalization and Health, 18*(1), 1–18.

Larsson, O. L. (2022). The Swedish Covid-19 strategy and voluntary compliance: Failed securitisation or constitutional security management? *European Journal of International Security, 7*(2), 226–247.

Leclercq-Vandelannoitte, A., & Aroles, J. (2020). Does the end justify the means? Information systems and control society in the age of pandemics. *European Journal of Information Systems, 29*(6), 746–761.

Lee, H., & Chung, K. H. (2023). Explaining South Korea's COVID-19 response through various levels of the institution. *Korea Observer, 54*(2), 205–225.

Lemke, T. (2019). *Foucault's analysis of modern government. A critique of political reason.* Verso.

Li, M. (2021). Biopolitical practices in Beijing. *European Review, 29*(6), 805–818.

Lindström, M. (2021). The New Totalitarians: The Swedish COVID-19 strategy and the implications of consensus culture and media policy for public health. *SSM-Population Health, 14*, Article 100788.

Lipscy, P. (2020). COVID-19 and politics of crisis. *International Organization*, (No. 74), 1–30.

Makarychev, A., & Romashko, T. (2020). Precarious sovereignty in a Post-liberal Europe: The COVID-19 Emergency in Estonia and Finland. *Chinese Political Science Review*, 1–23.

Makarychev, A., Goes, M., & Kuznetsova, A. (2020). The Covid biopolitics in Russia: Putin's sovereignty versus regional governmentality. *Mezinárodní Vztahy, 55*(4), 31–47.

Malm, A. (2020). *Corona, climate, chronic emergency: War communism in the twenty-first century*. Verso.

Mann, M. (1986). *The sources of social power. Volume 1. A history of power from the beginning to A.D. 1760*. Cambridge University Press.

Mann, M. (1993). *The sources of social power, volume II: The rise of classes and nation states*. Cambridge University Press.

Mann, M. (2012). *The sources of social power. Volume 3. Global empires and Revolution, 1890–1945*. Cambridge University Press.

Mann, M. (1984). The autonomous power of the state: Its origins, mechanisms and results. *European Journal of Sociology, 25*(2), 185–213.

Martinez, C. (2020). Karl Marx in Wuhan: How Chinese socialism is defeating COVID-19. *International Critical Thought, 10*(2), 311–322. https://doi.org/10.1080/21598282.2020.1779504

Merlingen, M. (2011). From governance to governmentality in CSDP: Towards a Foucauldian research agenda. *JCMS: Journal of Common Market Studies, 49*(1), 149–169.

Mhazo, A. T., & Maponga, C. C. (2022). Governing a pandemic: Biopower and the COVID-19 response in Zimbabwe. *BMJ Global Health, 7*(12), Article e009667.

Miller, P., & Rose, N. (2008). *Governing the present: Administering economic, social and political life*. Polity Press.

Moisio, S. (2020). 'State Power and the COVID-19 Pandemic: The Case of Finland'. *Eurasian Geography and Economics*, 1–8. https://doi.org/10.1080/15387216.2020.1782241.

Moss, S. M., & Sandbakken, E. M. (2021). "Everybody needs to do their part, so we can get this under control." Reactions to the norwegian government meta-narratives on COVID-19 measures. *Political Psychology, 42*(5), 881–898.

Nanda, M., Aashima, & Sharma, R. (2021). COVID-19: a comprehensive review of epidemiology and public health system response in Nordic region. *International Journal of Health Services*, *51*(3), 287–299.

Neumann, I. B., & Sending, O. J. (2021). Performing statehood through crises: Citizens, strangers, territory. *Journal of Global Security Studies*, *6*(1), ogz073.

Nielsen, J. H., & Lindvall, J. (2021). Trust in government in Sweden and Denmark during the COVID-19 epidemic. *West European Politics*, *44*(5–6), 1180–1204.

Nordlinger, E. (1981). *The autonomy of the democratic state*. Harvard University Press.

Ólafsson, J. G. (2021). Iceland: No lockdown and experts at the forefront. In D. Lilleker, I. Coman, M. Gregor, & E. Novelli (Eds.), *Political communication and COVID-19: Governance and rhetoric in times of crisis* (pp. 239–247). Routledge.

Onuh, P. A. (2021). Nigeria's response to COVID-19: Lockdown policy and human rights violations. *African Security*, *14*(4), 439–459.

Oppegaard, S. M. (2021). Kontrollsamfunnet og nyliberalismen: Makt og samtidsdiagnoser hos Deleuze og Foucault. *Agora*, *38*(3–4), 07–35.

Orlowski, E. J., & Goldsmith, D. J. (2020). Four months into the COVID-19 pandemic, Sweden's prized herd immunity is nowhere in sight. *Journal of the Royal Society of Medicine*, *113*(8), 292–298.

Pandey, A., & Galvani, A. P. (2019). The global burden of HIV and prospects for control. *The Lancet HIV*, *6*(12), e809–e811.

Pashakhanlou, A. H. (2022). Sweden's coronavirus strategy: The Public Health Agency and the sites of controversy. *World Medical & Health Policy*, *14*(3), 507–527.

Paterlini, M. (2020) Closing borders is ridiculous': the epidemiologist behind Sweden's controversial coronavirus strategy, https://www.nature.com/articles/d41586-020-01098-x

Petridou, E. (2020). Politics and administration in times of crisis: Explaining the Swedish response to the COVID-19 crisis. *European Policy Analysis*, *6*(2), 147–158.

Pierre, J. (2020). Nudges against pandemics: Sweden's COVID-19 containment strategy in perspective. *Policy and Society*, *39*(3), 478–493.

Porter, D. (1999). *Health, civilization, and the state: A history of public health from ancient to modern times*. Routledge.

Rawcliffe, C., & Weeda, C. (2019). Introduction. In C. Weeda (Ed.), *Carole Rawcliffe* (pp. 11–38). Amsterdam University Press.

Regeringen. (2020). Situationen kommer til at stille kæmpe krav til os alle sammen. https://www.regeringen.dk/nyheder/2020/statsminister-mette-frederiksens-indledning-paa-pressemoede-i-statsministeriet-om-corona-virus-den-11-marts-2020/

Rose, N. (1999). Powers of freedom: reframing political thought. Cambridge: Cambridge University Press.
Rosenberg, C. E. (1989). What is an epidemic? AIDS in historical perspective. *Daedalus*, 1–17.
Sandbakken, E. M., & Moss, S. M. (2021). "Now we are all in the same boat. At the same time, we are not." Meaning-making and coping under COVID-19 lockdown in Norway. *Human Arenas*, 1–25.
Sandset, T., & Villadsen, K. (2022). Pandemic modelling and model citizens: Governing COVID-19 through predictive models, sovereignty and discipline. *The Sociological Review*, 003802612211020.
Sandset, T., & Villadsen, K. (2023). Pandemic modelling and model citizens: Governing COVID-19 through predictive models, sovereignty and discipline. *The Sociological Review*, 00380261221102023.
Sarrazin, J.-P., & Aguirre. (2023). Governmentality, science and the media. Examining the "pandemic reality" with Foucault, Lyotard and Baudrillard. *Foucault Studies* (No. 35), 17–41. https://doi.org/10.22439/fs.i35.7073
Schmitt, S. (2020). *Political theology* (2nd ed.). Antelope Hill Publishing.
Schmitt, C. (1996). *The concept of the political.* University of Chicago Press.
Schmitt, C. (2008). *Leviathan in the state theory of Thomas Hobbes. Meaning and failure of a political system.* The University of Chicago Press.
Schmitt, C. (2014). *Dictatorship.* Polity Press.
Scott, J. C. (2017). *Against the grain: A deep history of the earliest state.* Yale University Press.
Skocpol, T. (1979). *States and social revolutions. A comparative analysis of France, Russia and China.* Cambridge University Press.
Slater, D. (2008). Can Leviathan be democratic? Competitive elections, robust mass politics, and state infrastructural power. *Studies in Comparative International Development, 43*, 252–272.
Snowden, F. M. (2020). *Epidemics and society: From the black death to the present.* Yale University Press.
Sotiris, P. (2020). Thinking beyond the lockdown: On the possibility of a democratic biopolitics. *Historical Materialism, 28*(3), 3–38.
SOU. (2008). *Krisberedskapen i grundlagen: Översyn och internationell utblick.* Fritzes Offentliga Publikationer.
Statista. (2023). Number of new coronavirus (COVID-19) deaths in Europe since February 2020 (as of January 13, 2023), by date of report. https://www.statista.com/statistics/1102288/coronavirus-deaths-development-europe/
Staupe-Delgado, R. (2021). Life in anticipation of the COVID-19 pandemic 'peak': Reflecting on 'strategies' for and variations in attempts at 'flattening the curve' and managing the crisis. *Journal of Extreme Events, 8*(01), 2150016. 27–470

Sun, Y., & Wang, W. Y. (2022). Governing with health code: Standardising China's data network systems during COVID-19. *Policy & Internet, 14*(3), 673–689.

Tegnell, A. (2021). The Swedish public health response to COVID-19. *Apmis, 129*(7), 320–323.

Tilly, C. (1992). *Coercion, capital, and European states, AD 990–1992*. Blackwell.

Tony See, S. H. (2022). Technology and biopolitics: A Deleuzian perspective. In S. S Das, A. R. Pratihar (Eds.), *Technology, urban space and the networked community* (pp, 51–70). Palgrave Macmillan.

Tréguer, F. (2021). The virus of surveillance: How the COVID-19 pandemic is fuelling technologies of control. *Political Anthropological Research on International Social Sciences (PARISS), 2*(1), 16–46.

Triantafillou, P. (2022). Biopower in the age of the pandemic: The politics of COVID-19 in Denmark. *European Societies, 24*(5), 657–681.

Tubi, O. (2022). Infrastructural capital in the Israeli vaccination campaign against COVID-19. *Social Science & Medicine, 303*, Article 115022.

Ursin, G., Skjesol, I., & Tritter, J. (2020). The COVID-19 pandemic in Norway: The dominance of social implications in framing the policy response. *Health policy and technology, 9*(4), 663–672.

Van Apeldoorn, B., & De Graaff, N. (2022). The state in global capitalism before and after the Covid-19 crisis. *Contemporary Politics, 28*(3), 306–327.

Varlik, N. (2015). *Plague and empire in the early modern Mediterranean world*. Cambridge University Press.

Walby, S. (2020). The COVID pandemic and social theory: Social democracy and public health in the crisis. *European Journal of Social Theory*, 1368431020970127.

Wallace, C., Mytna-Kurekova, L., Leon, M., O'Reilly, J., Blome, C., Bussi, M., … & Verdin, R. (2023). Governmentality versus community: The impact of the COVID lockdowns. *International Journal of Community Well-Being*, 1–18.

Weiss, L., & Thurbon, E. (2022). Explaining divergent national responses to Covid-19: An enhanced state capacity framework. *New Political Economy, 27*(4), 697–712.

Weber, M. (1978). *Economy and society*. New York: University of California Press.

White, S. (2010). Rethinking disease in Ottoman history. *International Journal of Middle East Studies, 42*(4), 549–567.

Winblad, U., Swenning, A. K., & Spangler, D. (2022). Soft law and individual responsibility: A review of the Swedish policy response to COVID-19. *Health Economics, Policy and Law, 17*(1), 48–61.

Zinn, J. O. (2020). A monstrous threat': How a state of exception turns into a 'new normal. *Journal of Risk Research, 23*(7–8), 1083–1091.

Žižek, S. (2020). *Pandemic! COVID-19 shakes the world*. Polity Press.

CHAPTER 3

The Question of the State and State Power: A Weberian-Foucauldian Theory

3.1 Introduction

To deal with the politics of COVID-19, we need a framework which addresses both the issue of power—a central aspect of the infection control regimes—and the state—as the state is the active part of the pandemic. For this purpose, and based on the aforementioned reflections, this study is *in primis* theoretically informed by two schools of thought. On the one hand, I have the Foucauldian theory of power, and the multitude of work within this tradition. The Foucauldian literature, including that on governmentality, is theoretically useful, as it invites scholars to conduct broad interrogations of the workings of power—as a relational force manifesting at the micro-level as mechanisms of power. Moreover, this perspective grants insights into the link between how a situation is perceived and how it is governed. This is the foundational framework of the book—which has Foucauldian origins (i.e. Gjerde, 2021a, 2021b, 2022). On the other hand, based on perceived analytical necessities, this framework seems to be in need of supplements, as the agential lens employed to understand the state's interventions in society in past Foucauldian studies of pandemic politics has remained implicit. The aforementioned studies define the state as acting, but *how* the state can act as such remains unexplored. To supplement the Foucauldian approach, I have the Weberian state theory and the multitude of work within this tradition, with the work of Michael Mann being my primary

L. E. L. Gjerde, *Nordic Leviathans*, International Political Theory,
https://doi.org/10.1007/978-3-032-00689-9_3

source. Mann's work offers a rich conceptual and analytical framework for exploring the state and the sources of its power. Can we, by combining these two approaches to the issue of power, have our cake and eat it, too?

To do so, I must overcome a hindrance, which relates to how the issues of the state and power are theorized. While Foucault's aim was 'putting [the state-centric theories] out for the garbage collector' (Jessop, 2001: 155), I shall illustrate theoretically and analytically how Foucault's insights are not just compatible with, but highly useful for, a state-centric approach (see also Jessen & von Eggers, 2020). Thus, I must find a way through which an agential approach to the state can handle the question of mechanisms of power, so as to formalize this framework. Here, the Weberian theory of the state, especially as discussed in Michael Mann's *The Sources of Social Power,* comes into play. Mann's work (1986, 1993, 2012, 2013) is about the sources of power, constructed around an 'organizational materialist' perspective, which posits that power is never free-floating, but dependent upon organization. This, I argue below, can complement the Foucauldian insights on the mechanisms of power, i.e. how power works. Note that, based on this 'organizational materialist' approach, I am interested in the agency of *organizations*, not individuals. Thus, contradicting Foucault (2003, 2009), who questioned if we even need a theory of state, I assert that state theory is essential for scholars investigating the many practices which states execute in contemporary societies, especially when covering empirical contexts where the state as an actor cannot be denied, as we must have some way of explaining how the state can act at all, if we are to use an agential lens.

While the Weberian-Foucauldian 'marriage' may appear strange with regard to the state, due to their different approaches to this question, Max Weber plays a key role in Foucault's theoretical development. The very notion of governmentality has roots in Weber's sociological thought on forms of different forms of rationality and rationalization (Colliot-Thélène, 2009; Flew, 2015; Szakolczai, 2000). Moreover, Foucault's work on discipline, rationalization and surveillance bears resemblance to Weber's work (Dandeker, 1990; van Krieken, 1990; Keyes, 2002; O'Neill, 1986). Weber (1978, 2015a, 2015b) discusses the rationalization of organizations, while Foucault (1991b, 2008a, 2009) studies the rationalization of power, how new models of governing emerge based on rationalization processes. The realist notion of the permanence of struggle is also shared by the two thinkers, through their common debt to the work of Friedrich Nietzsche (Dandeker, 1990; Jimenez-Anca 2013;

Owen, 2013; Szakolczai, 2013). Indeed, Arpad Szakolczai (2013) goes as far as to describe Weber and Foucault's relationship as 'parallel lifeworks'. Thus, the Weberian and Foucauldian approaches are highly compatible. Nonetheless, there are differences which must remedied along two axes: the question of power's *form*, where I opt for synthesizing the Weberian and Foucauldian approaches, and the question of the *nature* of the state, in which I opt for a Weberian approach.

While there is disagreement from a theoretical perspective, I find a certain symmetry which facilitates the union in question. First, Foucault was interested in the link between the microphysics and macrophysics of power (Jessen & von Eggers, 2020; Jessop, 2011). Lemke (2019: 123) writes that studying the macrophysics of power entails 'show[ing] how "macrostructures" more or less systematically (re)produce "micro-effects"' (cf Jessop, 2011: 64). This relates to Foucault's objective, as his studies constitute a 'genealogy of the state' (Lemke, 2002, 2019). Though interesting, this does not allow us to explore the state as an actor, as will be discussed below. I bracket the Foucauldian core issue of the institutionalization of power relations and macrostructures. Instead, as Raffnsøe et al. (2019: 167) recommend, I look towards governmental practices (or governance) and political rationalities, another Foucauldian way of speaking of macrophysical power. However, I break with their approach by (a) being state-centric, and (b) bringing the sources of power in as the macrophysics of power. This theoretical operation is based on the Foucauldian notion that theorizing should be based on tactical needs related to the analysis (Gutting, 2006). Bringing the sources of power into the analytical mixture adds ingredients, offering a new analytical field for theorizing on the issue of power, as the link between the microphysics and macrophysics can be explored in a new manner: what sources of power enable the mechanisms of power to manifest? Political rationalities become the concept for gluing these concepts together, as the ways the state reason decides how it seeks to use its power, and the exercise of power manifests in mechanisms of power at the micro-level.

Second, Mann's work focuses on the abstract—on power at the macro-level. Mann covers the history of power from the beginning until the twenty-first century—and his focus is the *sources* of power. Thus, Hillel Soifer (2008: 249) problematizes that, while the state is often analysed, few analytical tools remain for analysing state power. He calls for theory-building and empirical work based on the work of Mann. Related to this, Risto Heiskala (2016) recommends that Mann engage actively with

Foucault's work on power. Using the Foucauldian approach to the issue of power, scholars interested in the work of Mann can explore the manner which the sources of power manifest in mechanisms of power, thereby getting an analytical framework which can be combined with that of Mann. Thus, as stated in the literature review, this alliance may bear fruits for both Foucauldian and Weberian scholarship on (state) power.

The result should prove most useful, as the synthesis allows scholars to handle the most abstract macro-level and the most specific micro-level, and the connection between the two, combining a focus upon the functions of processes and relations of power, i.e. a structuralist and functionalist optic prioritizing the micro-level, with a Weberian organizational materialist perspective, prioritizing the macro-level, with state agency being the glue combining the micro-level and macro-level in practice. By combining these different but compatible and complementary theoretical traditions, and the different elements of power they prioritize, I engender a holistic approach to the question of the state, prioritizing state agency and how sources of power are accumulated to how they are used, and the consequences of such use, as the state (re)structures society in ways direct and indirect, vertical and horizontal.

This chapter is structured as follows. First, I discuss the question of power, leaning heavily on Foucauldian scholarship. Here, I also seek to address the possibility of combining the Foucauldian approach to power with a Weberian one, primarily motivated by the work of Michael Mann. This invites the state into the Foucauldian analytical framework, illustrating how defining organizations as containers or cages of power may enrich the Foucauldian tradition. Second, I discuss the Foucauldian approach to the state, its utility, and why we seek to move beyond it, inviting us to the Weberian-Foucauldian marriage. Third, I seek to make this marriage formal, albeit in an abstract manner. I present the Weberian-Foucauldian theory of the state, discussing compatibility and moving towards a coherent position. Fourth, after these abstract discussions, I move on to the issue of operationalizing these theoretical insights. I analyse examples with the theoretical framework covered above, so as to show how the Weberian-Foucauldian approach works as an analytical framework, as I combine the macrophysical and microphysical lenses. This operationalizes the marriage—setting the state for the coming empirical studies.

3.2 The Question of Power

The following reflections are largely Foucauldian in nature, basing themselves on Foucault's own work as well as insights from the governmentality tradition. The study of governmentality is a heterogenous approach to studying politics. It is a theoretical and analytical toolbox for empirical studies of governance and the political rationalities underpinning and enabling governance (Miller & Rose, 2008: 38). We supplement this Foucauldian literature with some primarily Weberian insights, leaning heavily on Mann's work, so as to enable our coming state-centric reflections.

To start with, we embrace insights from the governmentality tradition. From this perspective, to govern is to apply 'mechanisms and procedures intended to conduct men, to direct their conduct, to conduct their conduct' (Foucault, 2014: 12). Thus, governance is the more or less rationalized ways of applying technical means to structure, regulate, change, control or in other ways affect conduct (Dean, 1999: 14; Hindess, 1996: 106). The politics of COVID-19 is all about governing populations. To govern in turn relates to power, as one must exercise power to govern. Thus, a state incapable of exercising power, i.e. a powerless state, cannot govern. While power can be conceptualized in numerous ways, as it is a 'family resemblance' concept (Haugaard, 2010), we offer a synthesis of sorts. To avoid the 'overload-fallacy' where too many aspects of power are meshed together, thereby reducing the term's utility (Guzzini, 1993), we view power as a capacity for altering the course of actions, events, thoughts, moods, structures, etc. (Giddens, 1987; Lukes, 2004). While more Weberian than Foucauldian, both Weberians and Foucauldians assert that power is exercised (see Foucault, 1980, 1990, 1991a; Mann, 1984, 1986, 1993). Moreover, this definition encompasses both the microphysics and macrophysics of power. I now begin by discussing the former.

Foucauldians study power as a network existing relationally, in processes (Foucault, 1980: 98; Deleuze, 1988: 27). Power is the forces and strategies operating between and within social relations (Deleuze, 1988: 70). Power 'functions on the basis of particular powers, myriad issues, myriad effects of power' (Foucault, 1980: 188). The Foucauldian concept of power refers to the structural and institutional aspects of power, as a force existing in action. Foucauldians frequently refer to power as something which works through mechanisms (Sarr, 2011: 36).

The idea behind speaking about mechanisms of power is functionalist. A mechanism of power is an element in a larger whole, where a mechanism works side-by-side with other mechanisms, within a *social* machinery of power relations. These mechanisms may be positive or negative, i.e. they may produce, or they may destroy (Foucault, 1991a). The term 'mechanism of power' is useful as it centres the analysis around how power works, and thus, around power's *microphysics*. Below, we also include the macrophysics or sources of power into the theory, while seeking to avoid 'overloading' the concept of power. To better illustrate what we mean with mechanisms of power, we shall cover certain types of power below, and the mechanisms related to them. We shall use the term *mechanisms of power* when discussing the Foucauldian concept of power, and we shall offer some ontological reflections on this issue in the next chapter.

As power is exercised to deal with issues, in which the mechanisms of power manifest between and within relations, bodies, institutions, etc., so power is always exercised based on the ways reality is rendered governable, as governmentality scholars posit. The ways actors see the world determines how they govern (Dean, 1999; Foucault, 1985, 1990, 1991b, 2008a; C. Gordon, 1991; Miller & Rose, 2008). This occurs through political rationalities. Political rationalities are 'systemic way[s] of thinking about government' (Dean, 1999: 211). By rendering reality perceivable, political rationalities also render reality governable—enabling and restricting what governing actors can do (Foucault, 2008a; Miller & Rose, 2008; Rose, 1999).

The Foucauldian literature on power tends to study power beyond the state (i.e. Merlingen, 2011; Miller & Rose, 2008; Rose & Miller, 1992; for a critique, see Joseph, 2004). While taking the state seriously, Foucault (2003: 27–28) recommends that we examine power at its multiple, diverse and local points of manifestation—i.e. we must look at the *mechanisms* of power. Thinking 'anatomically', this means prioritizing the *microphysics* of power, even if Foucault spent considerable time on the macrophysics and the state (Jessop, 2001, 2011). To better understand this, we shall now discuss four key ways in which power can work, all highly significant within the Foucauldian literature, and pertaining to our cases.

Foucault (1980, 1990, 1991a) writes that the command of the sovereign, the prototype manner in which power worked during the ancient regimes and during the premodern era of monarchs and warlords, is displaced by discipline, the continuous, autonomous and diffuse channelling of forces to modify bodies and minds so as to produce individuals capable of conducting war, work and other activities in a highly regulated, almost automatic, uniform manner. Note that such changes are relative (Foucault, 1980, 1990, 1991a). What Foucault calls sovereign power, but which we shall label juridical-sovereign power, works through proscriptions grounded in law—by denying and repressing—whereas discipline works through producing and creating effects, identities, habits, thoughts, etc. (Foucault, 1980, 1991a, 2008b; Lea & Stenson, 2007; Stenson, 2005). Juridical-sovereignty stops individuals from doing something, for instance keeping a business open, i.e. a proscription. It manifests in a denial, in a negative manner. Discipline, on the other hand, works by altering habits and thoughts, such as through externally imposing infection control activities. In Foucault's (2008b: 22) words:

> whereas sovereign power is expressed through the symbols of the dazzling force of the individual who holds it, disciplinary power is a discreet, distributed power; it is a power which functions through networks and the visibility of which is only found in the obedience and submission of those on whom it is silently exercised.

Power, previously personalized around the person of the monarch or other notables, from whom it worked in ritualistic and spectacular ways through negative mechanisms such as public executions and torture, is now found to predominantly work in an impersonal and automatic manner through more complex and formal institutions, such as disciplinary mechanisms related to the separation of bodies or imposition of habits in prisons and schools.

This allows us to make some notes on our microphysical focus. A microphysical perspective on power pays close attention to these micro-level powers, the pieces which make up grander forms of power, like discipline. A form of power is studied as a whole made up of various mechanisms which function in a similar way, based on a specific political logic. Public executions and torture are juridical-sovereign mechanisms of power, working negatively through harming and destroying, seizing and denying, while having symbolic effects. Disciplinary mechanisms, such as isolation in cells, monitoring from the warden, systems of rewards and punishments, and the imposition of habits related to work, prayer, etc., work together within a disciplinary machinery within the prison, producing docile and modifiable subjects (Foucault, 1991a). While we refer to these elements of power as mechanisms, as they are meant to have certain effects within systems of power relations, we do not proclaim that these mechanisms have a fixed or regulated causality. Instead, their effects will vary based on how these mechanisms are imposed and upon resistance and interpretation from target populations (cf. Sayer, 2012).

Here, it should be noted that discipline entails the rationalization of conduct, a core element in Weber's sociology (Szakolczai, 2013). As Weber (2015a: 71) notes, discipline means adjusting and reprogramming the human being to the functions of society, so that the human being can be redirected and made part of the social machine, such as in the factory or army, or for the matters of this book, for purposes of infection control. Discipline creates uniformity through regulated, rationalized and predictable practices of commands and obedience (Foucault, 1991a, 2008b; Weber, 2015a, 2015b). There is however a main difference between the Weberian and Foucauldian approaches: Foucault (1991a) focuses on the *microphysics* of this rationalization, whereas Weber (2015a, 2015b) focuses on its *organizational* basis, something Foucault was less interested in (cf. Raffnsøe et al., 2019: 155).

Importantly, when I speak about *sovereignty*, I use the *Schmittian* terminology. Sovereignty is about the state's right to make decisions—far beyond the juridical-sovereign forms of governance Foucault (1980, 1991a) calls sovereignty. Essentially, this boils down to the issue of deciding whether a situation is normal or abnormal. This also involves determining what 'normal' entails. If the state determines that a situation is abnormal, then the state can suspend the legal and normative order of society, including democratic deliberation and/or various laws and rights. Declaring a situation to be exceptional justifies the use of extraordinary measures, for the purpose of protecting society. Legal and political norms presuppose a situation of normality, and in its absence, power is freed from formal restraints (Schmitt, 1996, 2020).

While this shows us the manner in which the state, through sovereignty, participates in creating conditions of (ab)normality through law, we should, as Dean (2007: 163) notes, avoid two problems: first, we should beware of presuming an exception/normal dichotomy, which we shall return to in the analysis. Second, we must also beware of assuming that state sovereignty is free-floating—as will be discussed in the conclusion, it is indeed fixed around cultural and social restraints. Nevertheless, we should understand sovereignty as a form of power structuring and enabling other mechanisms of power to emerge and work (Dean, 2007: 162). Indeed, sovereignty is 'a condition for effective internal government' (Dean, 2007: 134). From a Foucauldian perspective, we understand sovereignty as a meta-mechanism of power which affects and structures the room to act for political actors, which can be utilized to declare an exception and enable a multitude of microphysical powers to be imposed through the temporary suspension of various political restraints. Sovereignty is thus the core of the politics of COVID-19, both through the decision to declare the situation exceptional (or not), and more generally as the foundations of the two states' potential to govern more generally. However, I shall prioritize the mechanisms of power and the sources of power enacted to create these mechanisms.

While discipline was the predominant manner through which power worked in the early-modern era, neoliberal rule becomes increasingly dominant (C. Dean, 1999; Foucault, 2008a; Gordon, 1991; Miller & Rose, 2008; Rose, 1999). Liberal government works through the state-civil society distinction (Foucault, 2008a; Villadsen, 2016), in which the state demarcates a sphere beyond its formal interventions, where the state is not permitted to go. Civil society is meant to be a realm of indirect government, where government occurs through freedom. This means ruling through indirect forms of governance, based on responsibilizing individuals and altering the conditions under which individuals act, so as to foster and influence individuals' self-regulation (Foucault, 2008a; C. Gordon, 1991; Lemke, 2019; Miller & Rose, 2008). From this perspective, freedom is seen as a regulatory force (Foucault, 2008a; Rose, 1999), used to make individuals self-govern and self-police based on their self-interests which are to be aligned with that of the state. Liberal governmentality assumes that society and the individual both benefit from the individual's pursuit of rational self-interest, based on liberal philosophy (Foucault, 2008a), but the state (or other actors) can impose moral obligations to enable ethical conduct (Dean, 2007). Liberal mechanisms of power thus work in an indirect way, as the individual must be made to govern him- or herself according to certain criteria. For instance, the state can act to socialize the unemployed in order to activate them, so that they 'learn' how to govern themselves in accordance with the state's will (Lessenich, 2011).

From a Foucauldian perspective, exclusion is an important mechanism of power. While Foucault (2013) himself discusses exclusion more generically as a tactic for denying somebody access to spatial or social sites,

Deleuze (1992) discusses control (over access) as nowadays working on the basis of codes that mark individuals for inclusion or exclusion in an automatic manner, on abstract marks, such as (vaccination) passports, thus categorizing individuals as desirable or undesirable. While given less consideration in the Foucauldian literature than the core forms of rule discussed above, it is an important part of the politics of COVID-19. Control (over access) de-individualizes (Deleuze, 1992), as the person is reduced to a mark—such as 'green' or 'red' in the corona/green passports. Those marked 'right/green' are granted access, and those marked 'wrong/red' are denied access. Control (over access) manifests in mechanisms of exclusion as individuals seek to enter social and/or spatial sites where abstract conditions, such as registered address or the status as infected or non-infected, determine whether one can or cannot enter. However, exclusions can also occur in more disciplinary ways, for instance through isolation, which works by mixing control and discipline (cf Bowen, 2021).

These types of power are all highly relevant during the pandemic. Foucauldian scholarship invites scholars to investigate how power functions at the sites where it is exercised, where it manifests through different techniques, such as physical distancing or checkpoints where individuals must show corona passports. Through such techniques, individuals' bodies, habits, relations, minds, etc., are targeted by power, which manifest in mechanisms producing, hindering, moulding and in other ways affecting the object of power. These Foucauldian concepts invite us to inductively examine situations, such as classrooms and quarantine hotels, or abstract measures, such as the ban on the freedom of assembly and the metre/two-metres, to explore how power *works*. This means exploring the *microphysics* of power. While useful—indeed my analyses will prioritize the microphysics of power—the reduction of power to its exercise leads purely processual approaches to power to the *exercise fallacy*. The exercise fallacy entails the belief that power only exists in action, which veils how actors may refrain from exercising power, making analysts blind to real capacities, including these capacities' potential effects despite the absence of their activation (Lukes, 2004; Selg, 2016). For instance, the state's capacities to exercise different forms of power can suffice to pacify populations (Poulantzas, 1978) or regulate markets (Weiss, 1998). Beyond the passive effects of state power, state power can be kept dormant until the state identifies a need to exercise it (cf Gjerde, 2021b; Weiss & Thurbon,

2022). Therefore, reducing power to its activation may conceal both the powers and the effects of the state.

Moreover, a secondary issue is raised by Mark Haugaard (2022: 349), which asks 'yet if there is no center of power, as Foucault maintains, who or what is doing the disciplining?' While one can ignore the question for analytical or ontological reasons, or alternatively look locally at the individual teacher or prison ward, a more holistic solution is to examine how the very institutions' discipline works through and how it can be made to operate in the first place. A Foucauldian approach might in this regard entail exploring the institutionalization of power relations, struggles and strategies (Jessop, 2011), for instance, by exploring how discipline spreads throughout various institutions, becoming a paradigmatic form of governance (i.e. Foucault, 1991a). Eli Lichtenstein (2020: 87) makes clear how this can be accomplished from a Foucauldian perspective, noting that 'discipline does not spontaneously spread through society', as discipline 'requires the use of various political mechanisms', of which the state is the core 'tactic' and object of inquiry. While agreeing with Lichtenstein (2020), as I also want to look at the centre which makes disciplinary and other mechanisms of power possible on a societal scale, during the pandemic, my holistic approach entails looking towards the organizational basis of discipline, thereby breaking with the Foucauldian definition of the state, which Lichtenstein (2020) adheres to.

This brings us to a core Foucauldian concern—the *macrophysics* of power. While some recommend studying the macrophysics of power by studying the institutionalization of power relations and struggles (i.e. Jessop, 2011, 2015; Lemke, 2019), I prefer to look at governmental practices and rationalities (i.e. C. Gordon, 1991, 1994; Jessen & von Eggers, 2020; Raffnsøe et al., 2019). While partly a Foucauldian solution, I do break with the Foucauldian literature by bringing the state as an actor into the theory. This forces me to look at theoretical insights which can explain how the state acts. For this purpose, I take into account what Mann (1986, 1993, 2012, 2013) calls the *sources* of power.

As will be discussed further below, theoretically granting the state agency demands some justification. How can the state act? How can it exercise power? While studying the institutionalization of struggles in macrostructures (i.e. Jessop, 2011; Lemke, 2019) invites scholars to study how this becomes possible, this tells us little about how the state was able to act as it did, especially where institutionally similar states act differently. However, through mapping the *sources* of power, we can map the sources of the state's agency and autonomy. Mann (1986: 2–3) calls the sources of power 'generalized means' with the potential to manifest in the capacity 'to organize and control people, materials and territories'. Whereas the term mechanisms of power centre the analysis around how power works, the concept of sources of power centres the analysis around how power can be made to work through mediums, such as economic capital or organizational techniques, which enable power to be exercised.

Taking the insights of Mann (1984, 1986, 1993, 2012, 2013) seriously, seeing the macrophysics of power as a means which can be used, we can understand the state as a 'cage', or as Anthony Giddens (1981, 1987) writes, 'container' of power. Within the 'cage' or 'container', power can be dormant, until it is activated, as it was during the pandemic (Weiss & Thurbon, 2022). While agreeing that power should 'be analysed as something that circulates' (Foucault, 2003: 29) and is 'exercised' (Foucault, 1980: 89, 1990: 94; 1991: 26), economic, administrative and repressive resources are also accumulated and concentrated, for instance in castles during the medieval period, or the nation-state today (Giddens, 1981, 1987). Indeed, the Foucauldian theory of power as a dispersed network of forces may be seen as 'presuppose[ing] a concept of power as a potential possessed by all objects' (Sayer, 2012: 180). Taking the sources of power into account allows us to move beyond presupposing possession by linking together two different ways of conceptualizing and analysing power, without 'overloading' the concept (cf. Guzzini, 1993), while avoiding the exercise fallacy (cf. Lukes, 2004; Selg, 2016). After all, the concepts are codified in different but related concepts, bound together by the notion of power as capacity and how this capacity manifests in mechanisms of power based on the usage of sources of power. Sources of power as a concept simply refer to what makes it possible to exercise power, but sources are not power per se. The specific use of such sources is contingent upon numerous factors, precisely in the same way that a sword or capital can be used in different ways. A failure to apply sources of power strategically and pragmatically may make a seemingly powerful actor de facto powerless, just as a rich individual may waste immense resources through irrational investment. This perspective invites us to study how mechanisms of power can be created, allowing us to bring the state and other organizations into the picture, allowing us to study how sources of power can be possessed. This means seeing power as dependent upon organization—i.e. *organizational materialism* (Mann, 1993). The

Foucauldian structuralist[1] approach to power prioritizing the mechanisms of power is combined with a Weberian, agential approach prioritizing the organizations containing and channelling sources of power.

This means conceptualizing power as *pyramidical.* Power works by being contained and stored within centres of power, such as states or corporations, from which it can be exercised. While Foucault (1980, 1990) warns *against* top-down conceptions of power, calling them 'simplistic', a pyramidical conceptualization of power is not simplistic, as it includes the Foucauldian insights on the horizontal and bottom-up properties of power, while taking power's vertical or hierarchical nature seriously. The pyramidical conceptualization integrates Foucauldian imperatives of exploring power at the local context where it is exercised and therefore manifests, where power works and has effects (i.e. Foucault, 1980, 1991a, 2003, 2008a), while positing that this study of the microphysics of power can be enriched by exploring how the microphysics come into being, as the crystallization of the enactment of the macrophysics of power. This way, we can combine the Foucauldian understanding of power with state-centric lenses, such as that of Mann's work, reversing Foucault's (1990, 2003) decentring of power by recentring Foucauldian theorizing around the state.

3.3 The Foucauldian State

While leaning heavily upon Foucauldian notions on the mechanisms of power, appropriating the theoretical aim of exploring the link between the microphysics and macrophysics of power, as well as the governmentality literature's insights on the importance of exploring political rationalities and how they render reality governable, I do embrace a Weberian and thus non-Foucauldian definition of, and so approach to, the state, largely depending upon the work of Michael Mann for conceptualizing how the macrophysics of power works.

I must now interrogate the Foucauldian theory of the state, in order to integrate the Foucauldian theory of power with a Weberian state theory. As mentioned above, Foucault granted the state a privileged position within his work (Jessop, 2001, 2007, 2011). Much of Foucault's work is a

[1] While Foucault (1994d: 13) says that he is 'absolutely not' a structuralist, I label the Foucauldian approach to power as structuralist since it focuses upon the mechanisms of power and their functions, rather than on agency as such.

'genealogy of the state' (Lemke, 2002, 2019). This concern has, however, been discarded by much Foucauldian scholarship after Foucault, problematized as 'state phobic' by the Foucauldian scholars Mitchell Dean and Kaspar Villadsen (Dean & Villadsen, 2012; see also Jessop, 2011; J. Kim, 2021; Lessenich, 2011). On a similar note, Mathias Hein Jessen and Nicolai von Eggers (2020: 65) write that:

> Foucault believed that it was possible to combine the analysis of micro-powers with that of the state (Foucault, 2009: 358). Even though the 'governmentality-studies' recognize that Foucault developed the notion of governmentality to analyse both the macro- and micro-level of power (Burchell, 1991: 122; Gordon, 1991: 4; Rose, 1999: 5), the macro-level of the state – as well as the interrelation between micro and macro – is in effect abandoned in favour of a focus on the concrete practices and technologies of government, on political power 'beyond the state' (Rose & Miller, 1992).

Therefore, while Foucault takes the state seriously, labelling it 'one of the most redoubtable forms of human government' (Foucault, 1994c: 325), Foucauldians after Foucault, including most governmentality scholars, tend to prioritize power 'beyond the state' (Rose & Miller, 1992; see also Barry et al., 1996; Merlingen, 2011). Rather than looking *beyond* the state, it may be more beneficial to explore how power works within ***and*** beyond the state, and how the state governs beyond its formal apparatus, something several governmentality scholars have done (i.e. Arts, 2014; Lea & Stenson, 2007; Sending & Neumann, 2006). The latter solution is more in line with Foucault's own approach to governmentality, which, after all, entails the study *of* the state, partly by studying how relations and mechanisms of power beyond the state work and interweave with the state (Dean & Villadsen, 2012; Jessop, 2011)—a focus taken up in notable exceptions within the governmentality tradition (i.e. Arts, 2014; Lea & Stenson, 2007; Sending & Neumann, 2006).

Naturally, power beyond the state is imperative and it can be the main point of inquiry of individual scholars or even theories. Nevertheless, the argumentation behind this approach, that state-centric models 'obscure' how political power works (i.e. Miller & Rose, 2008; Rose & Miller, 1992), is hardly convincing, especially with regard to the pandemic, which reveals the great powers of the state. Nevertheless, the argument underpinning this approach—that government occurs through indirect means and often beyond the formal apparatus of the state—is central to my coming analysis. State power tends to work 'on the basis of an elaborate network of relations' between different parts of the state and between state and non-state institutions and organizations, through complex mechanisms of 'governing at a distance' (see Miller & Rose, 2008: 55). I fully accept the validity and utility of these insights. However, contrary to Rose's (1999: 4) claim that 'the state now appears simply as one element', or Miller and Rose's (2008: 35) argument that 'each of these diverse forces [the state, corporations, activist organizations etc.]... can translate the objectives and values of others into its own terms', (a) the state is not merely 'one element' among many, and (b) the autonomous powers of the state complicate the relations between forces within networks of power. Rather, the state is vertically positioned above non-state actors. As Dean (2007: 116) problematizes, one must not reduce the state to its juridical and constitutional form, and yet, governmentality scholars studying 'power beyond the state' reduce the state to its juridical and thus negative use of power (Bröckling et al., 2011). This neglects the state's infrastructural means and the manner in which the state can act through society (cf. Arts, 2014).

Moreover, the state's importance is currently increasing, not decreasing. Making this clear will, for my purposes, constitute a break with such notions, and position me with the literature of Dean and Villadsen (2012), Jessen and von Eggers (2020), Sending and Neumann (2006), etc. To further elucidate this position, it is useful to explore the concentration of power within the state apparatus over the last centuries. As briefly mentioned above, premodern states were embodied in the sovereign ruler rather than 'popular will', and supported by lacklustre technologies and organizational structures. The premodern state had limited capacities to intervene in citizens' daily lives, except next to centres of power, such as capitals, manors or castles. To extend their reach further, states depended upon autonomous non-state actors, such as clans, nobles, clergy or mercenaries (Giddens, 1987; Mann, 1984; Scott, 2017; Tilly, 1992). Over the last centuries, state autonomy and capacities have increased, as states monopolize the right to exercise violence and develop efficient state bureaucracies, militaries and other institutions (Elias, 1978, 1982; Mann, 1984, 1986, 1993; Giddens, 1987; Tilly, 1992; Scott, 2017).

The state has also increasingly concentrated ideological resources, inducing Pierre Bourdieu (1991, 2014) to speak of a state 'monopoly of symbolic violence'. Indeed, state power has also increased immensely in recent *decades* (Hegghammer, 2021; Mann, 2008). The state's extensive power—the power to organize large numbers of people and huge areas of land—and its intensive power—the ability to organize and command a high level of participation—continue to increase (Mann, 1986, 1993, 2008, 2012, 2013). Those Foucauldians who are not 'scared' of touching the state show how it increases its presence and potential for exercising power, also through non-state actors, through complex nexuses of power where the state is a centre of sorts, or at least the most important piece in a grand puzzle (i.e. Arts, 2014; Lea & Stenson, 2007; Lessenich, 2011; Sending & Neumann, 2006). As also covered by Weberians, power beyond the state can be informal state power, as will be discussed further below (cf. Evans, 1995; Mann, 2013; Weiss, 1998). The state is not 'one element', but the core element for scholars interested in power in our century, as also asserted by Foucault (1994a, 2008a, 2009) as well as more state-centric Foucauldians (i.e. Jessen & von Eggers, 2020; J. Kim, 2021). Thus, contrary to Miller and Rose's (2008: 56) argument that a state-centric approach referring to the autonomous state, such as Mann's (1984) work, 'obscures the characteristics of modern forms of political power', a state-centric view is likely to unveil the characteristics of contemporary political power, even if a) it must accept the importance of power beyond that state, which Mann (1986, 1993, 2012) does, and b) the state is not always the centre of importance.

Having positioned myself within the Foucauldian literature which takes the state seriously, I now move on to the core of our theoretical argument. As already stated above, I look to move beyond the Foucauldian approach to the state. This is not merely about perspective—many Foucauldians dismiss 'state phobia' (Dean & Villadsen, 2012). This is a question about the concept of the state. While I bracket the 'official' Foucauldian definition of the state, *at times,* Foucault (2013, 2019) himself operates with a similar conception to the state as I do in this book, even if this is a minor part of his scholarship on the state, and thus, an 'un-Foucauldian' approach. This can be explained by 'Foucault's approach [being] less a general theory of the state or even of governing', as it is an 'analytical attention to the mechanisms of government and rule and their manifestations in diverse practices' (Dean, 1994: 195). Foucault's dismissal of a theory of the state makes it obvious that his approach to the state will be based on utility, and thus, there are different *Foucaults*.

Stephan Sawyer (2015: 139), theorizing on the Foucauldian approach to the state, says that 'if one understands the state … as autonomous actors defined by diplomacy and warfare, then Foucault has little to tell us about the state'. On the surface, Foucault's work (2003, 2008a, 2009) on statecraft supports such an argument. Indeed, Foucault (2008a: 77) writes that the state is 'not… in itself an autonomous source of power', a notion dismissed as a 'myth' (Lemke, 2007: 53). Foucault (2003: 34) therefore asserts that power should be studied 'outside… the institution of the State', as '[while] I don't claim that the state apparatus is unimportant… power isn't localized in the state apparatus' (Foucault, 1980: 60).

This seemingly closes the door for scholars interested in the autonomous state. However, many Foucauldian insights on the state are valuable, also for scholars primarily interested in state agency and autonomy, but to unearth them, we must understand what the Foucauldian theory of the state entails. From a Foucauldian perspective, the state is generally defined as non-agential. This is both the case in Foucault's main work (2003, 2008a, 2009) on the state, as well as Foucauldian theorizing on the state (i.e. Jessen & von Eggers, 2020; Jessop, 2001, 2007, 2011; Lemke, 2007; Lichtenstein, 2020; Sarr, 2011; Sawyer, 2015). Foucauldians treat the state as a result, created by discourses, processes and practices, rather than an entity capable of acting in its own right (Foucault, 2009). Foucault (2008a: 7) calls the state 'the correlative of a particular of governing', and the state is seen as a form of governmentality (Jessen & von Eggers, 2020). The state is seen as an 'instrument' and 'effect' of governmental practices' (Lemke, 2007: 56; Rose, 1996: 43). Foucault (1991b: 103) argues that 'maybe, after all, the state is no more than a composite reality and a mythicized abstraction, whose importance is a lot more limited than many of us think'. In the words of Jessop (2011: 68), 'Foucault gave a privileged role to the state as the point of strategic codification of the multitude of power relations and as the apparatus in which the general line formed meta power', which means that the state 'invests' and 'colonizes' other power relations. From this position, the state has a structuring role, making it absolutely necessary for the workings of power in modern societies, as a meta-power (Foucault, 2008a, 2009). Based on such a definition of the state, we are told to study power 'outside of the model of Leviathan' (Foucault, 2009: 34). To summarize the Foucauldian approach to the state: Foucault (and Foucauldians) view the state as 'the outcome of processes which are both diverse and spatially scattered, without pre-determined boundaries, and of relations formed by people in society' (Colliot-Thélène, 2009: 175).

While an ontological issue, the Foucauldian definition also relates to empirical interest. Foucault (2003, 2008a, 2009) studies the genealogy and thus the history of the state. This entails studying processes of statification, statification being the process by which spheres, activities and institutions are placed within the state's domain. This also entails examining governmentalization, the rationalization processes by which reality is rendered governable in a manner delimiting state and non-state spheres (Foucault, 2009; Sending & Neumann, 2006; Villadsen, 2016). This enables the scholar to study the link between the microphysics and macrophysics of power (Jessen & von Eggers, 2020; Jessop, 2001, 2007, 2011; Lemke, 2002, 2007)—by studying how power works, how it is institutionalized, and thereafter, how it works in new ways based on the institutionalization of power relations and struggles.

Some of these Foucauldian insights are important to our study. As Weberians generally acknowledge, state power depends upon relations of power, institutions and practices beyond the state apparatus (i.e. Evans, 1995; Hobson, 1997; Mann, 1984, 2013; Weber, 1995). Appropriating insights from Foucauldians who take the state seriously while looking beyond it (i.e. Arts, 2014; Sending & Neumann, 2006), I can explore how the state uses non-state actors for infection control purposes, as I shall do in the analysis of both the Norwegian and Swedish cases. I also accept the importance of the processes of statification and governmentalization, which delimit and create state and non-state spheres. How does something become part of the state? For instance, 'civil society' as an exterior to the state, where the state is supposed to govern less formally does not necessarily *limit* the state. From a Foucauldian perspective, 'civil society' is a rationalizing instrument rather than a limitation as such, which allows for the demarcation of state and non-state realms, that are to be governed in different ways (Sending & Neumann, 2006; Villadsen, 2016). This insight allows me to explore how the Norwegian and Swedish states govern vis-à-vis, through and over formally non-state actors.

However, the Foucauldian stance on the processes by which the state is socially created, while not wrong, is partial. From a Foucauldian perspective, the state is generally defined as if created from the bottom-up through the institutionalization of struggles, relations and strategies (Jessop, 2011: 64). This is what Eric Nordlinger (1981) laments as society-centred explanations of the state. The state grows and shrinks based upon societal groups' interests, and these interests are external to the state, essentially colonizing it from beyond. While a useful strategy for denaturalizing the seemingly natural and universal nature of the state (i.e. Foucault, 2008a; Lemke, 2007), the refusal to acknowledge state autonomy means that the state's own role in political questions, including with regard to processes of statification, is veiled. The non-agential approaches to the state (i.e. Foucault, 2008a; Jessen & von Eggers, 2020; Mitchell, 1991) are right to assert that the state is a social construct, but wrong when this likewise entails denying that it is *also* a social constructor with autonomy from society at large. This processual ontological position dismisses the existence of the state beyond the social processes making it up, thereby becoming unable to handle how the state works in a relatively autonomous manner. Empirical insights show state autonomy and agency in diverse cases. Empirically, Skocpol (1979) shows the state's autonomy during revolutions. Evans (1995) and Weiss (1998) show state autonomy during economic transformations. Mann (2008) and Skocpol (2008) similarly reveal the state's autonomy in questions of rights and welfare. And of course, states have long been known to have significant autonomy regarding the questions of war and peace (Mann, 2012, 2013). Similarly, my two cases, as well as the politics of COVID-19 more generally (i.e. Weiss & Thurbon, 2022), show the autonomy and agency of the state. The state acts, relatively autonomously, through representatives, such as diplomats, soldiers or politicians. This is shown empirically, thereby demonstrating the theoretical and ontological issues with the Foucauldian approach to the state.

However, from a Foucauldian perspective, the main issue with this non-agential perspective is not (just) its (potential lack of) correspondence with reality, but its apparent lack of utility in a context where the state actively intervenes in society in a near-total manner (cf. Gutting, 2006). To understand massive collective actions, such as a total war or a lockdown, we must conceptualize the active state as a political organization, as an agent (see Wendt, 1999, 2004). Denying that the state is an actor with (potential) autonomy limits the analyst as there are numerous instances where the state and its preferences reign supreme, also against special interests and powerful non-state actors. As Neumann and Sending (2021) point out, the state should be conceptualized as an actor because it *performs* actions. Dismissing the agency of the state creates analytical blind-spots, whereas conceptualizing the state as an actor allows us to explore the increasingly dominant role of the state in questions of rule, also far beyond its formal apparatus. This is especially the case in crises, where the importance of political choices increases (Weiss & Thurbon, 2022), but the state has decision-making capacities which cannot be denied a priori (Nordlinger, 1981). As the Foucauldian core issue is the question of power and rule, so a theory about how the state exercises power appears useful—even if this demands theoretical heterodoxy and a rupture with both the tendency towards society-centrism and the predominance of a non-agential, processual definition of the state within the Foucauldian literature.

This does not mean that power beyond the state cannot be one, or even *the*, main focus. It also does not imply that studies of the state must explore the autonomous state and its agency. As Theda Skocpol (2008: 111) states, the objective is *not* to turn society-centred or economic-determinist accounts 'on their heads', through a reductionist state-centric approach. The aim of these theoretical reflections is not to substitute other research agendas. The objective is to bring the state into the theoretical and analytical framework as an *autonomous actor*, thereby opening new doors, building bridges. To do so, we break with the Foucauldian theory of the state, but we remain within the confines of Foucauldian scholarship. In *Penal Theories and Institutions,* Foucault (2019) discusses how the state, as a social body, exercises repressive power over society, with the emergence of new administrative institutions. The beginning of the end for feudalism sees the state apparatus concentrate on repressive resources, increasingly at the expense of local actors, offering the state new means for enforcing its will through violence. In *The Punitive Society,* Foucault (2013: 110) discusses the role of the police in 'exercising a whole set of controls of everyday life', which he finds makes the state 'the basic agent of morality' in society. Here, the state takes an active part in policing the conduct and morals of citizens. Moreover, Foucault (1994a: 138) calls the state a 'locus of acquisition of a special body of knowledge', indicating that the state is a 'cage' of knowledge/power. Such insights mirror Mann (1984) and Giddens' (1987) work on the state and state power.

This invites us to rethink the Foucauldian approach to the state—not through the non-agential lens discussed as 'Foucauldian' more generally, as well as within this text—but as an agent. Hence, we are called upon to combine the Weberian and Foucauldian approaches.

3.4 A Theory of State Power

As we seek to bring the state into the analytical framework as an autonomous actor, so we define the state in a *Weberian* manner. Here, we are concerned with the *modern* state. Basing myself on the work of Max Weber (1946, 1978), as well various Neo-Weberian scholars such as Theda Skocpol (1979, 1985, 2008), Norbert Elias (1978, 1982), Michael Mann (1984, 1986, 1993, 2008, 2012, 2013), Anthony Giddens (1981, 1987), Linda Weiss (1998) and Alexander Wendt (1999, 2004), as well as insights from Carl Schmitt (1996, 2008, 2014, 2020) I define the state as a *compulsory political organization claiming the right to make and apply binding decisions, consisting of a differentiated set of institutions and personnel, embodying the centre of a territorially demarcated area it claims ownership over, within which the state encompasses all individuals and all associations, as a consequence of its compulsory nature* (see also Gjerde, 2024b: 57). Within this area, the state claims authority over all associations, individuals and actions. It is therefore *de jure* positioned vertically above all other organizations existing within its territory, as the state is the provider of law. This establishes claims of a monopoly over the legitimate use of organizations of violence, such as military and police forces. With this monopoly, violence can only be permitted or prescribed by the state, otherwise, it is illegal, and thus punishable. This constitutes an institutional-legal order led by the state. The state is made up of administrative, policing and military institutions coordinated by an executive authority, institutionalizing political relations of protection and obedience. It is an intentional actor whose agency we can observe in its actions, for instance when it wages war, conducts diplomacy or pacifies internal regions. It is a collective actor, as it is made up of many individuals and institutions, and when it acts, it acts through the hands of state agents.

To understand the agency of the state, we must understand the capacities of the state, which all revolve around the issue of state power. If the state contains or cages power, it has the resources to act, also (potentially) independently. State power is relational—it is determined by the state's relations with, and position vis-à-vis, non-state actors as well as other states (Jessop & Morgan, 2022; Mann, 1984, 1986, 1993, 2008; Waltz, 1979), as Foucauldians also define it (see Villadsen, 2016). In practice, state power is grounded in the macrophysics of power, and thus the sources of power which the state contains, either formally within its apparatus, or informally throughout society. These sources are general means of power—means which can be used to exercise power in practice (Mann, 1984, 1986, 1993). State power is closely related to infrastructural and coercive power, which Mann (1984) calls the *autonomous powers of the state.* As Mann (1984, 1986, 1993, 2008, 2012, 2013) writes, coercive and infrastructural power grant the state autonomy. State autonomy refers to the degree the state can act in accordance with its will, with or without support from societal actors (Nordlinger, 1981). The existence of state autonomy, while relative, is seen in how states act in accordance with their own interests, also when faced with indifference or opposition (see Skocpol, 1979, 2008; Nordlinger, 1981; Mann, 2013). Moreover, beyond these two sources of autonomous power, we will make some reflections on the ideological power of the state.

First, on coercive power, which Mann calls *despotic* power. When we speak about coercive power, we speak about the coercive *sources* of power, as this relates to the *macrophysics* of power. Coercive power grants the state capacities to enforce its will unilaterally, without consulting groups in civil society. Coercive power is essentially the repressive or violent sources of power. Coercive power in modern societies is based on organizations capable of coordinating, concentrating and using violence, such as the police. Coercive sources of power let the state govern *over* society, through violence or the threat of violence. The more the state monopolizes the means of violence, and contains repressive resources, the more autonomous the state becomes vis-à-vis society (see Giddens, 1987; Mann, 1993, 2013; Tilly, 1992). I prefer the term *coercive* power over the term *despotic* power, to avoid blurring the line between legitimate and illegitimate state violence. As Weber (1946, 1978) would point out, violence is the very fundament of *political* order. Therefore, a term which refers to the use of, and capacity to use, state violence as despotic makes politics and despotism synonymous. Also, this blurs the lines between different forms of state coercion. The GULAG and COVID curfews are both instances of state violence. In both cases, individuals are forcefully confined to spatial areas by the state, and this is enforced through the legitimate means of violence. However, the degrees of violence applied towards individuals as well as the intentions behind them and the legitimacy of the measures differ greatly. Calling power 'despotic' if it is coercive conceals how state coercion may be desired, as it was during the pandemic (i.e. Buchanan 2022).

The concept of coercive power resembles Foucault's (1991a, 2019) theory about juridical-sovereignty. However, juridical-sovereignty works as a spectacular exercise of force manifesting in proscriptions, in an exclusively negative manner, whereas the functions of coercion *can* be more complex than juridical-sovereign forms of ruling. The state's *active* use of violence towards its own citizens generally diminishes in developed states, while the state's capabilities to regulate new spheres of life increase (Mann, 1984; Poulantzas, 1978; Weiss, 1998). This reduction in applied violence can be explained partly by the state increasingly monopolizing violence, which pacifies private individuals who cannot use violence without inviting state violence towards themselves (see Elias, 1978, 1982; Poulantzas, 1978; Weber, 1978). Moreover, discipline and other subtler forms of rule also depend upon coercive power, even if discipline cannot be enabled without immense institutional capacities. Thus, Foucauldian work on the coercive mechanisms of (state) power is useful, also for scholars interested in the autonomous state.

The monopolization of the right to conduct violence has constitutive effects (Poulantzas, 1978). The power of, and over, violence may or may not be used actively, but its constitutive effects depend only upon (perceived) capacities (Waltz, 1979). Coercion is institutionalized through law, which is 'the application of politically organized compulsion upon men's wills' (Novak 2008: 768), signalling the state's willingness to use violence towards those breaking the legal order. The more efficiently the law is upheld, the less private violence individuals practise and experience. Coercive resources are in the final instance not meant to be used for everyday purposes, as their constitutive effects are meant to pacify society, showing the importance of taking into account how unused power can work to affect action (cf Lukes, 2004).

Second, this brings us to infrastructural power. When I speak about infrastructural power, I speak about the infrastructural *sources* of power. Infrastructural power is defined by Mann (1984: 113) as 'the institutional capacity of the central state... to penetrate its territories and logistically implement decisions'. Infrastructural power is at the roots of states' capacities to 'build themselves into the lives of citizens in fundamental ways' (Rippa & Oakes, 2023: 6). Infrastructural power refers to the institutional resources which lets the state interfere with and regulate social life—control the border, demand taxation, socialize and educate children, distribute orders, obtain information about various social tendencies, etc. Infrastructural sources of power increase the state's autonomy as the state obtains means of controlling, overseeing and regulating society in an automatic, non-violent and highly efficient manner.

Infrastructural capacities relate to material infrastructure such as roads, technological development facilitates more efficient surveillance and the spread of information and orders, as well as organizational techniques (Giddens, 1987; Mann, 1984, 1986, 1993, 2008, 2012). Infrastructural sources of power enable the state to monitor society and implement its will, *through* rather than *over* society. Today the rationalization of political organizations is the core of this issue. This occurs through the establishment of modern, meritocratic bureaucracies. These organizations supersede individualist logics by granting individuals incentives to comply with the organization's goals, while socializing them into the norms of the bureaucracy, and separating the individual from 'the means of administration' (Weber, 2015a). This strengthens the collective and organizational basis of knowledge, granting organizations increased control over human resources, thereby increasing the power over and through knowledge (Dandeker, 1990; Weber, 1946, 1978, 2015a, 2015b). Similarly, enhanced surveillance technologies, both related to surveillance as the monitoring of individuals, and surveillance as the accumulation of information, allow for an increase in the quantity and quality of accumulated information (Mann, 2012, 2013; Rippa & Oakes, 2023).

Bureaucracies are containers of power and therefore potent instruments, especially when they—in the capacity of the means of administration—are placed under the control of the central state, becoming part of the state apparatus (Weber, 2015a, 2015b). Bureaucracies allow the state to administer entire populations and territories in ways impossible in the premodern world. Moreover, infrastructural sources of power are both enhanced and created by the state embedding itself into society. This enables the state to reach further, and it allows the state to govern through rather than over society (Evans, 1995; cf. Weber, 1995). Related to this, some governmentality scholars correctly show how such governance beyond the state is highly central to state power, as the relationship between state and non-state actors is not zero-sum (see Arts, 2014; McKee, 2009; Sending & Neumann, 2006). The state, governing in a liberal manner, seeks to govern through non-state actors. The expanding state is in this regard helped by democratic reforms and the emergence of new rights. As Mann (2008) writes, new gendered and ecological rights invite the state to expand deeper into previously non-state spheres, in order to provide these rights.

Much of Foucault's work handles the issue of infrastructural power. Foucault (1980: 39) reveals how power changes from primarily being power over the social body coming from above, to power within and through the social body. This is analogous to Mann's discussion of how coercive power is largely replaced by infrastructural power in modern democratic states, due to the latter's efficacy (Mann, 1993, 2012, 2013). As the state expands into society, and as it increases its technical and organizational capacities, so it can refrain from violence, governing through businesses, religious communities, families, etc., rather than over them.

This also means that Foucault's writings about the forms of power moving and working through society handle the issue of infrastructural power in action. Foucault's thoughts (1991a, 2008b) on discipline complement Mann's work, as they cover the issue of infrastructural power (Soifer, 2008). Philip Gorski (2003) has therefore written that Foucault's analysis of the capillary power of discipline can be seen as an attempt of exploring the state's infrastructure. Stephen W. Sawyer (2015) and Darren Byler (2023) have also discussed how discipline is related to infrastructural power. Discipline is a form of microphysical power manifesting as a result of the exercise of infrastructural sources of power, even if discipline sometimes depends upon coercive sources of power—as in the case of imprisonment. Immense infrastructural capacities, related to the rationalization and professionalization of organizations, surveillance capacities, ways of distributing and analysing information, and knowledge about the subject population, are necessary. Similarly, Foucault's writings (1980, 1990, 1991a) about power/knowledge handle the issue of infrastructural power. Power produces knowledge, as in disciplinary contexts where individuals are studied and monitored, and knowledge facilitates the exercise of power. Here, Foucault's work handles both how infrastructural power manifests at the micro-level and how the microphysics of power move back to enhance what we define as the state's infrastructural power. Supplementing Foucault with Mann, we can say that knowledge is contained within cages of power, such as the state bureaucracy (cf Gjerde, 2024a, 2024b).

Related to this, Foucault's writings (1990, 2008a) on biopolitics also bear resemblance to infrastructural power, as a concept. This link has also been made by other scholars (see Ayodele, 2019; Byler, 2023; Rippa & Oakes, 2023). Biopolitics entails biological life itself, for instance mortality rates, fertility rates, genetics, etc., becoming *objects* of political administration, as life and politics interweave (Foucault, 1990, 2008a; Rabinow & Rose, 2006; Rose, 2009; Shammas & Sandset, 2020; Villadsen & Wahlberg, 2015). Biopolitics revolves around optimizing the population's vitality (Foucault, 2003; Rose, 2009; Villadsen & Wahlberg, 2015). Biopolitics is enabled by knowledge, usually produced by scientific disciplines, like statistics, demography, epidemiology and biology (Foucault, 2008a; Lemke, 2019; Rose, 2009; Villadsen & Wahlberg, 2015). Such knowledge enables generalized action into the social body to correct and protect society from biological 'errors', like unhealthy habits (i.e. smoking), biological threats (i.e. 'bad genes') or external threats (pathogens). This knowledge renders populations and their tendencies knowable and thus governable in abstract ways. A core way in which this occurs is through what Foucault calls security mechanisms (Foucault, 2009; Sandset & Villadsen, 2023). I define security as revolving around the issue of safety and thus extraordinary measures to bring the situation back to normal (Opitz, 2011; Schmitt, 1996), meaning that we rather use the term *regulatory* mechanisms when referring to 'security mechanisms'. Regulation manifests in mechanisms meant to (re)direct forces, such as diseases, so as to alter their impact. Regulation operates at the macro-level through abstract measures, such as by changed levels of taxation on alcohol or by increasing the number of buses driving during rush hours during a pandemic to limit crowding.

These are infrastructural resources of the state, working through state power as the state seeks to improve its population biologically. Foucauldian studies explore how this occurs through various institutions where power manifests as it produces knowledge and works upon the biological bodies of individuals and populations, through regulative and predictive forms of governance, meant to affect the population, for instance by reducing smoking rates through increasing prices (Rose, 2009). The manner in which biopolitical forms of rule are enacted touch upon the issues of how knowledge enables complex logistical and infrastructural forms of rule. Thus, Foucault's writings are highly relevant for scholars interested in the autonomous state, including for those interested in the sources of power.

Moreover, a third form of power is of the utmost importance, both for our empirical context and for the state in general—ideological power, or in other words, ideological *sources* of power. Ideological power relates to the power of and through meaning, including the denoting of norms and rituals (Gorski, 2006; Mann, 1986, 1993, 2012, 2013). In this way, ideological power relates to the power over discourse, the power to impose 'regimes of truth' and thereby control what can be legitimately said (see Foucault, 1980, 1999). Through ideological power, power relations can be naturalized, and specific political measures can be justified. This is the passive utility of ideological power—offering support, a form of ideological infrastructure.

Ideological power relates to a core Weberian issue—legitimacy (Beetham, 1974; Weber, 1978). Legitimacy is the perceived appropriateness of governing arrangements and the relations between superordinate and subordinate (Weber, 1978). It relates to whether relations of power and authority are acknowledged as morally and socially acceptable by subject populations (Hurd, 1999). Legitimacy is a key resource for political actors, as institutionalizing power struggles and hierarchies reduces overt conflict, creating consensus around relations of rule. It relates partly to success, both with regard to the protection-obedience axiom, which posits that the state must protect society from threats (Hobbes, 1996; Schmitt, 1996), as well as the state's capacities in providing various other types of social good (Mann, 2012, 2013). Contemporary states are also highly dependent upon making their actions legal, i.e. based on the law, due to the rationalized modern criteria for legitimacy (Weber, 1978). The power of and over discourse—and thus meaning—increases legitimacy by construing the state's actions as legitimate (cf. Laclau & Mouffe, 1985). Without this resource, a political order is always threatened by the possibility of collapse (Bourdieu, 2014; Mann, 1984, 1993, 2012; Weber, 1946). Legitimacy is a central ideological resource as it grants leeway to legitimate actors. For instance, the legitimate state's commands are listened to, as we shall return to in the analysis, both when they are underpinned by threats of violence and when they are not.

Ideological power is also the power to define objects and situations, and thereby the active power to mobilize collective action (see Mann, 1986: 22). Typical examples are religious prophets or political demagogues mobilizing the masses (Mann, 1984), or states mobilizing society at large for war (Mironova & Whitt, 2020). By shaping how a situation is framed, those 'caging' ideological sources of power can mobilize the masses by shaping emotions and thoughts, so as to enable a collective action of an informal nature, such as protests, voluntary conscription into the army, or rebellion. Ideological sources of power are channelled through symbolic deeds. It may be a political action of symbolic significance, such as the Turkish state turning the Hagia Sophia back into a mosque (Oztig & Adisonmez, 2023), or closing down society due to a virus. It may be through ceremonies and rituals (Bourdieu, 1991). But the state can also simply speak—using the power of and over discourse (Bourdieu, 1991; Foucault, 1980)—for instance by construing the virus in a particular manner. Words are not *necessarily* cheaper than actions. Actions and articulations both carry symbolic content, meaning that they manifest ideological power.

In the contemporary world, including during the pandemic, propaganda is a core ideological instrument. Propaganda is not necessarily false/fake, (i.e. *disinformation*), even if disinformation is a propaganda instrument. Rather, propaganda is 'the management of mass communications for power purposes' (Lasswell, 1951: 66). It is weaponized information, utilized in campaigns where state and/or non-state actors seek to bias individuals and groups' attitudes, thoughts and affects (Lasswell, 1927). Doing so requires utilizing various rhetorical techniques, such as playing upon fear, guilt, envy, hope, self-interest, the national community and/or different values (Ingram, 2017; Wu, 2017). Note that while propaganda is a key ideological technique, legitimacy cannot be reduced to propaganda, as legitimacy entails legitimization processes in which those subject to power participate in complex series of negotiations (cf Migdal, 1988; Weber, 1978). Related to this, propaganda is facilitated by trust, as recipients of propaganda are more likely to comply and accept a vision of reality if they trust the provider, as seen in Norway during the pandemic (cf Christensen & Lægreid, 2020a).

Propaganda serves both passive purposes, i.e. it allows the state to shape public opinion towards accepting political arrangements, and it serves active purposes, as it is meant to mobilize masses towards action. As with the use of infrastructural and coercive sources of power, propaganda is effectively used by organizations which coordinate and contain knowledge about propaganda techniques, the human psyche and other pieces of relevant information, as well as the instruments needed to spread its message around society, so to enact communication campaigns capable of affecting the minds and emotions of entire populations. Using a Foucauldian lens, we can explore how propaganda works by exploring how it manifests at the level of emotions and thoughts, so as to change how reality is interpreted and thus, in the final instance, acted upon. Propaganda is a way of exercising ideological resources, manifesting in mechanisms of power at the level of emotions and thoughts, by altering how people think and feel.

We live in the era of propaganda (Wu, 2017). Just as infrastructural power has increased throughout the last century, so has the power of propaganda. Technological developments allow even the most private spheres to be colonized by the instruments of propaganda, through computers, televisions and mobile phones. Indeed, individuals reading through digital media in bed allow state (and non-state) actors to colonize even their bedrooms with sophisticated propaganda techniques. Improved possibilities of reaching private persons are coupled with an improved understanding of the human psyche, further increasing the potency of propaganda (Wu, 2017). It should be noted that while propaganda works on the basis of psychological and other techniques, the value of propaganda depends upon the ideological power of the wielder of this instrument. It is not merely about what is being said, or even how it is being said, but who says it.

Keeping propaganda as the exercise of ideological power in mind, the Foucauldian notion of liberal governance through self-regulation and freedom (see Foucault, 1991b, 2008a; C. Gordon, 1991; Miller & Rose, 2008; Rose, 1999)—can be state-mandated through the use of propaganda (cf. Lasswell, 1927, 1951; Wu, 2017). Self-regulation can be fostered and produced by propaganda, among other instruments, which seeks to make the individual act in a particular manner or for a particular objective. Importantly, we cannot reduce liberal governmentality to propaganda, but propaganda can be used to play upon knowledge and expertise, motivating individuals by convincing them, meaning that knowledge nexuses (psychiatry; medicine; economics) become abstract ideological sources of power which can be played upon and contested, among other things to legitimize political measures or nudge individuals into self-regulation based on political agendas, such as infection control.

Importantly, ideological power's efficiency is greatly enhanced by infrastructural power, as logistical, technological and organizational resources enable the prompt speed and creation of propaganda (see Mann, 1993, 2012, 2013). Legitimacy also interacts with coercive sources of power, as made clear by the issue of the state having a monopoly over the *legitimate* means of violence (Weber, 1978). Indeed, the Weberian focus upon political mastery or *Herrschaft*, which makes the state's commands and government in general appear legitimate, refers to legitimacy in general as a key element in political rule. Thus, the autonomous sources of state power can be understood as partly contingent upon legitimacy to work efficiently, but as Mann (1986, 1993, 2012) would point out, an autonomous state can also enforce its will over and through society against the will of non-state actors, and thus also to some extent in the absence of legitimacy, even if a state cannot survive indefinitely without legitimacy.

Reflecting on these sources of power, I can also explain how the state as a collective actor is *constituted*. The organizational configuration of the state—consisting of a rationalized state bureaucracy, a decision-making centre and numerous institutions—enables collective actions of a tightly regulated nature belonging to the state. Increased infrastructural powers are thus the core element enabling the state to move from being the instrument of a tyrant to being a depersonalized and abstract political entity which we can ascribe actions to. The institutional capacities of infrastructural power enable state autonomy, but also complex collective decision-making processes and thus actions more generally. Bringing the mechanisms of power into the picture, the macrostructures which make up the state can be seen as a result of the use of such sources of power in practice, which manifests in more or less regulated series of practices and institutional frameworks which make the state exist in action. In other words, the mechanisms of power which Foucauldians prioritize do indeed make up the state, as well as the state-society nexus which demarcates state from non-state spheres, a core element of liberal governmentality (cf Foucault, 2008a, 2009). However, the result of these mechanisms is more than a macrostructure. Rationalization, with its standardization of individual state agents and the normalization and regulation this produces at the micro-level, transforms the structure of the state into an organization and thus corporate agent.

Note that I impose upon Schmitt (1996, 2008) a Weberian understanding of state autonomy and state power: i.e. the state's right to declare the exception is dependent upon and constituted by its autonomy, and thus the autonomous sources of power, including state legitimacy and ideological capacities. From our Weberian perspective, a state will only be de facto capable of declaring an exception if it possesses the resources needed through a combination of the accumulation and use of coercive, infrastructural and ideological sources of power. Moreover, while my understanding of state autonomy is primarily Weberian, based on Mann's work, I take Schmitt's (1996, 2008) reflections on the exception seriously: state autonomy can perhaps best be observed in the exception, because the state more forcefully intervenes during the emergency than during everyday life—as seen with regard to Norway and Sweden, where similar populations accepted and supported different forms of state power based on the state's initial decision to declare the situation fully or only partly exceptional (cf Weiss & Thurbon, 2022).

A final note should be added before I seek to operationalize these somewhat abstract discussions. These theoretical reflections are state-centric. This is partly the case because our reality *is* state-centric. It is also motivated by the particular context of the pandemic being *extremely* state-centric. The two states in question unilaterally decide, and society must obey. Nonetheless, state-society relations are important. There are constant conflicts over the legitimate reach of the state, and these conflicts are ancient (cf. Migdal, 1988; Scott 2017; Tilly, 1992). Moreover, states embedding themselves within society enhance their capacities to act (Evans, 1995). Indeed, the state has always existed within society (Migdal, 1988; Seabrooke, 2002; Sabry, 2022). While the state can transgress state-non-state boundaries, as the coming chapters will show the state is not omnipotent. The state cannot colonize non-state spaces indefinitely. The COVID-19 pandemic revealed the might of the state, but it also hinted at the limits of its power. Even in China, state coercion and the state's expansion into society to deal with COVID-19 led to massive protests in late 2022 (Yang, 2022). The state's vertical position vis-à-vis society lets it expand into society, transgressing boundaries, especially if the state can declare a situation exceptional and have this definition accepted by large sections of society, but such actions may have unknown consequences, and such actions can produce counter-actions, including resistance and even rebellion. This nevertheless justifies my focus upon the state within this particular empirical context.

3.5 Operationalizing the Weberian-Foucauldian Marriage

The aforementioned theoretical discussions serve a purpose—to marry the Weberian theory of the state, heavily dependent upon the work of Mann and the sources of power, and the Foucauldian theory of the mechanisms of power, so as to create an analytical framework for exploring the politics of COVID-19 in Norway and Sweden, and thus cover the aforementioned gaps, while laying the groundwork for a new theoretical synthesis for exploring state power more generally. This synthesizing has until now been abstract. It is time to clarify how this theoretical framework can be analytically used, thereby operationalizing the marriage.

This is all based on tactical needs. When exploring the politics of COVID-19 from a Foucauldian perspective, exploring the mechanisms of power through an agential lens defining the state as subject, a question arises: *how* do these mechanisms of power come into being? Through a pyramidical conception of power, we perceive power as working as follows: power flows from the top of organizations, based on the sources of power they cage and thereafter use. For the state, I am mostly interested in coercive, infrastructural and ideological sources of power. These sources can be enacted, for instance through the monopoly over legitimate means of violence, the state bureaucracy, or targeted communication campaigns. When these sources are used, they impact institutions, relations and individuals in different ways, depending on how they are used, and how their usage is interpreted, felt and accepted or resisted by target populations. When power manifests in various local settings and institutions, such as pupil-teacher or doctor-patient interaction, it creates both effects within the interaction, and equally important, it produces knowledge about the subject population and utility of techniques of power, which thereafter allows for the increased potency of power from above.

To operationalize the theoretical framework, I now look at the Ottoman politics of the plague, before moving on to the politics of COVID-19 in Norway and Sweden. I explore the mechanisms of power of the Ottoman Empire, before discussing the sources of power and thereafter, the political reasoning of the state and how it underpinned its agency. Following my anatomical perspective on power, I address both the macrophysics or sources, and the microphysics or mechanisms, of power. Scholars can start with their main inquiry of interest, thereby choosing strategically according to their theoretical and empirical focus. However, it will generally be useful to first look at how power manifests in mechanisms of power. In line with Foucault's research strategy (1990, 1991a), we seek to study how bodies, thoughts, relations, habits, etc., are handled. Thereafter, we seek to explore how these mechanisms of power came into being by looking towards their organizational and thus agential origins, in order to explore the sources of power enacted to constitute said mechanisms.

The following reflections will be based on Ottoman scholarship (i.e. Balmus, 2012; Bolaños, 2019; Varlik, 2015). As stated earlier in the chapter, the Ottoman state sought to control the material and spiritual hygiene of the population, especially within the centre of the Empire. Controlling material and spiritual hygiene became a state responsibility, and the state acted swiftly to ensure that its will manifested in reality. New spheres became affairs of the state, and the state expanded into new social sites. Slaughterhouses and the sizes, locations, etc., of new buildings were increasingly regulated, in the predictive manner of biopolitical regulation, where abstract criteria are crafted and imposed. Similarly, the state would determine how and where funerals could be held, exercising biopolitical forms of regulation based on its predictions and generalizations (cf. Sandset & Villadsen, 2023). This would manifest in changed behaviour at the micro-level, with rituals carried out in new ways, or alternatively, with the risk of state violence. Moreover, the somatically or morally 'impure' were placed under tight control of a disciplinary and juridical-sovereign nature. They experienced techniques of power regarding their bodies, relations, practices and moralities, as they would be disciplined as well as excluded from certain areas, and in some cases, they experienced juridical-sovereign repression, in the form of prohibiting activities considered immoral, such as prostitution. As Nükhet Varlik (2015: 283) writes:

> it is unmistakable that the powers of governance now went beyond regulating bodies and sought to infiltrate on moral conduct and lifestyle. Perhaps it should not come as a surprise that these regulations especially targeted perceived danger zones, where disordered interactions were imagined to take place.

Moreover, the Ottoman Empire closed its border, placing travellers in quarantine and isolation on islands and in other facilities. Power was exercised at the level of the body, as bodies were distributed and confined in space. Bodies were not handled as individuals, but as groups or crews, as most would arrive by ship. The body was regulated, monitored and confined, for instance by being quarantined in a specifically designated area, or alternatively aboard the ship. Time also became a political instrument, regulating bodies for days, controlling the individual through time. Mechanisms of power manifested in practice at the locations where bodies, practices, relations, thoughts, etc., were to be shaped and moulded, produced and destroyed. The Ottoman Empire, by implementing quarantine, obtained increased control over travellers, and could regulate their bodies through the rationalization of time, i.e. a given period, and control over the border, i.e. the spatialization of power, making entry into the city a tightly regulated affair.

However, how are these mechanisms of power, which regulate 'impure' buildings and rituals, targeting 'immoral' conduct and thoughts, and confining 'dangerous' bodies, possible? This is a question also raised in the literature review. From a Foucauldian perspective, power is to be studied as mechanisms manifesting in and enabled by institutional arrangements. Therefore, agency is no core concern, and it may be bracketed for analytical and ontological reasons. However, the aforementioned studies on the issue of COVID-19 did include an agential lens, exploring how the state exercised power—as I do now. If a scholar brings organizational agency into the picture, then said scholar needs some way of accounting for how this agency leads to said mechanisms of power. It is not enough to say that the state exercises discipline. Discipline is after all a mechanism, which is not fully under somebody's control (i.e. Foucault, 1991a, 2008b). Therefore, bringing the agency of the state into the picture demands some sense of theorizing on the sources of power that enable the state to act in a way to create the disciplinary arrangements manifesting in said mechanisms. After all, while the Ottoman Empire did exercise power in these various ways, gaps still remain in the argument, as how the Ottoman Empire could act as such is unexplained.

This is where our microphysical lens is supplemented by a macrophysical lens. Moving beyond the mechanisms of power, I can trace the origins of said mechanisms to the state apparatus. The Ottoman politics of the plague was enabled by various infrastructural resources. The state administration, which regulated and controlled state agents for this purpose, had to be sophisticated. Moreover, it became increasingly so when the state implemented the politics of the plague. The state depended upon a professional corps of agents employed specifically to implement its will in practice. This also required a certain level of embeddedness—the state had to be present in society to actually regulate it. Beyond the trained, uniform and professional personnel, the state necessitated means of accumulating and distributing information. Thus, the state had to have means of surveillance, to monitor the border as well as those in quarantine. Also, the state needed knowledge about how plagues work and how they spread. They also had to know their own populations, including the 'dangerous', i.e. the morally and somatically 'impure', and their whereabouts, characteristics and practices. These are no small feats prior to the technological revolution of the last century—and we cannot begin to understand the politics of plague in the Ottoman Empire if we ignore these infrastructural resources (cf. Varlik, 2015).

To connect the issue of the macrophysics and microphysics of power, I must bring the state's agency into the picture, which also entails exploring the rationalizations and problematizations underpinning government. As an actor, the state must have preferences. State preferences are the result of a complex series of deliberations, contestations and negotiations (Nordlinger, 1981; Wendt, 1999, 2004). As the politics of plague had both medical and moral components, so the state's biopolitical objectives revolved around more than regulating bodies. The *morals* of individuals also became objects of governance. The state 'infiltrated' society in new ways, becoming the 'basic agent of morality' and hygiene (cf. Foucault, 2013), as happened in Britain and France, also for biopolitical reasons (Foucault, 1994a, 1994b). The state increasingly policed the bodies and morals of individuals, seeking to discipline them, to change them. This statification—numerous new aspects of life were placed under state control—is best explored by conceptualizing the state as an agent which imposes itself upon society—based on the aforementioned governmentalization which renders reality governable in such a manner to begin with. Modernist and conservative philosophies converged as official Ottoman state doctrine, together with economic and geopolitical considerations. Taking the questions of governmentalization and statification seriously, we can enhance an agential approach to the state by exploring how the state colonizes or embeds itself within parts of society where previously it was absent, or vice-versa, why it leaves parts of society which were previously statified. The politics of the plague in the Ottoman Empire shows how statification and governmentalization occur. Concerns of a medical *and* spiritual nature, together with geopolitical considerations, manifested in a form of ethico-biopolitics. The Ottoman state combined different concerns and objects of rule into a political framework, and the political measures manifesting in statification were the result of governmentalization.

I can similarly operationalize the theoretical marriage by making similar reflections on the politics of COVID-19 in Norway and Sweden, where I discuss the link between the microphysics and macrophysics of power, as well as the importance of political rationalities. As with the Ottomans, I start by looking at mechanisms of power, before I seek to contextualize them as being enabled by sources of power which the state enacts on the basis of political reasoning. To do so, I shall briefly discuss the three core ways the Norwegian and Swedish state governed, and the core of our analytical focus below—voluntarism, juridical-sovereignty and conscription, the latter being a form of 'government at a distance' which enables the state to act through individuals transformed into infection control agents, as briefly discussed in the last chapter.

First, as stated above, the politics of COVID-19 in Norway and Sweden worked partly through voluntarism and responsibilization (see Girtli Nygren & Olofsson, 2020; Sandset & Villadsen, 2023). This shows power working through the state that mobilizes individuals to voluntarily comply. This occurred largely through communication campaigns meant to activate citizens as responsible subjects (Almlund et al., 2023). As we shall discuss further below, power manifested at the micro-level of hearts and minds through complex communication campaigns where the state attempted to alter how the situation was perceived. A Foucauldian lens on this issue will focus upon the communication as it manifests at the level of thoughts and feelings, and thereafter in potentially altered conduct. Such studies of indirect government and how it manifests in self-governance are useful. However, numerous questions arise from such studies. How can the state communicate a totalizing message, spread through society? Why cannot a private individual or organization accomplish such a feat? Why was the state's message largely accepted in Norway and Sweden, despite their messages being contradictory, justifying different strategies? The answer must lie within the state, and more accurately, in the ideological sources of power which the state cages and enacts when it finds it necessary. We can explain the microphysics of power—communication as it manifests at the level of thoughts and feelings so as to constitute self-regulation—by looking at how the state uses and relies upon material technologies, legitimacy, citizen's trust in the state, organizational knowledge and propaganda techniques. The communication campaigns first and foremost make sense when we contextualize them as enactments of ideological sources of power, moving between the micro- and the macro-level. The agency of the state creates the link between the two by translating sources into mechanisms of power.

Similarly, both states worked partly through juridical-sovereign measures related to law (Gjerde, 2021b; Winblad et al., 2022). The Norwegian state closed down, while the Swedish state opted for a softer use of law, which in rarer cases manifested in local close-downs. In both countries, this entailed confiscating various rights and liberties, such as the right to assemble, or for certain businesses, the right to operate. While there were several differences that we shall touch upon below, this manifested in negative mechanisms of power, i.e. closures, denials, fines, etc. However, how can the state as an actor exercise power in this way? A macrophysical perspective allows us to explain how these juridical-sovereign mechanisms of power can be made to operate. The state cages vast coercive sources of power within itself, monopolizing the legal right to use violence through the police and military corps. This makes the state's commands binding, as the state can impose its will through force, thereby enabling these negative mechanisms of power to operate. The coercive sources of power, underpinned and supported by institutional capacities we shall cover below, formed the roots of these juridical-sovereign mechanisms, as the state enacted these sources when it acted forcefully over society by saying 'no'.

Moreover, as discussed above, the mobilization of society through conscription into the infection control machinery was a key technique in both countries. The Norwegian and Swedish states allocated responsibilities to people as infection control agents. Those individuals had either to withdraw from roles such as that of employer, or to accept mandatory responsibilities in enforcing the state's will on the state's behalf. While there are numerous differences in practice between the two states, they both exercised power in such an indirect manner, governing at a distance, in formalized ways. Conscription worked as an abstract mechanism of power, which made the active exercise of power on the state's behalf compulsory. Thus, conscription manifested in practice when conscripts acted in accordance with the state's will by exercising power over others. This exercise of power manifested in exclusionary and disciplinary mechanisms, such as isolation, distancing, etc. To mobilize tens or even hundreds of thousands of individuals, these states depended upon numerous infrastructural sources of power: embeddedness within society, a highly competent and professionalized bureaucracy and administration, vast surveillance capacities rooted in technology and organization and knowledge about their populations. The strength of this mobilization lies in the state's capacities to formalize it, making conscription into the state machinery obligatory for vast numbers of individuals. Naturally, this mobilization was supported both by the immense ideological sources of power, making the state's conscriptions legitimate, and the coercive sources of power, which enabled the state to punish those disobeying formal commands.

This way, we can study how the state acted through and over society by enacting these sources of power, and this enactment of its sources of power manifested at the micro-level in mechanisms of power, within and beyond the state apparatus. We must however move beyond discussing the mechanisms and sources of power, as I did in the Ottoman example. While this has afforded useful insights into how the state's actions link sources and mechanisms of power together, by translating the former into the latter, another question remains unanswered. Why did the two states act to deal with COVID-19? As stated above, the 'Spanish flu' killed scores in a way that made COVID-19 appear relatively mild, merely a century ago. Why did states during the coronavirus pandemic feel a need to act? And why did the Swedish state act in a soft manner compared to the 'COVID consensus' (Green, 2021)? A governmentality perspective posits that we must explore the rationalizations and the problematizations underpinning government.

In both countries, COVID-19 has been interpreted through a biopolitical frame, which granted the issue of life itself as a priority. In Norway, the state subordinated all problems to the imperative of infection control, also if further problems were created by the infection control regime (Gjerde 2022). This made it necessary for the state to act with severity—the situation called for severe measures—due to the abnormality of the situation. The Swedish state's vision somewhat clashes with this. As others have pointed out, the Swedish state reasoned in a more liberal manner (Larsson, 2022; Nygren & Olofsson, 2020). The Swedish state saw a great biopolitical crisis *and* worried about the effects of state intervention, combining liberal *and* biopolitical considerations. This helps us understand the political responses of the two states. The Norwegian state acted with the greatest severity because it perceived the situation to be a great crisis, subordinating other concerns to biopolitical problematizations and rationalizations. In contrast, the Swedish state tried to limit its own interventions in society, because it perceived the situation through biopolitical *and* liberal lenses. It is not institutional or cultural factors which determined the strategies of these two states, but rather, different forms of problematizations and rationalizations of the situation.

Exploring the link between the sources and mechanisms of power, we can explain how mechanisms of power work and how they can be made to work, thereby studying power in a manner combining a macrophysical and microphysical lens. Contrary to Foucault's (2008b: 16) claim that:

> we cannot use the notion of State apparatus because it is much too broad, much too abstract to designate these immediate, tiny, capillary powers that

> are exerted on the body, behavior, actions, and time of individuals. The State apparatus does not take this microphysics of power into account [,]

we may in fact benefit from exploring the state and its role in designating mechanisms of power towards individuals' bodies, actions, time, behaviour, etc., as the state apparatus seems to indeed take the microphysics of power into account (cf. Lichtenstein, 2020). To do so, we must however move *beyond* the microphysics of powers, as we must explain how the state can participate in designating these 'tiny' powers exerted in local contexts, also far beyond the state's formal apparatus. Studying the link between the mechanisms and sources of power, between how power can be contained and how it works, and between how political reasoning underpins political actions, I blend the Foucauldian understanding of government and the mechanisms of power with a Weberian understanding of the state as an autonomous actor and a container of sources of power. This invites us to study the state, and more importantly the state's agency, as the active component.

I can now conclude this *preliminary* operationalization. During the pandemic, different mechanisms of power emerged, related to control, discipline, juridical-sovereignty and self-regulation. These mechanisms were the direct result of the states exercising power, thereby being contingent upon state agency, and the sources of powers states can cage and thereafter use. This occurred based on a primarily biopolitical reasoning in Norway, and a mixture of biopolitical and liberal reasonings in Sweden: different quantities of these sources of power were utilized. These culturally, ideologically and institutionally similar states acted differently on the basis of how they perceived the situation. The reasoning of the two states provided justifications for different strategies, but in both cases, power operated in a pyramidical manner. Power moved from the top and down, both when it manifested in explicit exercises of state power and when it manifested in various subtle and horizontal mechanisms of power, such as disciplinary mechanisms imposed by formally non-state actors or even private individuals voluntarily policing fellow citizens due to the communitarian spirit both states sought to foster. The Weberian-Foucauldian synthesis allows us to explore these different dimensions of power, moving to holistic understanding of the state.

References

Almlund, P., E Kjeldsen, J., & Mølster, R. (2023). Expressions of governance, risk, and responsibility: Public campaigns in the crisis and risk management of Covid-19 in Denmark, Norway, and Sweden. In B. Johansson, Ø. Ihlen, J. Lindholm, & M. Blach-Ørsten (Eds.), *Communicating a pandemic: Crisis management and Covid-19 in the Nordic countries* (pp. 121–149). University of Gothenburg.

Arts, B. (2014). Assessing forest governance from a 'Triple G' perspective: Government, governance, governmentality. *Forest Policy and Economics, 49*, 17–22.

Ayodele, O. (2019). Information infrastructures: The conduit power of ICTs in Africa. *The Strategic Review for Southern Africa, 41*(2).

Balmus, B. (2012). *Plague, quarantines and geopolitics in the Ottoman Empire.* Edinburgh University Press.

Barry, A., Osborne, T., & Rose, N. (1996) Introduction. In A. Barry, T. Osborne, & N. Rose, *Foucault and political Reason* (pp. 1–18). Routledge.

Beetham, D. (1974). *Max Weber and the theory of modern politics.* George Allen & Unwin LTd.

Bröckling, U., Krasmann, S., & Lemke, T (2011). From Foucault's lectures at the College de France to studies of governmentality: An introduction. In Bröckling, S. Krasmann, & T. Lemke (Eds.), *Governmentality: Current issues and future challenges* (p. 54). Routledge.

Bolaños, I. A. (2019). The Ottomans during the global crises of cholera and plague: The view from Iraq and the Gulf. *International Journal of Middle East Studies, 51*(4), 603–620.

Bourdieu, P. (1991). *Language and ideological power.* Polity Press.

Bourdieu, P. (2014). *On the state: Lectures at the Collège de France, 1989–1992.* Polity.

Bowen, C. (2021). Discipline and control and Covid-19. *La Deleuziana, 13*, 164–175.

Buchanan, I. (2022). Biopolitics, Discipline and Governmentality. In: Das, S. S., and Pratihar, A. R. (eds.). Technology, *Urban Space and the Networked Community.* Cham: Palgrave Macmillan (1–28).

Burchell, G. (1991). Peculiar interests: Civil society and governing 'the system of natural liberty'. In: Burchell, Graham, Gordon, Colin and Miller, Peter (eds). The Foucault Effect: Studies in Governmentality. Chicago: Chicago University Press, pp. 119–150.

Byler, D. (2023). The camp fix: Infrastructural power and the "re-education labour regime" in Turkic Muslim industrial parks in north-west China. *The China Quarterly, 255*, 628–643.

Christensen, T., & Lægreid, P. (2020a). Balancing governance capacity and legitimacy: How the Norwegian Government handled the COVID−19 crisis as a high performer. *Public Administration Review, 80*(5), 774–779. https://doi.org/10.1111/puar.13241

Colliot-Thélène, C. (2009). Modern rationalities of the political: From Foucault to Weber. *Max Weber Studies, 9*(1), 165–187.

Dandeker, C. (1990). *Surveillance, Power and Modernity*. Polity Press.

Dean, M. (1994). *Critical and effective histories. Foucault's methods and historical sociology*. Routledge.

Dean, M. (1999). *Governmentality: Power and rule in modern society*. Sage.

Dean, M. (2007). *Governing societies. Political perspectives on domestic and international rule*. Open University Press.

Dean, M., & Villadsen, K. (2012). *Statsfobi og Civilsamfund. Foucault og hans arvingers blik på staten*. Nyt fra Samfundsvidernskaberne.

Deleuze, G. (1988). *Foucault*. University of Minnesota Press.

Deleuze, G. (1992). Postscript on the society of control. *October, 59*, 3–8.

Elias, N. (1978). *The history of Manners. The civilizing process, volume 1*. Basil Blackwell.

Elias, N. (1982). *Power and civility. The civilizing process volume 2*. Basil Blackwell.

Evans, P. B. (1995). *Embedded autonomy: States and industrial transformation*. Princeton University Press.

Flew, T. (2015). Foucault, Weber, neoliberalism and the politics of governmentality. *Theory, Culture & Society, 32*(7–8), 317–326.

Foucault, M. (1980). *Power/knowledge*. Pantheon books.

Foucault, M. (1985). *Discourse and truth: The problematization of Parrhesia*. Northwestern University Press.

Foucault, M. (1990). *The history of sexuality, volume 1. An introduction*. Penguin Books.

Foucault, M. (1991a). *Discipline and punish: The birth of the prison*. Penguin Books.

Foucault. (1991b). Governmentality. In G. Burchell, C. Gordon, & P. Miller (Eds.), *The Foucault effect: Studies in governmentality*. The University of Chicago Press.

Foucault, M. (1994a). *The birth of social medicine*. In F. D. Faubion, M. Foucault (Eds.), *Power. Essential works of Foucault 1954–1984 volume* 3 (pp. 134–156). New York: The New Press.

Foucault, M. (1994b). The politics of health in the eighteenth century. In F. D. Faubion, M. Foucault (Eds.), *Power. Essential works of Foucault 1954–1984 volume* 3 (pp. 90–105). New York: The New Press.

Foucault, M. (1994c). Omnes et Sungulatim. In F. D. Faubion, M. Foucault (Eds). *Power. Essential works of Foucault 1954–1984 volume 3* (pp. 298–325). New York: The New Press.

Foucault, M. (2003). *Society must be defended: Lectures at Collège De France, 1975–1976*. Pidacor.

Foucault, M. (2008a). *The birth of biopolitics - Lectures at the Collège de France, 1978–1979*. Palgrave Macmillan.

Foucault, M. (2008b). *Psychiatric power: Lectures at the College de France, 1973–1974*. Macmillan.

Foucault, M. (2009). *Security, territory, population: Lectures at Collège de France, 1977–1978*. Palgrave Macmillan.

Foucault, M. (2013). *The punitive society*. Picador.

Foucault, M. (2014). *The government of the living*. Picador.

Foucault, M. (2019). *Penal theories and institutions*. Picador.

Giddens, A. (1981). *A contemporary critique of historical materialism. Volume 1: Power, property and the state*. Macmillan Press LTD.

Giddens, A. (1987). *A contemporary critique of historical materialism. Volume 2: The nation-state and violence*. University of California Press.

Gjerde, L. E. L. (2021a). From liberalism to biopolitics: Investigating the Norwegian government's two responses to COVID-19. *European Societies, 23*(sup1), S262–S274. https://doi.org/10.1080/14616696.2020.1824003

Gjerde, L. E. L. (2021b). Governing humans and 'things': Power and rule in Norway during the Covid-19 pandemic. *Journal of Political Power, 14*(3), 472–492. https://doi.org/10.1080/2158379X.2020.1870264

Gjerde, L. E. L. (2022). Den norske regjeringens diskursive muliggjøring av koronapolitikken: Et Foucauldiansk perspektiv. *Norsk sosiologisk tidsskrift*, (3), 29–45.

Gjerde, L. E. L. (2024a). Marrying the sources and mechanisms of power? Understanding the quarantine hotel through Michel Foucault and Michael Mann. *Journal of Political Power*. https://doi.org/10.1080/2158379X.2024.2337617

Gjerde, L. E. L. (2024b). Biopolitical Leviathan: Understanding state power in the era of COVID-19 through the Weberian-Foucauldian theory of the state. *Theoria: A Journal of Social and Political Theory, 71*(1), 48–74. https://doi.org/10.3167/th.2024.7117803

Gutting, G. (2006). Introduction: Michel Foucault: A user's manual. In G. Cutting (Ed.), *The Cambridge companion to Foucault. 2nd edition* (pp. 1–28). Cambridge University Press.

Guzzini, S. (1993). Structural power: The limits of neorealist power analysis. *International Organization, 47*(3), 443–478.

Gordon, C. (1994). Introductio'n. In F. D. Faubion & M. Foucault (Eds.), *Power. Essential works of Foucault 1954–1984 volume* 3 (pp. xi–xli). The New Press.

Gordon, C. (1991). Governmental rationality: An introduction. In G. Burchell, C. Gordon, & P. Miller (Eds.), *The Foucault effect: Studies in governmentality* (pp. 1–51). University of Chicago Press.

Gorski, P. S. (2003). The disciplinary revolution: Calvinism and the rise of the state in early modern Europe. University of Chicago Press.

Gorski, P. S. (2006). Mann's theory of ideological power: Sources, applications and elaborations. In J. A. Hall & R. Schroeder (Eds.), *An anatomy of power: The social theory of Michael Mann* (pp. 101–134). Cambridge University Press.

Green, T. (2021). *The Covid consensus: The new politics of global inequality*. Hurst.

Heiskala, R. (2016). The evolution of the sources of social power, and some extensions. In R. Schroeder (Ed.), *Global powers. Michael Mann's anatomy of the twentieth century and beyond* (pp. 11–37). Cambridge University Press.

Hobbes, T. (1996). *Leviathan*. Oxford University Press.

Hurd, I. (1999). Legitimacy and authority in international politics. *International Organization, 53*(2), 379–408.

Haugaard, M. (2010). Power: A 'family resemblance' concept. *European Journal of Cultural Studies, 13*(4), 419–438.

Haugaard, M. (2022). Foucault and power: A critique and retheorization. *Critical Review, 34*(3–4), 341–371.

Hegghammer, T. (2021). Resistance is futile: The war on terror supercharged state power. *Foreign Affairs, 100*, 44.

Hindess, B. (1996). *Discourses of power: From Hobbes to Foucault*. Blackwell.

Hobson J, M. (1997). *The wealth of states: A comparative sociology of international economic and political change* Cambridge University Press.

Ingram, H. J. (2017). An analysis of inspire and Dabiq: Lessons from AQAP and Islamic State's propaganda war. *Studies in Conflict & Terrorism, 40*(5), 357–375.

Jimenez-Anca, J. J. (2013). Beyond power: unbridging Foucault and Weber. *European Journal of Social Theory, 16*(1), 36–50.

Joseph, J. (2004). Foucault and reality. *Capital & Class, 28*(1), 143–165.

Jessen, M. H., & von Eggers, N. (2020). Governmentality and statification: Towards a Foucauldian theory of the state. *Theory, Culture & Society, 37*(1), 53–72.

Jessop, B. (2001). Bringing the state back in (yet again): Reviews, revisions, rejections, and redirections. *International Review of Sociology/Revue internationale de sociologie, 11*(2), 149–173.

Jessop, B. (2007). From micro-powers to governmentality: Foucault's work on statehood, state formation, statecraft and state power. *Political Geography, 26*, 34–40.

Jessop, B. (2011) Constituting another Foucault Effect. Foucault on states and Statecraft . In Bröckling, S. Krasmann, & T. Lemke (Eds.), *Governmentality: Current issues and future challenges* (pp. 54–73). New York: Routledge.

Jessop, B. (2015). *The State: Past, Present, Future*. Wiley.
Jessop, B., & Morgan, J. (2022). The strategic-relational approach, realism and the state: From regulation theory to neoliberalism via Marx and Poulantzas, an interview with Bob Jessop. *Journal of Critical Realism, 21*(1), 83–118.
Keyes, C. F. (2002). Weber and anthropology. *Annual Review of Anthropology, 31*(1), 233–255.
Kim, J. (2021). Rethinking public administration and the state: A Foucauldian governmentality perspective. *International Review of Public Administration, 26*(2), 175–191. https://doi.org/10.1080/12294659.2021.1889102
Laclau, E., & Mouffe, C. (1985). *Hegemony and Socialist Strategy. Towards a Radical Democratic Politics*. Verso.
Larsson, O. L. (2022). The Swedish Covid-19 strategy and voluntary compliance: Failed securitisation or constitutional security management? *European Journal of International Security, 7*(2), 226–247.
Lasswell, H. D. (1927). The theory of political propaganda. *American Political Science Review, 21*(3), 627–631.
Lasswell, H. D. (1951). The strategy of Soviet propaganda. *Proceedings of the Academy of Political Science, 24*(2), 66–78.
Lea, J., & Stenson, K. (2007). Security, sovereignty, and non-state governance from below. *Can. JL & Soc., 22*, 9.
Lemke, T. (2002). Foucault, governmentality, and critique. *Rethinking Marxism, 14*(3), 49–64. https://doi.org/10.1080/089356902101242288
Lemke, T. (2007). An indigestible meal? Foucault, governmentality and state theory. *Distinktion: Scandinavian Journal of Social Theory, 8*(2), 43–64. https://doi.org/10.1163/9789087909857_004
Lemke, T. (2019). *Foucault's analysis of modern government. A critique of political reason*. Verso.
Lessenich, S. (2011). Constructing the socialized self. Mobilization and control in the "active society". In Bröckling, S. Krasmann, T. Lemke (Eds.), *Governmentality: Current issues and future challenges* (pp. 304–319). Routledge.
Lichtenstein, E. B. (2020). On the ways of writing the history of the state. *Foucault Studies*, 71–95.
Lukes, S. (2004). *Power: A radical view*. Macmillan.
Mann, M. (1984). The autonomous power of the state: Its origins, mechanisms and results. *European Journal of Sociology, 25*(2), 185–213.
Mann, M. (1986). *The sources of social power. Volume 1. A history of power from the beginning to A.D. 1760*. Cambridge University Press
Mann, M. (1993). *The sources of social power, volume II: The rise of classes and nation states*. Cambridge University Press.
Mann, M. (2008). Infrastructural power revisited. *Studies in Comparative International Development, 43*(3), 355–365.

Mann, M. (2012) *The sources of social power. Volume 3. Global empires and Revolution, 1890–1945.* Cambridge University Press.

Mann, M. (2013). *The sources of social power. Volume 4, globalizations, 1945–2011.* Cambridge University Press.

McKee, K. (2009). Post-Foucauldian governmentality: What does it offer critical social policy analysis? *Critical Social Policy, 29*(3), 465–486.

Merlingen, M. (2011). From governance to governmentality in CSDP: Towards a Foucauldian research agenda. *JCMS: Journal of Common Market Studies, 49*(1), 149–169.

Migdal, J. S. (1988). *Strong societies and weak states: State-society relations and state capabilities in the Third World.* Princeton University Press.

Miller, P., & Rose, N. (2008). *Governing the present: Administering economic, social and political life.* Cambridge: Polity Press.

Mironova, V., & Whitt, S. (2020). Mobilizing civilians into high-risk forms of violent collective action. *Journal of Peace Research, 57*(3), 391–405.

Mitchell, T. (1991). The limits of the state: Beyond statist approaches and their critics. *The American Political Science Review, 85*(1), 77–96.

Nordlinger, E. (1981). *The autonomy of the democratic state.* Harvard University Press.

Novak, W. J. (2008). The myth of the "weak" American state. *The American historical review, 113*(3), 752–772.

Poulantzas, N. (1978). *State, power.* New Left Books.

O'Neill, J. (1986). The disciplinary society: From Weber to Foucault. *British Journal of Sociology*, 42–60.

Opitz, S. (2011). Government unlimited. The security Dispositif of illiberal governmentality. In Bröckling, S. Krasmann, & T. Lemke (Eds.), *Governmentality: Current issues and future challenges* (pp. 93–114).

Oztig, L. I., & Adisonmez, U. C. (2023). Sovereignty, power, and authority: Understanding the conversion of Hagia Sophia from a performative perspective. *Southeast European and Black Sea Studies.* https://doi.org/10.1080/14683857.2023.2189543

Owen, D. (2013). *Maturity and modernity: Nietzsche, Weber, Foucault and the ambivalence of reason.* Routledge.

Sabry, M. I. (2022). The institutional origins of state–society relations. *Fulbright Review of Economics and Policy, 2*(2), 161–183.

Sandset, T., & Villadsen, K. (2023). Pandemic modelling and model citizens: Governing COVID-19 through predictive models, sovereignty and discipline. *The Sociological Review*, 00380261221102023.

Sarr, M. (2011). Relocating the modern state: Governmentality and the history of political ideas. In Bröckling, S. Krasmann, & T. Lemke (Eds.), *Governmentality: Current issues and future challenges* (pp. 34–55). Routledge.

Sayer, A. (2012). Power, causality and normativity: A critical realist critique of Foucault. *Journal of Political Power, 5*(2), 179–194.
Sawyer, S. W. (2015). Foucault and the state. *The Tocqueville Review/la Revue Tocqueville, 36*(1), 135–164.
Schmitt, C. (1996). *The concept of the political*. University of Chicago Press.
Schmitt, C. (2008). *Leviathan in the state theory of Thomas Hobbes. Meaning and failure of a political system*. The University of Chicago Press.
Schmitt, C. (2014). *Dictatorship*. Polity Press.
Schmitt, S. (2020). *Political theology* (2nd ed.). Antelope Hill Publishing.
Scott, J. C. (2017). *Against the Grain: A Deep History of the Earliest State*. New Haven: Yale University Press
Seabrooke, L. (2002). Bringing legitimacy back into Neo-Weberian state theory and international relations. Australian National University, Department of International Relations, Working Paper 2002/6.
Selg, P. (2016). 'The fable of the Bs': Between substantialism and deep relational thinking about power. *Journal of Political Power, 9*(2), 183–205.
Sending, O. J., & Neumann, I. B. (2006). Governance to governmentality: Analyzing NGOs, states, and power. *International Studies Quarterly, 50*(3), 651–672.
Shammas, V. L., & Sandset, T. J. (2020). Reproduction and the welfare state: Notes on Norwegian biopolitics. *Nordic Journal of Social Research, 11*(1), 1–18.
Skocpol, T. (1979). *States and social revolutions. A comparative analysis of France, Russia and China*. Cambridge University Press.
Skocpol T. (1985). Bringing the state back in: Strategies of analysis in current research. In P. B. Evans, D. Rueschemeyer, T. Skocpol (Eds.), *Bringing the state back in* (pp. 3–37). Cambridge University Press.
Skocpol, T. (2008). Bringing the state back in: Retrospect and prospect the 2007 Johan Skytte prize lecture. *Scandinavian Political Studies, 31*(2), 109–124.
Soifer, H. (2008). State infrastructural power: Approaches to conceptualization and measurement. *Studies in Comparative International Development, 43*, 231–251.
Stenson, K. (2005). Sovereignty, biopolitics and the local government of crime in Britain. *Theoretical Criminology, 9*, 265–287.
Szakolczai, A. (2000). *Reflexive historical sociology*. Routledge.
Szakolczai, A. (2013). *Max Weber and Michel Foucault: Parallel life-works*. Routledge.
Rabinow, P., & Rose, N. (2006). Biopower today. *BioSocieties, 1*(2), 195–217.
Raffnsøe, S., Mennicken, A., & Miller, P. (2019). The Foucault effect in organization studies. *Organization Studies, 40*(2), 155–182.
Rippa, A., & Oakes, T. (2023). Infrastructural thinking in China: A research agenda. *The China Quarterly*, 1–13.

Rose, N. (1996). Governing "advanced" liberal democracies. In A. Barry, T. Osborne, & N. Rose (Eds.), *Foucault and political reason* (pp. 37–64). Routledge.

Rose, N. (1999). *Powers of freedom: Reframing political thought*. Cambridge University Press.

Rose, N. (2009). *Livets politik. Biomedicin, Magt og Subjecktivitiet i det 21. århundrede*. Dansk Filosofisk forlag.

Rose, N., & Miller, P. (1992). Political power beyond the state: Problematics of government. *British Journal of Sociology, 22*(3), 283–299.

Tilly, C. (1992). *Coercion, capital, and European states, AD 990–1992*. Blackwell.

Van Krieken, R. (1990). The organization of the soul: Elias and Foucault on discipline and the self. *European Journal of Sociology/Archives Européennes de Sociologie, 31*(2), 353–371.

Varlik, N. (2015). *Plague and empire in the early modern Mediterranean world*. Cambridge University Press.

Villadsen, K. (2016). Michel Foucault and the forces of civil society. *Theory, Culture & Society, 33*(3), 3–26.

Villadsen, K., & Wahlberg, A. (2015). The government of life: Managing populations, health and scarcity. *Economy and Society, 44*(1), 1–17.

Waltz, K. H. (1979). *Theory of international politics*. McGraw-Hill.

Weber, M. (1946). *From Max Weber: essays in sociology*. Oxford University Press.

Weber, M. (1978). *Economy and society*. University of California Press.

Weber, M. (1995). *The Russian revolutions* (G. C. Wells & P. Baehr, Trans. and Ed.). Cambridge: Polity Press.

Weber, M. (2015a). Discipline and charisma. In T. Waters & D. Waters (Eds.), *Weber's rationalism and modern society: New translations on politics, bureaucracy, and social stratification* (pp. 59–72). Palgrave Macmillan.

Weber, M. (2015b). Bureaucracy. In T. Waters & D. Waters (Eds.), *Weber's rationalism and modern society: New translations on politics, bureaucracy, and social stratification* (pp. 73–127). Palgrave Macmillan.

Weiss, L. (1998). *The myth of the powerless state: Governing the economy in a global era*. Blackwell Publishers.

Weiss, L., & Thurbon, E. (2022). Explaining divergent national responses to Covid-19: An enhanced state capacity framework. *New Political Economy, 27*(4), 697 712.

Wendt, A. (1999). *Social theory of international politics*. Cambridge University Press.

Wendt, A. (2004). The state as person in international theory. *Review of International Studies, 30*(2), 289–316.

Winblad, U., Swenning, A. K., & Spangler, D. (2022). Soft law and individual responsibility: A review of the Swedish policy response to COVID-19. *Health Economics, Policy and Law, 17*(1), 48–61.

Wu, T. (2017). *Attention merchants*. Vintage books.
Yang, W. (2022). China's zero-COVID policy pushes society to the limit. *DW*. https://www.dw.com/en/chinas-zero-covid-policy-pushes-society-to-the-limit/a-63862471

CHAPTER 4

Norwegian Leviathan Lives! Exploring the Anatomy of the Politics of COVID-19 in Norway

4.1 Introduction

Decades of infection control policymaking based on softer measures, both worldwide and especially in the West (Green, 2021), and the liberal political rationality emphasizing voluntarism over coercion in contemporary Western societies (Foucault, 2008; Miller & Rose, 2008), were replaced in Norway within a matter of *days* in mid-March 2020 (Gjerde 2021a). Norway, while the strictest Scandinavian country during the pandemic (Conyon et al. 2020; Nanda et al. 2021), was, if the scope of the analysis is global rather than merely Scandinavian, comparatively moderate and relatively liberal (see Cheibub et al., 2020; Nanda et al. 2021).

However, how can we best explore this political context? While much has been said about the Norwegian politics of COVID-19 (Christensen & Lægreid, 2020a, 2020b, 2022; Gulbrandsen, 2022; Staupe-Delgado, 2021), also from a Foucauldian perspective (i.e. Gjerde, 2021a, 2021b, 2022, 2023; Sandset & Villadsen, 2023), several gaps can be identified. From a Foucauldian perspective, the inclusion of the state as an actor introduces a certain black box, as it is not explained how the state can discipline populations or forcefully close-down society. Mechanisms are touched upon as originating from an actor, but how this actor has the capacities to enforce such mechanisms of power remains relatively untouched. This is a result of the state, including its autonomy, powers and form, being left relatively untouched. Empirically, the mobilization

L. E. L. Gjerde, *Nordic Leviathans*, International Political Theory,
https://doi.org/10.1007/978-3-032-00689-9_4

of society has only been covered in its informal, not formal, form, how the border control regime works as a mechanism of control over access has not been developed, beyond how the closed border denies access, while the issue of quarantine and isolation has been left understudied. The manner in which the lockdown works has also only been touched upon in a brief manner. To remedy these theoretical and empirical issues, I utilize the Weberian-Foucauldian state theory, preliminarily developed in chapter 3, to analyse a concrete empirical context. Using Mann's conceptual framework on the sources of power, and Foucault's conceptual framework on the mechanisms of power, combined with a Weberian definition of the state, I study the anatomy of power during the pandemic.

This chapter is framed by a single research question*: how did the Norwegian state govern its territory and population during the pandemic?* To answer this question, I explore 21 interviews, based on the interview guide (see Gjerde, 2024c) and countless public sources from the Norwegian state, i.e. the Norwegian government, the Directorate of Health and the Institute of Public Health. The public data sources will be provided in the section 'empirical references: chapter 4', beneath the bibliography. Interview data will be referred to in the text. Generally speaking, the interviews grant us thicker descriptions of how power was exercised as mechanisms, whereas the sources of power are covered by the state's public documents, even if there will be some overlapping. More information on the methodology is accessible in the digital appendix (see Gjerde, 2025).

The coming analysis will be theoretically driven by the Weberian-Foucauldian analytical framework. Besides briefly covering law, a coercive resource, I will move between the sources and mechanisms of power, as we explore the macrophysics and microphysics of power, and importantly, their relationship. The objective is to explore how the Norwegian state governed, and how it could govern as such, by exploring the Norwegian state as an actor with various means at its disposal, which it used to govern. I start by exploring the soft, symbolic forms of governance of the Norwegian state. This entails investigating the communication campaign and how it related to calls to self-govern. I study how the state's ideological resources—its legitimacy, rhetoric, communication technologies—were put to use, and how these sources of power manifested as mechanisms of power at two levels—the level of hearts and minds, i.e. the target of the communication campaign, and thereafter, in changed conduct, the primary objective of affecting the individual on an emotional and cognitive level.

After exploring the Norwegian state's soft and indirect governance, I move on to the formal measures it adopted, and thus its autonomous powers. A brief description of the legal context is called for here, to clarify the legal resources enabling the state to intervene in society in the first place. This paves the way for an analysis of four different aspects of the politics of COVID-19: the internal lockdown, the mobilization of society, control over dangerous and vulnerable bodies and the closure of the border (i.e. the external lockdown). I explore how these formal forms of governance occurred at the local level, as mechanisms of power, which targeted habits, thoughts, relations, bodies, etc., in spatial and social space, and I increase the level of abstraction by discussing the sources of power the state used as it exercised power to create the said mechanisms. I shall explore how juridical-sovereignty, discipline and control (over access) manifested in different ways in different parts of society, based on how the state exercised power through its means.

4.2 The Symbolic Might of Norwegian Leviathans

4.2.1 Ideological Techniques

A major part of the state's strategy entailed convincing citizens and residents about a) the fact that COVID-19 is a great danger, and b) that they must comply and subordinate to the moral needs of the national community. This necessitated producing consent along two axes—*passive* acceptance of restrictions and *active* participation in infection control through self-regulation going beyond the formal demands of the state. This generating of consent was to be achieved through a communication campaign enabled by the Norwegian state's infrastructural power, meaning that both the state bureaucracy as well as the logistical and technological resources made it possible to spread the state's message throughout society.

The rhetorical politics of crisis, community and expertise were the core of this strategy. The state played upon fear by representing the situation as a crisis, upon morality by referring to the need for a national *dugnad*, and upon expertise by referring to science and medical knowledge (see also Almlund et al., 2023; Christensen & Lægreid, 2020b; Sandset &

Villadsen, 2023). The state instrumentalized fear, communitarian values and science to secure compliance. This communication campaign was de facto an instrument of power and rule, articulated to affect the moods, thoughts and actions of the population.

The basis of the communication campaign was the representation of the situation as a crisis. The situation was stated to be the gravest since WW2 (Regjeringen.no., 2020a), warnings were made about the risk of societal collapse and mass death (Regjeringen.no., 2020b), and references to EU countries with graver situations were made, followed by warnings that Norway would reach that point unless the right measures were implemented (Regjeringen.no., 2020c). Such references were combined with the explicit assertion that the situation was 'a health crisis and a biological crisis which became a national crisis affecting all sectors' (Regjeringen, 2020d). Warning about potential societal collapse and mass deaths, where a third of the population was labelled at risk due to age and/or chronic diseases and referring to the death toll on a daily basis, while using war metaphors such as 'invisible enemy' or 'mobilize', made the situation tense and grave (Gjerde, 2022).

Defining COVID-19 as a 'public health threat', thus justifying measures based on the infection control law, declaring the situation as a pandemic and labelling the pandemic a national crisis and public health threat (Regjeringen, 2020e, 2020f), were also symbolic operations representing the situation as severe. Similarly, implementing a 'corona law' and referring to the need of suspending/ignoring democratic practices and even potentially parts of the Constitution (Lovdata, 2020a), had symbolic effects, revealing the gravity of the situation. The state sought to instil fear to ensure compliance (Christensen & Lægreid, 2020a). This generating of fear was a political operation, justifying the lockdown and making individuals comply with recommendations due to the exceptional nature of the situation. Indeed, the lockdown itself carried significant symbolic meaning, spreading fear: 'right before the lockdown, a friend and I spoke about the possibility of a lockdown, my friend wanted to return home [to their family] because we feared the lockdown' (Teacher 7).

The politics of crisis was combined with the politics of community—and more specifically of ***dugnad***. The state utilized the communitarian spirit of the dugnad to mobilize individuals into the formally voluntary but morally obligatory role of infection controller (cf. Gjerde, 2021b, 2022; Sandset & Villadsen, 2023). In the words of the Prime Minister Erna Solberg, 'this is not the time for "me". It is the time for "us"'

(Regjeringen.no., 2020a). The entire population was asked to participate in the dugnad, to show 'solidarity' (Regjeringen, 2020g, 2020h, 2020i). The state utilized the dugnad to make it formally voluntary and yet morally obligatory to comply with the state's vision as well as with legal and moral orders, unifying the population into an ethical whole (cf. Gross, 2023; Sandset & Villadsen, 2023).

The state also played upon the politics of expertise and science. Government officials referred to expertise to legitimize its approach and articulations as scientific and thus as objectively accurate (Sandset & Villadsen, 2023). As the Minister of Health Bent Inge Høie said on March 10, all measures would be 'based on a clear medical foundation' (Regjeringen.no, 2020j). The measures, including the closure of society, were to be based on 'scientific knowledge' (Regjeringen, 2020k). Moreover, references were constantly made to the analyses of the Institute of Public Health and the Directorate of Health, which underpinned and supported the measures (Regjeringen, 2020l). References to 'scientific' and 'medical' aspects allowed the state to combine the authority of science with its own political authority, making it not merely moral, but also rational, to agree with the state. Moreover, restrictions had to be 'evidence-based' measures according to Norwegian law (Lovdata, 2022)—making references to science necessary to justify them. As Sandset and Villadsen (2023: 625) note, predictive models on mortality rates, infection rates and other abstract information about the virus did not merely enable governance. Such models also produced self-governance and affected how citizens interpreted the situation. Thus, scientific models and references to expertise implicate, in our societies, a necessary reference to 'truth'. The truth of how the state exercised its power was legitimized and backed by the truth of science (cf. Foucault, 2014: 9), thus becoming an ideological resource. Scientific authority was also comprised of politicians and experts standing together, presenting a united front, at press conferences (VG, 2020). This revealed unity as officials proclaimed the state's vision and direction. It also transferred experts' scientific credentials onto politicians as they spoke, whereas the stage, being a serious state setting, symbolized political authority.

The state's vision was spread throughout various infrastructural resources, such as the mass media (Kristensen & Hartley, 2023), customarily responsible for promulgating the government's narrative, offering few alternative voices (Christensen & Lægreid, 2020b; Graver, 2020b; Gjerde, 2022). Also, speakers were used at public sites, such as trains or bus stations, while posters were placed everywhere to inform citizens. By means of smartphones, computers and television, the state's vision followed the individual everywhere, from the toilet to the bus, from the bed to the kitchen. Logistical capacities enabled the prompt distribution of propaganda throughout society.

This communication campaign manifested at the micro-level, at the level of hearts and minds. Therefore, nine people out of ten supported the continuation of the lockdown in late March 2020 (NTB, 2020), and support for measures remained high into 2021 (see Norsk koronamonitor, 2020a, 2020b, 2020c, 2020d, 2020e, 2021a, 2021b). The majority of Norwegians complied with, and internalized, the state's vision, by trusting the state, fearing COVID-19 and embracing the moral sentiments of dugnad (Moss & Sandbakken, 2021; Sandbakken & Moss, 2021; Sætrevik et al., 2021; Scharffscher & Engen, 2022; Stenøien & Tønseth, 2022). Trust is an important ideological resource, and here it increased the impact of communication and strengthened the legitimacy of infection control measures.

My informants confirmed such findings. For instance: 'Some pupils stopped coming [to school] due to fear' (Teacher 8). Such fears cannot be separated from the state's active representation of the situation as an exceptional crisis with potentially horrifying consequences for society and the individual (cf. Christensen & Lægreid, 2020b; Gjerde, 2022). The communitarian ethics of the state was embraced by the population, which felt moral and communitarian obligations, compelling them to reduce the likelihood that they infected others. Whether adult or child, all had to do their part: 'it [compliance with infection control rules] has gone very well… we have spoken a lot [to the pupils] about how we must do our part' (Teacher 6). Moreover, trust in the authorities was common (Christensen & Lægreid, 2020a; Helsingen et al., 2020), as also explicitly stated by an informant: 'we trust the authorities' (Psychiatric worker 10). *Even* sceptics initially supported the Norwegian state's interventions in society, including the lockdown: 'it was so serious… the first week we [my partner and I] cleaned everything [with anti-bacterial disinfectants], but it didn't last long, not at all' (Journalist 19). While the state's communication campaign had a strong impact upon the minds and hearts of the population, compliance weakened as the pandemic evolved: 'There's a red thread. At the start, it was like, we'll do whatever it takes! However, it has started becoming a bit more like, "and so what"?' (Office 9). The state's legitimizing capacities weakened when citizens obtained information from different sources, and when the situation was normalized.

While the state's communication campaign has been studied, the sources of power which enabled the state to get its vision accepted has remained untouched. The ideological sources of power, related to both legitimacy and trust, enabled the state to impose its vision through propaganda, meaning that old negotiations and performances producing legitimacy and trust could be harvested during this crisis. The state generated consent by speaking, socially creating the situation as it defined it. Ideological sources of power, consisting of the authority of science, political legitimacy, trust and other resources, made the state's voice matter when it was exercised through propaganda techniques fostered and improved over the last century. This communication was spread throughout society via various infrastructural instruments, such as television, digital media, newspapers and speakers, as well as daily discussions and other informal means of communication, allowing the state's vision to spread everywhere. This manifested at the micro-level, at the level of citizens' feelings and thoughts, both legitimizing the state's strategy, rendering previously unheard-of state coercion both legitimate and desired and imposing responsibilities upon the private individual.

4.2.2 Self-Govern, Please

The communication strategy was not merely about legitimizing restrictions and imposing compliance with the state's *perception* of the situation. Communication manifested not only at the level of hearts and minds, but at the level of conduct, as the state sought to mobilize individuals as active participants in the infection control regime, partly by making them voluntarily self-govern (Almlund et al., 2023; Sandset & Villadsen, 2023). The communication campaign created informal but morally obligatory roles for citizens as informal infection controllers—a form of liberal governance through self-regulation (cf. Dean, 2007; Foucault, 2008; Miller & Rose, 2008; Rose, 1999).

This revolved around producing voluntary compliance. Voluntarism was seen as an important part of the strategy—also in the aftermath of the lockdown (Helsedirektoratet, 2020a; Regjeringen, 2020o). The state used the aforementioned communication strategy to instil urgency and moral sentiments, in order to alter people's behaviour. Therefore, recommendations were articulated as a soft and informal form of governance, disseminated throughout society via the state's communication campaign, providing citizens with guidelines and normative standards for self-governing (Almlund et al., 2023; Sandset & Villadsen, 2023). A multitude of recommendations were articulated. Citizens were advised to follow sanitary recommendations, wash hands frequently, for at least 30 seconds with soap, or use anti-bacterial spirits if hand-wash was unavailable. Facemasks, while initially not recommended, became recommended during the autumn of 2020, for cases where distancing could not be practised such as on buses and trains, as well as in the most sensitive contexts, such as hospitals, to then become mandatory in such contexts. Citizens were told to avoid public transportation and crowds, to test themselves and stay away from people outside of the household if they had symptoms, or if one for other reasons could be contagious, to stay at home whenever possible and generally reduce contacts and activities outside the household, preferably even refraining from having visitors. Citizens were also recommended to refrain from travelling within the country if possible, and to avoid travelling abroad (Regjeringen, 2020m, 2020n; FHI, 2021a). Particular recommendations were also articulated to vulnerable persons, who had to be especially careful (FHI, 2021b). This made mundane bodily activities and social activities objects of self-regulation. The individual became morally obliged to self-govern according to the will of the state.

These recommendations were accepted and practised by the vast majority of Norwegians (see Helsingen et al., 2020; Wollebæk et al., 2022). In the words of an informant:

> It's a bit ironic, I had a friend over to work on a dress… we were told to only have 2 visitors [per week] …. And so my mother came to pick up something, and that was that two visits… so later, when my friend needed a bit of assistance from a third party, I had to go out for that hour, since my two close contacts were already used... While I had 18 close contacts at work daily (Kindergarten 1).

Thus, compliance with recommendations manifested not just in individuals placing limitations upon themselves, but in certain cases, with individuals engaging in self-restraint of a moral nature which they found dubious in practice, for instance due to the high number of contacts the informant interacted with daily in any case. Self-regulation manifested in individuals voluntarily limiting their lives by imposing restrictions upon themselves, such as by leaving their private homes to avoid breaking the recommendation to have no more than two close contacts per week. The state imposed moral obligations through its communication campaign, which made individuals change the manner their lives were conducted. This included policing their homes, ensuring that family, including children, complied with recommendations, i.e. reducing the sizes of their social circles: 'We worked a bit with regard to how many visitors we [the informant and partner, plus two children] could have at home at a given time… we were very strict' (Psychiatric worker 10). Even the smallest children were supposed to self-regulate, as personal responsibility became universal: 'I was taking my child to a birthday party…. When we came to the door, two children were standing there talking… as we approached, they disengaged… gave us lots of space… it seemed like a habit' (Rector 4). At the micro-level, power manifested in self-regulating behaviour related to hygiene, reduced social contact, distancing and other practices of infection control, in all kinds of social contexts. Voluntarism was practised by individuals formally and voluntarily engaging in the infection control behaviour which the state recommended and morally demanded compliance with.

State propaganda manifested in more than self-governance. It also manifested in informal state agents voluntarily imposing social control (Moss & Sandbakken, 2021). The rhetorical politics produced a disciplinary context where citizens had to follow 'pandemic norms' related to the national dugnad and the state's recommendations (Sandset & Villadsen, 2023). My informants illustrated the logic of this social control: 'I have a cousin who is anti-vaccination. I haven't met up with him since I found out' (Kindergarten 1), and 'there has been so much vaccination pressure in the healthcare services… I experienced extreme pressure… it was also dehumanizing and humiliating' (Doctor 13). The sources of ideological power exercised through the communication campaign manifested in conscripted individuals subscribing to the state's vision, excluding and disciplining others at the micro-level, so as to enforce pandemic norms. Defiant family members or colleagues faced pressure to comply, as the combination of communitarian ethics and fear, played upon by the state, created bottom-up and horizontal exercises of power when individuals accepted the state's vision and policed others in accordance with it.

This way, the state expanded morally and informally into all spheres of life, through a liberal form of rule. While liberal self-governance is often seen working through rational self-interest (Foucault, 2008), it can also operate through 'ethical self-governance', which functions by imposing moral obligations upon the individual (Dean, 2007: 61). This was the case here, as it was in the *moral* common interests of the state and the individual for the individual to self-govern during the pandemic (Sandset & Villadsen, 2023), even if the vulnerable also had *personal* interests in complying. This was a form of communitarian liberal rule. The autonomous, free individual was to act in accordance with common moral values and interests—as self-regulation and informal discipline merged together in a complex and informal strategy—the mobilization of the private individual.

By making citizens accept its narrative, the state fostered self-governance according to its own interests, and tendencies towards social control of perceived dissidents and sceptics. The state showed its capacities to govern in extensive and intensive ways through the sheer force of its moral authority and the ideological powers it cages. By utilizing propaganda to channel its meaning-making throughout society, with the aforementioned communication devices, the state produced (and produces) affective and ethical conditions under which voluntarism can manifest in self-regulatory mechanisms. The state acted upon and through the Norwegian traditions of dugnad and communitarianism to make compliance with the state's vision a moral obligation. The individual henceforth had to handle his or her daily life in a manner befitting a moral and good citizen whose body would be self-regulated in a myriad of minor, almost imperceptible, ways, such as coughing correctly or keeping at a distance when passing others. I not only confirm this self-regulation, covered extensively in previous research as a process of government (i.e. Gjerde, 2021b; Sandset & Villadsen, 2023), with a new set of data, i.e. interviews, but I also develop it further by illustrating how this self-governance came into being as the state enacted its ideological sources of power through the communication campaign. The state governed the individual at a distance through its voice, to enable this self-regulation at the micro-level. Thus, even self-regulation during the pandemic appears to best be explained through a pyramidic understanding of power, and a state-centric lens, exploring how power diffused from the centre of the state and into the most mundane everyday situations governed through voluntarism, also hinting at the possibility that neoliberalization and the rise of liberal governmentality, far from moving the state out of people's lives (i.e. Miller & Rose, 2008; Rose, 1999), simply entails a subtler form of government by the state.

4.3 The Autonomous Powers of Norwegian Leviathan

4.3.1 For My Enemies, the Law

Some lawyers may discuss the legality of the politics of COVID-19 (i.e. Graver, 2020a, 2020b; cf Gjerde, 2023). While ethically interesting, from a sociological standpoint, law originates in the *sword* of the state (Hobbes, 1996; Schmitt, 1996; Foucault, 2013, 2019). While laws will be illegitimate if customs are ignored (Seabrooke, 2002), exceptional situations change the picture. If a situation is dangerous enough, even a democratic state can, and will, suspend its legal and democratic norms (Schmitt, 1996).

This was also the case in Norway during the pandemic. Two laws were central to the Norwegian politics of COVID-19. First, the most central law was the infection control law (Smittevernloven). This law grants the state a wide range of responsibilities with regard to protecting the population's health, and the rights to implement measures to ensure that these responsibilities are fulfilled—if a disease is classified as a public health threat (Lovdata, 2022). The state may ban social events, including business meetings, cultural events or social interaction between households. This law grants the state rights and duties to act decisively if a disease threatens the social body, as the state has responsibilities to protect the population from disease.

Second, the Norwegian state implemented a 'corona law' in March 2020, which lasted until May 2020. This emergency law gave the government 'increased powers', allowing it to implement laws without parliamentary voting or deliberation, also when/if measures would bypass the Constitution. A one-third minority of parliament could however cancel this law and the proscriptions and prescriptions imposed through it (Lovdata, 2020a). This emergency law's primary purpose was to suspend democratic practices related to deliberation for the time being, while offering safeguards to ensure that the law would not be abused. This effectively suspended the political norms regulating Norwegian politics during 'normal' times, even if parliament remained sovereign, as a one-third minority could suspend the emergency law's measures. The executive functioned as *acting* sovereign, but actual sovereignty never left parliament.

These laws have been briefly discussed (i.e. Graver, 2020a, 2020b), but not as coercive sources of power. Essentially, they should be conceptualized as coercive sources of power because they allowed the state to back up *legal* commands with *legitimate* threats of violence, given that breaking the state's law entails fines and imprisonment. Fines and imprisonment for up to 6 months are the potential punishments for breaking the law (Lovdata, 2020b). In other words, the laws formalized the state's biopolitical will, making non-compliance illegal and thus punishable. Beyond coercion, these laws had symbolic effects, signalling the gravity of the situation. Indeed, these laws declared the situation to be abnormal and exceptional. The state used its sovereignty to suspend legal norms. This was the root of the lockdown and the various forms of state coercion which we shall now turn our attention to, which were enabled by the state suspending pre-pandemic norms, thereby opening the door to exceptional political operations that would have been impossible during a normal situation.

4.3.2 Anatomy of the Lockdown

The most (in)famous measure implemented against COVID-19 was the lockdown—a forceful measure utilized in Norway to formalize social distancing, i.e. both reducing the amount of people socially interacting and increasing the physical distance between those actually interacting. The lockdown was an exceptional measure entailing the closing down of society. While the lockdown started as a national measure, it could also be local/regional (Regjeringen, 2020p, 2021a, 2021b). The authorities differentiated between regions in late 2020 and early 2021, implementing stricter measures in regions where infection rates were higher. For instance, the Ring (Ringen), i.e. Oslo and neighbouring areas, had high contagion rates due to the 'British' variant in early 2021. This was also the case for central areas in the region Telemark and Vestfold, as well as the city of Bergen (Regjeringen, 2020p, 2021a, 2021b). Stricter measures were therefore implemented in these areas. This occurred in collaboration with local authorities, who were advised by the Directorate and the Institute to impose stricter rules (Helsedirektoratet, 2020b). While local authorities could implement stricter rules—in collaboration with national experts—they could not implement softer rules than those the state imposed nationally (Helse- og omsorgsdepartementet, 2021).

The lockdown has been discussed as a juridical-sovereign measure resulting in the closing down of huge wedges of society (i.e. Gjerde, 2021b; Sandset & Villadsen, 2023). However, the lockdown has only been analysed in a preliminary manner, leaving untouched both how power worked at the micro-level, and how power was enabled at the macro-level. Therefore, we need an in-depth analysis of how power manifested and was made to manifest. The lockdown should be understood as a series of mechanisms of power, consisting of internal and external parts. The core of the *internal* lockdown consisted of a series of close-downs, i.e. juridical-sovereign seizures of rights and liberties, which were mostly backed by a) the metre/two-metre, the legal dictate that social distancing had to be practised throughout the entire social body, and b) the ban on the freedom of assembly, which prohibited most social gatherings from taking place if more than a certain number of people entered the social site. This is revealed by how certain workplaces like cafeterias could remain open if they could practise social distancing for employees and customers while respecting the ban on gatherings (Helsedirektoratet, 2020a).

Nevertheless, regardless of the metre/two-metres and the ban on gatherings, close-downs were enforced. Some, such as psychologists, could have practised their profession without breaking the distancing or crowding criteria, and yet they were closed down, too. Combining the metre/two-metres and restrictions on freedom of assembly, the state regulated not merely individuals and their activities, but the entirety of the social body, including various public and private organizations, from schools to churches to businesses. Those not part of 'crucial' sectors like grocery stores were generally given home working or, when this was impossible, laid-off and potentially fired as they had no tasks to fulfil, and the state, while offering massive financial support (see Greve et al., 2021), could not or would not pay indefinitely. With the implementation of the lockdown, businesses, schools, cultural institutions, bars, gyms and a multitude of other social spaces were ordered to close (Helsedirektoratet, 2020a; Regjeringen, 2021a, 2021b).

I now look more closely at the two core parts of the internal lockdown. First, the close-downs were rooted in the ban on gatherings (Helsedirektoratet, 2020a; Regjeringen, 2021a, 2021b). The ban on gatherings was a general measure, restricting the size of formal and informal social gatherings. This annihilated individuals' right to assemble by prohibiting gatherings to take place in private or public. On the one hand, the ban manifested in the close-down of social sites where too many individuals gather, such as universities, offices and schools. If more than 5, 8, 10, 20 or 50 people had to meet at a given place, depending on time and space, as the severity of measures varied, then this measure manifested in activities ceasing and sites closing. The ban functioned in a juridical-sovereign manner by closing down sites such as nightclubs, events like concerts and political gatherings where situations could potentially degenerate.

On the other hand, prohibiting gatherings above a certain limit had exclusionary effects when gatherings were still allowed to take place, i.e. regarding funerals, or during later lockdowns, education in primary and secondary schools. This made groups objects of governance in their own right. Below, we shall return to the responsibilities this allocated organizers, and how this worked as a form of power through society, which was especially predominant when the lockdown was lifted. Notably, the ban on gatherings targeted social rather than spatial space. Huge numbers of unrelated people could wait at the train station together, yet the same number of people could not meet in a park or a private home. Larger social gatherings were banned, the scope of others reduced. Some formal and informal social sites were allowed to remain open, given that mobilized state actors policed events and ensured that gatherings complied with restrictions, thereby constituting a form of 'governing at a distance' (Miller & Rose, 2008).

Second, on the metre/two-metres. Establishments had to close if they could not maintain distances between customers within their locales (Helsedirektoratet, 2020a; Regjeringen, 2021a, 2021b). The metre/two-metres was a social distancing measure separating bodies. It worked as a generalized restriction, affecting all of society. It resulted in spatial space becoming manageable through the body, which became a point of reference, inviting interventions whenever bodies got too close to one another. This political instrument worked in two different ways. On the one hand, this was a juridical-sovereign form of governance manifesting as activities ceased and sites closed—i.e. a negative mechanism of power. Hairdressers, tattoo-artists and similar businesses were ordered to close, while boxing, football and similar activities were prohibited (Helsedirektoratet, 2020a). The impossibility of staying physically apart meant that such sites and activities broke the metre/two-metre, thereby being prohibited by default. On the other hand, the metre/two-metres worked as a disciplinary measure, dividing people in spatial space, imposing demands that individuals comply by regulating their own bodies. The body became an object to regulate throughout all of society, in mundane contexts from standing in line at the store to sitting at the bus. Personal relations and interactions were altered, as bodies were meant to remain apart unless they lived in a common household. Individuals were virtually always under the gaze of formal and informal state agents, whether on the train, at school, or in the park. Below, we shall cover how this worked as a form of power through society.

The lockdown worked through mechanisms of closing down, denying and stopping. The lockdown was the result of the state exercising immense powers over society, resulting from a spectacular juridical-sovereign show of force. This had significant symbolic and ritualistic characteristics, as it revealed the coercive powers of the state and the gravity of the situation (Sandset & Villadsen, 2023). The spectacular nature of the lockdown created a symbolic 'shock effect', one of its *primary* aims, as the director of the Directorate of Health himself acknowledged in its aftermath (Myrvang, 2021). The lockdown was supposed to shock the population into voluntarily participating in the dugnad and complying with infection control legislation.

The lockdown can thus be defined as the closing down of society through a series of primarily juridical-sovereign mechanisms of power, supported by disciplinary and exclusionary mechanisms also working beyond and beside the lockdown. Thus, the lockdown is 'much more than confinement alone' (Bhowmick & Alam, 2023: 156). This series of measures was enabled by the state's coercive, infrastructural and ideological resources. As already established, the state's successful communication campaign and its high degree of legitimacy made its coercion accepted (cf Christensen & Lægreid, 2020a: 774). The lockdown was legitimate—as seen by 90% supporting the continuation of the lockdown in late March 2020 (NTB, 2020)—and thus enabled by the state's ideological sources of power. Moreover, the legitimate lockdown had to be enforced, or at least the threat of enforcement had to be made, towards those not accepting the state's vision. The law, as a coercive resource, compels. As stated by an informant: 'I ensured distances between my pupils, to keep my hands clean. I am no lawbreaker, but I have learned the difference between law and recommendation' (Teacher 12). The state's repressive capacities, rooted in organizations caging violent capacities, i.e. the police and the penal system (Mann, 1993, 2013), produced compliance (cf.

Elias, 1978, 1982). However, it was not enough to have sets of repressive institutions. The lockdown depended on the state's infrastructural resources enabling the effective employment of coercion in the face of dissidence. The lockdown was a complex political operation, not a show of brute force. This was partly a biopolitical question of knowledge, calculations and predictions. The lockdown was grounded in knowledge, which the state accumulated and obtained on the basis of tests and diagnoses related to mortality rates, contagion rates, inoculation risks, etc. (Sandset & Villadsen, 2023).

The lockdown therefore depended upon the state's accumulation of information. The state accumulated information about the population (impersonal surveillance) and surveilled the activities, health statuses and whereabouts of individuals (monitoring). This partly occurred through the app 'smittestopp', which was a voluntarily installable app tracing movement (automatically if one's phone is connected to internet), symptoms (through self-reporting) and potential contact with people self-reporting positive diagnoses (Regjeringen, 2020q). It was a control device in the Deleuzian terminology, revolving around de-individualized, aggregated data (Gjerde, 2021b: 484). The most important surveillance instrument was however the Corona Centre, which to date has remained unanalysed. The Corona Centre was an administrative organ created to deal with the pandemic, organized locally based on orders from above. It surveilled individuals by tracing contagion patterns, and enforced compliance with the compulsory testing regime. This allowed the state to obtain and accumulate abstract information about contagion patterns and chains. Thereafter, the state could make decisions, such as whether regionalized measures were needed, or whether the lockdown should be tightened or slackened (FHI, 2020; Helsedirektoratet, 2022).

The infrastructural powers of the state, based around rationalized bureaucracies, and especially the expert institutions of the Directorate of Health and the Institute of Public Health, with their techniques for both accumulating information and interpreting this information, were core resources. They not only surveilled the virus, but also studied mortality and hospitalization rates, virus mutations and other issues, basing recommendations and commands on their expertise. Such biopolitical techniques of obtaining, storing and analysing information strengthened the infrastructural capacities of the state, showing the link between the concepts of biopolitics and infrastructural power, as the former is a subgroup of the latter (cf. Ayodele, 2019; Byler, 2023; Rippa & Oakes,

2023). With its administrative apparatus and surveillance capacities, the state monitored the situation as well as citizens and their conduct at an abstract level, as a population. This set of infrastructural resources worked together with the coercive resources of law and the monopoly over the legitimate means of violence to enable the lockdown.

When the state locked down society, it exercised power in a pyramidical manner. From the parliament, government and Directorate of Health, orders were created and dispensed throughout the state bureaucracy. Sources of power manifested in mechanisms of power, as power moved through the institutions of the state and into society. The state penetrated society in numerous dimensions and angles, coercively, infrastructurally and ideologically: the lockdown was a totalizing political measure, affecting the entirety of Norway. Civil society ceased to be a field beyond formal state interventions. In contrast with the Swedish approach that will be covered below, the Norwegian state's approach should not be described as (partly) liberal, even if this has been done in the past (i.e. Gjerde, 2021b; Sandset & Villadsen, 2023). While voluntarism was employed, the lockdown entailed the suspension of civil society as a sphere formally beyond state control, thereby suspending liberal governmentality as a core principle of government. This way, the lockdown reveals the extensiveness and the intensity of the state's power, as *everything* was *formally* subjugated to the state and its biopolitical agenda.

4.3.3 Mobilizing Society

The politics of COVID-19 in Norway was more complex than the lockdown. This has partly been covered, for instance by studies taking into account the *moral* mobilization of individuals, which we covered above (cf. Gjerde, 2021b; Sandset & Villadsen, 2023). However, the *formal* mobilization of society has remained untouched. This mobilization depended upon power beyond the formal apparatus of the state and 'government at a distance' (Miller & Rose, 2008). The state utilized non-state actors for political purposes (cf. Arts, 2014; Sending & Neumann, 2006). This makes the mobilization of society a core Foucauldian issue.

The internal lockdown was lifted as the state increasingly mobilized society instead of closing it down, moving from predominantly exercising coercive power *over* society, to predominantly exercising infrastructural power *through* society. However, restrictions remained in place when the lockdown was lifted (Regjeringen, 2020s). There was no absolute shift. The state depended upon a fluid mixture of mobilizing and closing down society—as the state switched from suppression to control strategies (Christensen & Lægreid, 2020a). Power through society was channelled by the state through formal demands that conscripted individuals should enforce compliance. To accomplish this in practice, the state formalized the mobilization of society, making it obligatory by imposing the responsibility of enforcing the state's political objectives upon teachers, managers, security guards, police officers, etc.

The school is an excellent example of a formal context where the state mobilized personnel for infection control objectives. As most schools in Norway are public, so their personnel tend to be public servants employed by the state. Nevertheless, the case of the school reveals the logic of mobilization, and how infection control responsibilities were imposed upon abstract roles like 'teacher' and 'rector'. During the initial lockdown, all educational facilities were closed down. However, the state reopened such facilities after the initial lockdown, even if higher and secondary education facilities were closed during later lockdowns. When these facilities were reopened, the state mobilized their staff. Personnel were tasked with ensuring that students, pupils and others could (a) keep their distance, (b) wash and/or sanitize hands frequently, (c) stay within specific groups so as to not interact beyond their classes and potentially their age-groups, formalized as the cohort system. They were tasked with sanitizing and restructuring classrooms to make them safer, to facilitate distancing (Helsedirektoratet, 2020a, 2021a), as informants from the educational sector attest to. For instance, teachers were allocated the responsibility for ensuring that distancing rules were enforced: 'in the neighbouring school, one teacher walked around with a metre-stick to ensure that children kept the proper distances' (Teacher 12).

In cases where distancing could not be enforced within a given locale, social reorganizing became necessary, something supervised by rectors (see A. Harris & Jones, 2020, 2022). In the words of an informant: 'It was hard to make people stay a metre apart inside the classrooms as we have double desks, so it could only be one pupil per table. Only half the pupils could be here at a given time' (Rector 2). Moreover, to avoid gatherings, pupils were governed through the cohort, an ad hoc ban on gatherings. Cohorts distributed pupils, but also potentially employees, students and others, within groups. An individual was not allowed to interact with individuals outside of the assigned groups while inside specific locales, such as schools or offices: 'a normal cohort consists of up to 8 children and 3 adults' (Kindergarten 1), and 'a cohort consists of 20–30 pupils... during breaks, there is no intermingling' (Principal 2). Cohorts manifested at the micro-level through exclusion, as individuals could not interact across cohorts. This was sometimes enforced with physical barriers: 'We had areas, and pupils were divided on the basis of whether they were in the 8th, 9th or 10th grade' (Teacher 14). Segregation by class in schools and kindergartens limited social contact without hindering children from entering the institution.

This manifested in mobilized infection control agents restructuring the spatial spaces of their locales to hinder social interaction across cohorts, banning cross-cohort interaction. This segregation manifested in control over access to social groups, where individuals were to be *socially* confined, sometimes through spatial segregation, a disciplinary technique which divided up spatial space and allocated different spaces to different groups. The cohort was a 'dividing practice' by which groups were objectivized, as they were (temporarily) *created* through their isolation (cf. Foucault, 1994a: 326). The educational facilities and their personnel were mobilized as infection control agents, responsible for enforcing discipline, through mechanisms related to the supervision of the teacher, who had to surveil whether or not infection control regulations were followed. Bodies were to be kept apart, as teachers controlled bodily activities such as handwashing and where bodies sat in classrooms, etc. In the absence of compliance, the teacher had to intervene: 'I felt a bit like a police officer!' (Teacher 8).

The state mobilized conscripts well beyond the public sector. Funerals constituted an informal and private example of something the state turned into a biopolitical device, with disciplinary and exclusionary characteristics. The organizer of the funeral was allocated a role with infection control responsibilities, in a manner similar to that described above with the roles of 'rector' and 'teacher'. Funerals were never disallowed, but they were tightly regulated. Funerals were generally allowed to take place with a maximum of 20 to 50 people. Therefore, 84% of Norwegians experiencing the death of their child during the pandemic had to arrange the funeral with limits on who they could invite to the funeral. Moreover, 75% were disallowed from standard funeral practices, like hugging (see Dyregrov & Kristensen, 2021). As experienced by two informants: 'We could enter the church, but every second row was closed off and we had to keep our distance' (Pensioner 15), and:

> We could have 50 guests and a small memorial service… we invited the 50 who could enter so that we didn't risk there being 53 people at the funeral… some cancelled at the last moment, and then we invited a few more to the funeral' (Lives and works abroad 18).

While the state did not send formal state agents to the funeral, it nevertheless governed *through* the mourning subject organizing the funeral. The mourning parent, sibling or partner became *formally* responsible for overseeing the funeral in line with commands from the state, on the state's behalf. This meant excluding individuals, even (potential) family and loved ones, to ensure that physical contact did not occur. This made one of the most sensitive social rituals a tightly regulated affair of the state, as the mourner became a mobilized state agent, and the ritual of mourning became a context of state power. Power manifested in mandatory distancing criteria, including the ban on hugging and other ritualistic forms of tenderness customary during funerals. Every mourner had to micro-manage their own bodies, to abide by the infection control rules, which the organizer was responsible for enforcing in practice. Funerals, like all those social activities still allowed to occur, became an infection control instrument.

Similarly, the state demanded that social sites previously closed down had to be restructured so to facilitate infection control behaviour. For instance, tables and chairs at offices, cantinas and other social sites were moved around, to limit the number of people entering and ensure that the distance between individual chairs was appropriate. Thus, 'the cantina was closed' (Teacher 5), and 'people had to use the stairs instead of the elevator!' (Office 11). Such restructuring of spatial and social spaces was carried out in numerous ways. It could entail closing certain spaces (i.e. elevators, cantinas), or places that had frequently been closed outright which were allowed to remain open could do so only with restrictions regarding the number of people allowed to enter, having breaks at the same time, etc. Opening and closing hours, where individuals could sit in the bar or nightclub, how many guests an establishment could allow to enter, bans on dancing and so on, were also implemented (Helsedirektoratet, 2020e). Workers at offices, hospitals and bars had to restructure their social sites to ensure that infection control protocols were followed by employees, patients, guests, etc.

The mobilization of society was the result of a series of conscriptions. Conscription functioned as a subtle mechanism of power where individuals in roles like 'teacher' or 'funeral organizer' were subjugated to various formal responsibilities. Thereafter, conscription manifested in practice whenever individuals complied by enforcing the state's will through diverse policing responsibilities, within contexts such as funerals or classrooms. Conscription was an automatic, anonymous form of power that de-individualized the conscript, transforming him/her into a component of the infection control machinery, easily replaceable by others (cf. Foucault, 1991). Formal mobilization of society is the result of numerous individuals becoming parts of the state's formal infection control regime through their roles within given social contexts. Public servants and private employees were transmuted into instruments of the state through the state's formal and informal ties with state-owned and private institutions. The mobilization of society was the formalization of infection control requirements on a societal scale, allowing the state to impose numerous mechanisms of power upon the bodies, thoughts, habits, relations, etc., of individuals, through the hands of conscripted infection control agents, rather than simply closing down sites. This meant shifting from the negative power of denying people the freedom to pursue activities to the positive and productive power of creating and shaping activities through conscripted agents (cf. Foucault, 1990, 1991). As with the lockdown, power worked in a pyramidical manner. Power moved downwards, from the centre of the state and through numerous joints of the state, including both formal state institutions and institutions and agents far beyond the formal state apparatus, even encroaching upon the most intimate, private contexts, such as funerals. The state exercised power over those it formally conscripted, subjugating them to formalized demands, so that they exercised power upon others on the state's behalf.

This form of rule was primarily infrastructural. The mobilization of society was enabled by the state's embeddedness in society, as well as the fact that numerous public institutions which could be rearranged for various purposes, such as schools and kindergartens. State-owned institutions could be rearranged for biopolitical purposes without much controversy, making it possible for disciplinary mechanisms to be enforced through teachers, rectors, etc. Embeddedness and surveillance capacities, combined with coercive sources of power, also turned the organizers of funerals and other social events into state agents. Infrastructural sources of power enabled the state to monitor how its orders were followed, thereby making compliance automatic due to knowledge that non-compliance carried risks, as these infrastructural resources were underpinned by the threat of punishment and thus the coercive sources of power. The state's capacities to implement policy through society were at the roots of the mobilization of society—allowing the state to redirect the primary purposes of institutions and organizations—both public and private—to infection control. This rearranging was upheld by the great legitimacy of the Norwegian state and the massive popular support for its response.

By mobilizing society, the state governed both through its formal apparatus and beyond it, in line with contemporary governmentalities (Miller & Rose, 2008). However, the use of non-state actors of a liberal nature is based on a certain level of reciprocity, as non-state actors need a certain level of autonomy (Arts, 2014; Sending & Neumann, 2006). As this autonomy was suspended during the pandemic, so civil society became a formal state instrument. This illustrates the utility of discussing power 'beyond the state'. The state depends upon relations of power and governmental practices well beyond its formal apparatus (Foucault, 1991; Miller & Rose, 2008). However, the state worked as a centre when it coordinated, regulated and controlled its agents, whether public employees or private individuals, using them as infection control agents. Therefore, the mobilization of society was a temporary process of statification, enabled by the state caging, and thereafter using, numerous sources of power, primarily of an infrastructural nature. New spheres and individuals became domains and parts of the state, enabled by the autonomous powers of the state, which allowed the state to govern through conscripted agents. This statification manifested as power worked pyramidically, vertically and horizontally, originating from the centre of the state, yet moving far beyond its formal boundaries. The lowest units, such as pupils in schools, mourners at funerals or patients at hospitals, were governed by the state through a multitude of joints, but they all experienced state power at the level of their minds, bodies and feelings, through these various conscripts.

4.3.4 Dangerous and Vulnerable Bodies

While the lockdown and mobilization of society were general political measures, targeting the entirety of the social body, certain physical bodies were handled in more elaborate ways than others. The state was especially interested in two types of bodies: the (potentially) dangerous and the vulnerable. These bodies were managed through a) quarantine, b) isolation and c) shielding—issues only alluded to in past research (i.e. Gjerde,

2021b; Sandset & Villadsen, 2023). Whereas the former two related to excluding the (potentially) dangerous, the latter related to protecting the (potentially) vulnerable. These measures supplemented the lockdown, but a) and b) were active throughout the period in hand. This section explores how the state exercised control over bodies and access to spatial and social sites, and how coercive and infrastructural power manifested in control and discipline at the micro-level.

First, quarantines. Quarantines targeted the *potentially* dangerous, i.e. those *suspected* of being infected and therefore contagious. There were different types of quarantine. 'Waiting' quarantine affected those having interacted with diagnosed individuals. 'Travelling' quarantine affected those entering Norway from abroad. 'Household' quarantine affected those whose household members were diagnosed. Importantly, quarantining did not *confine* bodies to specific locations. Quarantine was a strict form of social distancing. It manifested in exclusion from *social* sites, formalized in a legal duty to not have visitors, not go to work, etc. The state refused individuals access to certain social sites. Besides social interaction within the household, one could go outside for a walk, and if necessary, enter grocery stores or pharmacies (Helsedirektoratet, 2020a, 2020c, 2022).

Second, isolation. Isolation was imposed by the state on those diagnosed with COVID-19. Isolation manifested as confinement within the home, or alternatively at quarantine hotels if one requested this, or if one's house was deemed unsuitable. The purpose of isolation was to exclude the individual from social *and* spatial spaces outside the location of isolation. It manifested at the level of the body, in confinement within the locale of isolation, which became 'a segmented, immobile, frozen space' from which individuals could not leave (Foucault, 1991: 195). The state kept the contagious individual away from society to 'purify' it from contagious bodies (cf. Foucault, 1994b: 146). Moreover, whereas quarantining was an individualized social distancing technology, isolation worked both as an instrument of confinement and a *collectivized* social distancing measure, affecting the households and close contacts of the diagnosed, who were quarantined as a result of this diagnosis (see Helsedirektoratet, 2020a, 2020c, 2022).

The individual was legally obliged to comply. To ensure compliance, the state monitored the population, through the TISK-strategy (test, isolate, contagion-trace, quarantine). The strategy worked as follows: after a positive diagnosis, the diagnosed individual was isolated. The contacts of the diagnosed individual were traced to place them in quarantine. They would then be tested, and if positive, the cycle continued until the chain of contagion was broken (Helsedirektoratet, 2020c). Thus, testing served purposes beyond producing information. Testing also enabled the tracing of the contagion and thus (potentially) dangerous bodies throughout Norway. Formally, contagion tracing occurred through the 'Corona Centre', where individuals were ordered to test themselves and comply with orders. The Corona Centre was, as mentioned earlier, a temporary biopolitical organ created by the Norwegian state to systematize surveillance of (potentially) dangerous bodies and discipline and coerce (potentially) dangerous dissidents, based primarily on local testing and tracing (Helsedirektoratet, 2020d, 2021b). It was staffed by regular employees: '[at the corona centre], we were not only healthcare workers, but also property brokers, firemen, store workers' (Nurse/corona centre 17). The state conscripted diverse sets of citizens to staff this disciplinary apparatus, which functioned in an almost automatic manner, as 'it does not matter who exercises [disciplinary] power' (Foucault, 1991: 202). The state could conscript anyone to replace anyone in the disciplinary machinery, as it conscripted individuals to surveil the population in a formal manner.

The infection controllers at the centre had diverse responsibilities, such as calling to inform individuals about their in-quarantine status, telling them to come to the centre to test themselves and pass on information about their last days activities with the controllers. If diagnosed as dangerous, the staff at the Corona Centre traced potentially contaminated bodies throughout the network of those isolated, so as to end the contagion chain: 'we went to the houses of those who could not come [to the centre]. We'd test them and their household members' (Nurse/Corona Centre 17). The state identified (potentially) dangerous bodies by tracing the diagnosed body's network of interaction, testing those parts of these networks when they were located. While quarantine and isolation manifested in exclusion from social and spatial spaces, it was enforced disciplinarily by those conscripted to work at the centre. These infection control agents distributed orders to (potentially) dangerous bodies and made sure that they complied, cooperating with the police to ensure that dissidents were brought into line:

> one would [sometimes] need to tell people that, either you show up here for the test at hour x, or we'll come to your house with the police. … most

asked "are you serious?" and we'd have to say, "yes we're serious". Most got scared when we mentioned the police (Nurse/Corona Centre 17).

The caller became the eyes and mouth of the state. The worker at the Corona Centre both monitored and commanded individuals. The state made individuals comply with orders, through an abstract and complex institutional arrangement where some called, others tested and yet others analysed the tests, so as to identify dangerous bodies to isolate. Through the call, the (potentially) dangerous individuals were made aware that 'they were seen but could not see', and this 'visibility... assures the automatic functioning of power' (Foucault, 1991: 200–201). Indeed, the explicit threat of state violence was an exception rather than a rule. Individuals generally complied prior to, and almost always after, the threat of the police. The call served an important disciplinary function, making power visible but unverifiable. As with the panopticon model, individuals could always potentially be under the gaze of those supervising them, but the individual could never know if or when the gaze was upon them (Foucault, 1991). The Corona Centre worked as an abstract panopticon, where the Corona Centre made it impossible for the (potentially) dangerous to know when those who wielded the power could examine and potentially report wrongdoings.

Contagion tracing also occurred in a less formal manner. The state moved beyond the organ of the Corona Centre—by mobilizing huge numbers of people, such as rectors and teachers. They were allocated tracing responsibilities as part of their everyday duties during the pandemic: 'I've spent so much time, my weekends, my evenings, conducting contagion tracing, calling around' (Rector 2), as 'contagion tracing occurred when a pupil was infected, then we'd trace to find out where it came from' (Teacher 14). Personnel within schools were mobilized as they had to ensure that (potentially) infected individuals did not enter the school, and that they were made aware of their status as 'in quarantine' until further notice. However, these contagion tracers lacked the coercive instruments of the state. They could inform the sick, but not give them orders.

Thus, quarantine and isolation worked through a rigorous infection control regime, manifesting in social and spatial confinement and hence exclusion: 'I've been quarantined twice... the first time wasn't so bad, but the second one felt a bit like a restriction on our freedom' (Rector 2). This restriction on individual freedom worked through exclusion due to an abstract status, in the same manner as through the formalized 'corona passport' (cf. Stefanizzi et al. 2022; Tazzioli, 2021). The (potentially) dangerous individual was handled as an abstract (potential) bearer of infection, through a biopolitical form of control. While the Norwegian state did not *institutionalize* the corona passport, its politics of quarantine and isolation entailed coding every member of the population either as green (not suspected), orange (suspected) or red (diagnosed). Those coded orange were socially excluded, those red were also spatially confined, while people coded green were free to move around in society. While quarantine and isolation manifested as forms of control (over access), the existence of such measures were disciplinary, as individuals were 'corrected' if they failed to avoid infectious individuals. Moreover, quarantine and isolation were supported and enabled by a disciplinary apparatus of surveillance, as well as through criteria imposed on the body. Sometimes, a negative test was demanded in the aftermath of this period of 7, 10 or 14 days. Thereafter, the individual could freely enter social and spatial sites from which he/she had previously been excluded. Quarantine and isolation were made up of a combination of control (over access) and discipline, showing how these two forms of power were closely interwoven during the pandemic (cf. Bowen, 2021).

Third, there was shielding—excluding bodies from entering spatial and social sites considered at risk. A famous example was the shielding of the elderly, which initially entailed suspending their rights to receive visitors as well as those of others living in medical institutions, such as nursing homes. Some exemptions were granted if there were 'good' reasons for having visitors, such as imminent death (Stortinget, 2020), leaving many to live out their final days in isolation, until it was time to say goodbye:

> My parent was a bit ill before, but then the pandemic came. My parent was such a social person,... but nobody could visit any more. My parent got so depressed, sitting alone in the room, that my parent stopped eating and drinking. We knew where it was going.... we were allowed to visit when my parent got terminal (Pensioner 15).

Making old people's homes an object of protection, the state closed down medical facilities from visitors, denying the elderly their right to social contact with loved ones. This manifested in the social isolation of the elderly, who were kept physically apart from family and loved ones by dividing them, objectifying them as vulnerable objects to protect. To achieve this, the state governed through the personnel of such sites, conscripting them into the state's infection control machinery, regardless of whether they were civil servants or belonged to private institutions. This way, the state controlled access and imposed exclusion and isolation. The elderly could (legally, if not necessarily *actually*) leave their homes.

The state started easing and thereafter lifting the ban in May 2020 (Regjeringen, 2020r). Thereafter, visits were permitted, but restricted:

> Only the closest relatives could come, and only two at a time... They couldn't hug etc. If it was raining, they would need to call us, so that we could ensure that all other residents/patients were in their rooms so that we could meet the family [inside] while distancing... we'd follow them to the room... the resident/patient would need to call us so we could escort them out to the exit. Then we'd sanitize everything (Nurse/Corona Centre 17).

While easing its grip, the state nevertheless continued governing through various disciplinary measures, manifesting in altered social contact, as disciplinary measures such as banning hugs, limiting the numbers of people allowed to enter, restrictions on whom the state allowed to enter, and tight control over where the bodies of visitors moved in spatial spaces, were implemented. The inclusion of outsiders into the medical facility was coupled with numerous proscriptions and prescriptions of a disciplinary nature, which conscripted medical personnel imposed upon guests.

Similarly, the infamous 'cabin ban' banned individuals from staying overnight at recreational houses outside the municipality where they live. Largely rural municipalities with fewer infrastructures for dealing with a pandemic were shielded from the influx of residents, because they were seen as both potentially bringing disease and potentially absorbing these places' limited healthcare services. The state mobilized the Norwegian civil defence to ensure that people obeyed this juridical-sovereign seizure of property rights (Regjeringen, 2020f). Control (over access) was interwoven with juridical-sovereignty, as the state used law to enforce this seizure of rights, which worked through territorially based exclusion. Thus, shielding made the vulnerable, such as the elderly living in nursing homes or vulnerable areas, such as rural municipalities, objects to protect. Shielding manifested in various forms of exclusion, and for some who had to be protected, such as the elderly in medical facilities, in their isolation.

In these heterogenous cases, power moved pyramidically down from the top of the state and into society. The state mobilized its social and human resources for the purpose of controlling bodies and their access to different social and spatial spaces. The very term 'private' was temporarily abolished. This became manifest as dangerous bodies diagnosed with COVID-19 were perceived as breaking the law if they received visitors, while the elderly and vulnerable in medical facilities were prevented from having visitors and certain forms of property rights were suspended. Henceforth, when individuals were allowed to leave their homes or visit loved ones, it was the state *granting* this access, as the state carefully considered how to govern. The control and discipline exercised over bodies, their whereabouts and their social interaction depended upon massive institutional capacities, manifesting in dividing practices which kept individuals spatially and socially apart (Foucault, 1994a).

The core of this form of government was the state's embeddedness in society, seen especially through its control over medical facilities, in which personnel could be promptly mobilized for infection control purposes. Embeddedness made it possible for the state to quickly reorganize such facilities, making it possible to exclude family and close ones from visiting the elderly, or alternatively, imposing disciplinary measures on those permitted to do so. Similarly, the possibility of mobilizing the civil guard to stop people from using private property beyond one's place of residency demanded grand infrastructural capacities. Indeed, embeddedness enabled the state to create this new biopolitical apparatus—the Corona Centre—which was both the result of immense institutional capacities, and a source of infrastructural power, producing information which it distributed alongside orders. Infrastructural power, based on the state's massive quantity of professionalized staff and its efficient state bureaucracy, enabled the state to mobilize and thereafter organize huge numbers of individuals as infection control agents as the state-controlled bodies and their access to different spaces.

Doing this, the state could use numerous institutions and actors to produce, analyse and distribute information, which made it possible to rigidly control (potentially) dangerous bodies. Control and discipline converged in a complex governing operation where the state-administered (potentially) dangerous bodies through its infrastructural and coercive capacities, the former enhancing and enabling the latter, whereas the latter served as a supplement supporting the effective use of the former. The state sought to protect society from (potentially) dangerous propagators of infection by tracing them and thereafter confining them socially and/or spatially, which, beyond disciplining (potentially) dangerous bodies, also generated information about the target population, thereby enhancing the state's capacities to act through and over society. To do so, the state had to know whom to confine, whom to exclude from social settings, and their whereabouts. Therefore, the Corona Centre was the infrastructural source of power underpinning quarantine and isolation in Norway.

Control over bodies was thus first and foremost enabled by the state governing through conscripts. The state mobilized huge numbers of individuals to monitor (potentially) dangerous bodies and guard vulnerable bodies (and places). This shows the institutional capacities of the Norwegian state, as its embeddedness and bureaucratic capacities enabled the quick restructuring of different institutions and the creation of new ones, for infection control purposes. And again, this all rested partly upon ideological power, as the Norwegian state's capacities to get its vision accepted meant that its measures were legitimate and thus produced less dissent than past pandemic restrictions (cf. Snowden, 2020), making both the mobilization of society and the coercive sources supporting this mobilization legitimate, as the state acted with severity to restrict the (potentially) dangerous and protect vulnerable bodies and sites.

4.3.5 *Close the Border!*

The closed border represented the lockdown's *external* feature. This revolved around handling (potentially) dangerous bodies. The border regime consisted of attempts to limit border crossings, both through direct, blunt exclusions, as well as more subtle political operations making border crossing inconvenient and awkward, by making more complicated the conditions under which border crossing could take place. While the closed border has been briefly discussed (Gjerde, 2021b; Sandset & Villadsen, 2023), the conditions imposed upon those allowed to enter together with their significance have only been studied with regard to the quarantine hotel (i.e. Gjerde, 2024a), whereas the border itself as a site of power has remained relatively understudied.

Borders are governing instruments 'delimit[ing] territories', which can be 'utilize[d] in various ways to define what stays inside and outside, and to address different types of threats and problems' (Dean, 2007: 39). By closing the border, the state defined the outside as dangerous. The border closure was accomplished with the coercive power of the state, which was utilized to ensure the integrity of the command. Norway had to be defended from (potentially) dangerous bodies crossing the border. When COVID-19 arrived, the state closed its borders to those lacking citizenship or resident permits, including de facto residents if they lacked such documents, something common to EU and EEA-citizens living in Norway, since they do not need to apply for documents to actually live in Norway. If they sought to re-enter Norway, they risked deportation (Gjerde, 2023). Military units were deployed to block the roads into Norway and ensure that nobody crossed the border illegally during the spring of 2020 (Regjeringen, 2020f). The very presence of military forces worked in a juridical-sovereign manner, signalling the state's coercive capacities and the gravity of the situation (cf. Davenport, 2007). The closed border was the result of the negative assertion of power, which could lead to deportation and other forms of punishment if individuals ignored the state's will. This was an overt expression of force, dependent primarily on coercive sources of power, supported by infrastructural power and surveillance capacities that allowed the state to monitor the border and would-be travellers. This juridical-sovereign exercise of power also had symbolic effects, signalling the gravity of the situation.

Citizens and residents could however not be denied entry. Nevertheless, power was exercised upon those still allowed to enter—indeed power may be channelled at the border in more productive ways than refusing entry (cf. Foucault, 1990, 1991). Travellers still allowed to enter Norway were initially placed in quarantine in a manner similar to other potentially dangerous bodies. However, measures were tightened during the autumn of 2020, limiting border crossings by making the conditions of travel awkward and difficult (Regjeringen.no, 2020t). First, travellers had to fill in extensive documents about their previous whereabouts, where they were to quarantine, their reasons for entering Norway, show a recent negative test, and sometimes be tested again:

> They [the state] only accepted Norwegian corona passports, so I had to pay to have mine translated! [At the border] they accepted my Norwegian corona passport but not my partner's Danish one… we felt importuned by the fact that my partner had to be tested in Norway and in Denmark (Lives and works abroad 21).

These were the conditions for entering Norway, which were in effect throughout most of the pandemic, albeit to different degrees as the level of severity varied based on contagion numbers in the country one travelled from. There was no unconditional right to enter Norway, and during the periods when relatives could enter, conditions were imposed upon them, too. Individuals were obliged to submit information in various forms and prove their 'safe' status, both by being tested prior to, and frequently after, crossing the border, as well as taking further steps to obtain the right documents, such as furnishing proof of a foreign vaccination accepted by the Norwegian authorities.

Second, the state created the National Communication Centre in early 2021. This was a surveillance organ, tasked with monitoring travellers in quarantine in private homes. State agents would contact those placed in quarantine via SMS and phone calls, disciplining travellers. Staff would ask those in quarantine about their whereabouts, whether they knew their obligations, the facilities available, such as whether they had separate toilets and access to food, mandatory requirements to avoid quarantine hotels (Helsedirektoratet, 2021c):

> as soon as we registered as having entered Norway, they [the National Communication Centre] called us [my partner and I], terrorizing us! We heard about people receiving 20,000 kroner [2,000 euros] fines for being in the wrong place at the wrong time (Engineer 20).

A newly formed political organ was created to distribute information and monitor those receiving it. Like the Corona Centre, the caller became the eyes and mouth of the state, surveilling and commanding the traveller. Travellers were contacted via SMS and phone calls. The state made clear to travellers that they were monitored, and furthermore, that reports of suspected wrong-doing would go to those in charge of infection control at a given municipality, who would in turn delegate policing responsibilities down the hierarchy, for instance to 'corona police officers', often pensioners with past experience in the police force, who would then enforce compliance and potentially fine rule-breakers (Helsedirektoratet, 2021c). As at the aforementioned Corona Centre, power at the National Communication Centre worked in an automatic manner, making itself visible but unverifiable. Power operated from a digital panopticon, where the state could always *potentially* see and the disciplined individual could never verify (cf. Foucault, 1991), thereby forcing the traveller to comply with quarantine obligations. This biopolitical apparatus was an infrastructural resource, generating knowledge, allowing the state to distribute information about dissidents, so as to punish them through law. The state used its infrastructural power to create the conditions for the effective application of coercion, if dissent was suspected, spreading fear to potential dissidents. As mentioned earlier, violence was not to be used frequently, but the threat of punishment was to discipline would-be dissidents.

Third, the state created the quarantine hotel, with various criteria for exemptions, in November 2020. The quarantine hotel was the strictest measure imposed upon those actually allowed to cross the border (Regjeringen.no, 2021c; Helsedirektoratet, 2021d). Unlike standard quarantine, the rules of the quarantine hotel were unclear. Whether one could leave the hotel or not, for how long, and the rules with regard to registration, were confusingly varied and vague, making it hard to understand the rules (Gjerde, 2024a). The quarantine hotel, like the quarantine more generally, targeted a (potentially) dangerous body. Yet, the traveller's body was considered *more* dangerous than other bodies. Therefore, the state excluded the traveller not just from social spaces, but also from his/her own home or that of loved ones, until proven safe, in order to keep Norway 'pure' from the dangers brought from abroad (cf. Foucault, 1994b). This increased the severity of the quarantine, making travel increasingly difficult and inconvenient. First, the traveller was forced to remain at a chosen location, being denied access to his or her home. Second, he had to pay a fee of 50 euros per night for this stay, as the state seized resources alongside rights, reducing individuals' actual possibility of entering Norway, also when this was not formally prohibited, such as to citizens and residents: 'I could neither afford nor take time to sit in a quarantine hotel' (Lives and works abroad 21). Third, inside the quarantine hotel, the traveller was monitored closely. Individuals had to register when they checked in, when leaving the hotel for a walk, when returning, and at times they were only allowed to leave for two hours at a time. Travellers needed the approval of a municipality representative to return home after a given numbers of days had passed and a negative test (Gjerde, 2024a).

The 'guest' of the quarantine hotel was disciplined, as mundane activities like entering or leaving were monitored and submitted to formalized criteria, as was the bed they slept in and their daily activities in general (see Regjeringen.no, 2021c, 2021d). Constant monitoring of travellers' activities, including the times of departure and arrival at the hotel after going for walks, constituted a constant reminder that the state's eye was upon the individual. Travellers were treated with measures that were meant to dissuade people from travelling altogether. When travellers arrived, a firm grip was imposed upon their bodies and minds, so as to limit the likelihood of people not complying with obligations and, more generally, feeling the desire to travel again during the pandemic. From increased surveillance and paperwork to the quarantine hotel itself, the traveller experienced a multitude of measures whose purpose was to make travel difficult and unenjoyable, and thus undesirable.

The state's border policies were made possible through the sources of power which the state depends upon to control *access* to its territory. The state exercised power by enacting infrastructural and coercive sources of power. These powers moved from the centre of the state and down, manifesting at the border, where various forms of discipline and control were exerted, in private homes, where state agents called and monitored (potentially) dangerous bodies, and in quarantine hotels, where some travellers were forced to remain for a period of 3–10 days, depending upon the rules at a given time. These powers were frequently enacted by formally non-state actors, such as former police officers or hotel employees, who governed on the state's behalf. Power moved from the centre and downwards, until it reached bodies, minds and relations at the micro-level, both at the border and in people's homes or the quarantine hotel, thereby working in a pyramidical manner. This was made possible by the state redirecting political institutions, such as the border control apparatus, for its biopolitical objectives of limiting travel and controlling travellers. The border control regime, including testing stations and tight border control for biopolitical purposes, was a re-articulation of the general border control apparatus towards tighter forms of control, supplemented by new biopolitical arrangements like the testing apparatus and infection control protocols.

However, the state did more than depend upon pre-existing institutions. The state created two new biopolitical organs—the quarantine hotel and the National Communication Centre. These organs were institutional resources. They were both results of the state's infrastructural power, and enhanced the state's institutional capacities, as the state could tightly regulate the bodies of those entering Norway through these novel instruments. This allowed the state to monitor travellers through calls, and to place people in the quarantine hotel, where bodies could be controlled more extensively. The state conscripted both public servants and private employees, transforming them into infection control agents, something especially interesting in the scenario of quarantine hotels, where workers from the service industry were conscripted. The state embedded itself deeper within society, appropriating the hotel as a political instrument. Coercive power—and the threat of punishment—underpinned all of these measures—but this was primarily a question of institutional rather than coercive capacities.

These microphysical powers, as they manifested on the body of the 'guest' of the quarantine hotel and the traveller at the border, as well as in the mind of the *potential* traveller, were coordinated and designated by the state, which acted through its autonomous powers as it sought to 'nudge' people away from travelling altogether. The state acted upon and through society, through formal and informal state agents, enforcing conditions which had to be satisfied for access to be granted to would-be travellers. The state went beyond blunt and linear action. Controlling the border allowed the state to change the conditions under which access was granted. This was a regulatory mechanism. While border control worked through exclusions and discipline, its primary objective was to limit the numbers of people crossing the border. The measures were direct and specific, although their purpose went beyond the actual traveller upon whom power was exerted. The main target was not the individual quarantined, but the would-be traveller not yet travelling, as the state sought to reduce entries by more tightly governing the bodies of those who could still enter.

4.4 Handling the Social Body

The politics of COVID-19 in Norway has been studied utilizing the Weberian-Foucauldian theory of the state, which includes the combination of Mann's theory of the sources of power as the macrophysics of power, with a Foucauldian framework of the mechanisms of power as its microphysics. The politics of COVID-19 in Norway consisted of a complex series of political operations where life in its entirety was placed under the state's direct or indirect, formal or moral, control. This occurred along various dimensions, from the internal lockdown to the handling of dangerous bodies, from the closed border to the mobilization of society, from the surveillance of society to the monitoring of (potentially) dangerous bodies.

I have studied novel aspects of the politics of COVID-19 in Norway. For instance, the logic of the border control regime was more complex than its closure—it worked through a multitude of political measures imposed to limit entries, manifesting in more complex mechanisms of power than juridical-sovereignty. Similarly, how quarantine and isolation works as mechanisms of power, and how the mobilization of society and lockdown worked at the micro-level, have been studied. Likewise, the study has explained these processes by discussing the sources of power making them possible.

The result of the Norwegian politics of COVID-19 was essentially the suspension of state-non-state and public–private distinctions. This suspension is made possible by the massive and diverse set of sources of power concentrated within the state apparatus, which the state is capable of utilizing in practice to govern. During the pandemic, we could see power working in a pyramidical fashion, from the centre of the state and down into society itself. Power originated at a centre from which it diffused, showing that, while Foucault (1991, 2003, 2009) is right that power should be studied where it works, we cannot understand power if we fail to trace its origins. Power is not free-floating. In our state-centred era, power will likely to originate in, and be regulated by and fixated around, the state. Beyond showing the problem of analysing mechanisms of power without taking into account the sources of power enabling power to be exercised, and the agency involved, this also hints at a theoretical issue: the Foucauldian literature indeed ought to become state-centred, as also argued by others (cf J. Kim, 2021; Lessenich, 2011).

The pyramidical manner power worked during the pandemic, and the ways civil society was essentially annexed as everything became a matter of state, shows how it is somewhat misleading to label the Norwegian approach as liberal biopolitics (i.e. Gjerde, 2021b; Sandset & Villadsen, 2023). Liberal governmentality revolves around 'a domain outside "politics"' which should keep 'its existence and its autonomy' (Miller & Rose, 2008: 60). However, the state suspended civil society and the private realm as sites beyond formal intervention, cancelling out the autonomy of this space. This discontinued liberal governmentality as a form of ruling and thinking, in favour of the security thinking related to the state of exception (Agamben, 2008: 50). This is seen as the state intervening in all kinds of private affairs, such as whether individuals could use their property, sleep at home or in a quarantine locale, have visitors, leave home if sick, and so on. This signals a decisive suspension of liberalism as a dominant principle of governing, even if, as Dean notes (2007: 110), governing liberally may require the use of authoritarian measures. The

Norwegian state remained a liberal democracy throughout the pandemic, but the measures implemented within this liberal democracy were non-liberal. Liberal governmentality was temporarily subordinated to biopolitical interventionism. Importantly, the ease by which the Norwegian state cancelled liberal governmentality, moving towards interventionist biopolitics in the manner of days (cf Gjerde, 2021a), shows how the state's capacities were never weakened, despite arguments to the contrary (i.e. Miller & Rose, 2008). Thinking as a state-centric Foucauldian, the turn towards neoliberalism, while allowing power to decentralize in practice (i.e. Foucault, 2008), never challenged the hierarchical position of the state, or its potential reach into society, as proven by how quickly the state could move from liberalism to interventionism.

The Norwegian state's suspension of state-non-state boundaries is not merely empirically interesting, but also carries theoretical significance regarding the question of the form and nature of the state itself. A common critique of state-centric approaches defining the state as an actor revolves around the idea that the state and society have unclear boundaries. For instance, Mitchell (1991), Foucault (2008, 2009) and Jessop (2011, 2015) argue that the unclear boundaries between the state and society prove the problematic nature of state-centric approaches, which define the state as an actor. In the words of Mitchell (1991: 90), 'the boundary of the state never marks a real exterior', making him argue that 'the line between state and society is not the perimeter of an intrinsic entity, which can be thought of as a free standing object or actor'. In other words, the state is defined as non-agential due to its unclear boundaries to its exterior, society at large.

While Mitchell is proven partly right by the pandemic—as the Norwegian state proves how state/society boundaries are indeed flexible and can be transgressed—his conclusions on the ontological and theoretical lessons this supposedly brings forth regarding the form of the state appear disproven by the politics of COVID-19. Contrary to Mitchell's arguments, the Norwegian state, as an intrinsic entity, acted upon this boundary, moving or even suspending it at will. This is not unique, and it can be explained from a state-centric perspective defining the state as an actor, contrary to argumentation of the aforementioned scholars. The state itself is able to act beyond the liberal boundaries separating it from civil society. If we want to understand how these boundaries are both (re)produced and potentially transgressed or cancelled altogether, we need an agential theory of the state. After all, the state is capable of acting upon the society which it is intertwined deeply with. The Norwegian state decided to transgress these boundaries, which, while not set in stone, are political constructs produced by the agency of the state. The agency of the state, which Foucauldian and other non-agential approaches to the state dismiss, is enabled by the sources of power which the state accumulates, concentrating within itself. These sources allow the state to act upon and through society. State power is essentially a question of state agency, and while the boundaries of the state are indeed unclear, the agency of the state is made clear by, among other things, how the state can act upon these boundaries. Failing to account for state agency, state autonomy similarly becomes opaque. The powers of the state escape analytical attention.

While non-state actors will participate in determining the state's scope (i.e. Migdal, 1988), the state has the final right through might, especially during crises (i.e. Schmitt, 1996). The state's very definition of a situation, and of the state-society boundaries, deeply affect how citizens think about them, especially if the state is legitimate in the eyes of its population, like in Norway. The boundaries between the state and society are not merely potentially analysable from a state-centric perspective, but indeed, may potentially only fully make sense once we embrace an agential theory of the state. The state (re)produces or destroys the boundaries based on its own actions, making clear that the unclarity of these boundaries in no way disproves state-centric approaches. This will be made clearer when we move beyond the context of Norway, where we can observe a state (re)producing boundaries which the Norwegian state preferred to transgress.

References

Agamben, G. (2008). *State of exception*. Chicago: University of Chicago Press.

Almlund, P., E Kjeldsen, J., & Mølster, R. (2023). Expressions of governance, risk, and responsibility: Public campaigns in the crisis and risk management of Covid-19 in Denmark, Norway, and Sweden. In B. Johansson, Ø. Ihlen, J. Lindholm, & M. Blach-Ørsten (Eds.), *Communicating a pandemic: Crisis management and Covid-19 in the Nordic countries* (pp. 121–149). University of Gothenburg.

Arts, B. (2014). Assessing forest governance from a 'Triple G' perspective: Government, governance, governmentality. *Forest Policy and Economics, 49*, 17–22.

Ayodele, O. (2019). Information infrastructures: The conduit power of ICTs in Africa. *The Strategic Review for Southern Africa, 41*(2).

Bhowmick, S., & Alam, M. (2023) Foucault meets novel coronavirus: Biosociality, excesses of governmentality and the "will to live" of the pandemicariat. *Foucault Studies* (No. 35), 145–166. https://doi.org/10.22439/fs.i35.7088

Bowen, C. (2021). Discipline and control and Covid-19. *La deleuziana, 13*, 164–175.

Byler, D. (2023). The camp fix: Infrastructural power and the "re-education labour regime" in Turkic Muslim industrial parks in North-west China. *The China Quarterly, 255*, 628–643.

Cheibub, J. A., Hong, J. Y. J., & Przeworski, A. (2020). Rights and deaths: Government reactions to the pandemic. Working paper. https://doi.org/10.2139/ssrn.3645410

Christensen, T., & Lægreid, P. (2020). Balancing governance capacity and legitimacy: how the Norwegian Government handled the COVID−19 crisis as a high performer. *Public Administration Review, 80*(5), 774–779. https://doi.org/10.1111/puar.13241

Christensen, T., & Lægreid, P. (2020). The coronavirus crisis—Crisis communication, meaning-making, and reputation management. *International Public Management Journal, 23*(5), 713–729.

Christensen, T., & Lægreid, P. (2022). Scientization under pressure—the problematic role of expert bodies during the handling of the COVID-19 pandemic. *Public Organization Review, 22*(2), 291–307.

Conyon, M., He, L., & Thomsen, S. (2020). Lockdowns and COVID-19 deaths in Scandinavia.*Available at SSRN 3616969.*

Davenport, C. (2007). State repression and the tyrannical peace. *Journal of Peace Research, 44*(4), 485–504.

Dean, M. (2007). *Governing societies. Political perspectives on domestic and international rule.* Open University Press.

Dyregrov, A., & Kristensen, P. (2021) Koronapandemiens innvirkning på ritualer blant foreldre som har mistet barn. Rapport- og artikkelserie ved senter for krisepsykologi 3(2021) Universitet i Bergen. ISSN 2703-7800-4 https://www.uib.no/sites/www.uib.no/files/attachments/ritualrapport_etterlatte_foreldre_issn_2703-7800-4_.pdf

Elias, N. (1978). *The history of manners. The civilizing process, volume 1.* Basil Blackwell.

Elias, N. (1982). *Power and civility. The civilizing process volume 2.* Basil Blackwell.

Foucault, M. (1990). *The history of sexuality, volume 1. An introduction*. Penguin Books.

Foucault, M. (1991). *Discipline and punish: The birth of the prison.* Penguin Books.

Foucault, M. (1994a). Subject and power. In F. D. Faubion & M. Foucault (Eds.), *Power. Essential works of Foucault 1954–1984 volume 3* (pp. 326–349). The New Press.

Foucault, M. (1994b). *The birth of social medicine*. In F. D. Faubion & M. Foucault (Eds.), *Power. Essential works of Foucault 1954–1984 volume* 3 (pp. 134–156). The New Press.

Foucault, M. (2008). *The birth of biopolitics - Lectures at the Collège de France, 1978–1979*. Palgrave Macmillan.

Foucault, M. (2013). *The punitive society*. Picador.

Foucault, M. (2014). *The government of the living*. Picador.

Foucault, M. (2019). *Penal Theories and Institutions*. Picador

Gjerde, L. E. L. (2021). From liberalism to biopolitics: Investigating the Norwegian government's two responses to COVID-19. *European Societies, 23*(sup1), S262–S274. https://doi.org/10.1080/14616696.2020.1824003

Gjerde, L. E. L. (2021). Governing humans and 'things': Power and rule in Norway during the Covid-19 pandemic. *Journal of Political Power, 14*(3), 472–492. https://doi.org/10.1080/2158379X.2020.1870264

Gjerde, L. E. L. (2022). Den norske regjeringens diskursive muliggjøring av koronapolitikken: Et Foucauldiansk perspektiv. *Norsk Sosiologisk Tidsskrift* (3), 29–45. https://doi.org/10.18261/nost.6.3.3

Gjerde, L. E. L. (2023). Biopolitical and juridical creations of the quarantine hotel: A discourse analysis of the Norwegian case. *Acta Sociologica, 66*(4), 357–371. https://doi.org/10.1177/00016993221136038

Gjerde, L. E. L. (2024a). Marrying the sources and mechanisms of power? Understanding the quarantine hotel through Michel Foucault and Michael Mann. *Journal of Political Power*. https://doi.org/10.1080/2158379X.2024.2337617

Gjerde, L. E. L. (2024c). Interview guide: Online appendix. https://doi.org/10.13140/RG.2.2.24808.69126

Gjerde, L. E. L. (2025). Methodology: Digital appendix. *Research Gate*. https://www.researchgate.net/publication/387958773_Methodology_Digital_Appendix

Gulbrandsen, K. S. (2022). Centre–periphery contestation and the spatialization of Covid-19 discourse in Norway. *Territory, Politics, Governance, 10*(6), 759–778.

Graver, H. P. (2020a). COVID-19 regulation in Norway and state of exception. COVID-19 and Constitutional Law. Universidad Nacional Autónoma de México, 167–175.

Graver, H. P. (2020b). *Pandemi og unntakstilstand. Hva covid-19 sier om den norske rettstaten*. Dreyers Forlag.

Green, T. (2021). *The Covid consensus: The new politics of global inequality*. Hurst.

Greve, B., Blomquist, P., Hvinden, B., & Van Gerven, M. (2021). Nordic welfare states—Still standing or changed by the COVID-19 crisis? *Social Policy & Administration, 55*(2), 295–311.

Gross, L. (2023). "Not a major or complicated task": Activating Dugnad under COVID-19 and the imagination of equality in the Norwegian Welfare State. *Anthropologica, 65*(1).

Harris, A., & Jones, M. (2020). COVID 19 – School leadership in disruptive times. *School Leadership & Management, 40*(4), 243–247.

Harris, A., & Jones, M. (2022). Leading during a pandemic – What the evidence tells us. *School Leadership & Management, 42*(2), 105–109.

Helsingen, L. M., Refsum, E., Gjøstein, D. K., Løberg, M., Bretthauer, M., Kalager, M., & Emilsson, L. (2020). The COVID-19 pandemic in Norway and Sweden–threats, trust, and impact on daily life: A comparative survey. *BMC Public Health, 20*(1), 1–10.

Hobbes, T. (1996). *Leviathan*. Oxford University Press.

Jessop, B. (2011). Constituting another Foucault Effect. Foucault on states and Statecraft In Bröckling, Krasmann, S., & Lemke, T (Eds.), *Governmentality: Current Issues and Future Challenges* (pp. 54–73). Routledge.

Jessop, B. (2015). *The state: Past, present, future*. Wiley.

Kim, J. (2021). Rethinking public administration and the state: A Foucauldian governmentality perspective. *International Review of Public Administration, 26*(2), 175–191. https://doi.org/10.1080/12294659.2021.1889102

Kristensen, L. M., & Hartley, J. M. (2023). The infrastructure of news: Negotiating infrastructural capture and autonomy in data-driven news distribution. *Media and Communication, 11*(2), 307–318.

Lessenich, S. (2011). Constructing the socialized self. Mobilization and control in the "active society". In Bröckling, S. Krasmann, & T. Lemke (Eds.), *Governmentality: Current issues and future challenges* (pp. 304–319). Routledge.

Mann, M. (2008). Infrastructural power revisited. Studies in Comparative International Development, 43(3), 355–365.

Mann, M. (1993). *The sources of social power, volume II: The rise of classes and nation states*. Cambridge University Press.

Mann, M. (2012). *The sources of social power. Volume 3. Global empires and Revolution, 1890–1945*. Cambridge University Press.

Mann, M. (2013). *The sources of social power. Volume 4, globalizations, 1945–2011*. Cambridge University Press.

Migdal, J. S. (1988). *Strong societies and weak states: State-society relations and state capabilities in the Third World*. Princeton University Press.

Miller, P., & Rose, N. (2008). *Governing the present: Administering economic, social and political life*. Polity Press.

Mitchell, T. (1991). The limits of the state: Beyond statist approaches and their critics. *The American Political Science Review, 85*(1), 77–96.

Moss, S. M., & Sandbakken, E. M. (2021). "Everybody needs to do their part, so we can get this under control." Reactions to the Norwegian government meta-narratives on COVID-19 measures. *Political Psychology, 42*(5), 881–898.

Nanda, M., Aashima, & Sharma, R. (2021). COVID-19: A comprehensive review of epidemiology and public health system response in Nordic region. *International Journal of Health Services, 51(3)*, 287–299.

Sandbakken, E. M., & Moss, S. M. (2021). "Now we are all in the same boat. at the same time, we are not." Meaning-making and coping under COVID-19 lockdown in Norway. *Human Arenas,* 1–25.

Sandset, T., & Villadsen, K. (2023). Pandemic modelling and model citizens: Governing COVID-19 through predictive models, sovereignty and discipline. *The Sociological Review,* 00380261221102023.

Scharffscher, K. S., & Engen, O. A. (2022). Pandemi, tillit og kommunikasjon. *Stat & Styring, 32*(2), 6–9.

Schmitt, C. (1996). *The concept of the political.* University of Chicago Press.

Seabrooke, L. (2002). Bringing legitimacy back into Neo-Weberian state theory and international relations. Australian National University, Department of International Relations, Working Paper 2002/6.

Sending, O. J., & Neumann, I. B. (2006). Governance to governmentality: Analyzing NGOs, states, and power. *International Studies Quarterly, 50*(3), 651–672.

Snowden, F. M. (2020). *Epidemics and society: From the black death to the present.* Yale University Press.

Stefanizzi, P., Bianchi, F. P., Brescia, N., Ferorelli, D., & Tafuri, S. (2022). Vaccination strategies between compulsion and incentives. The Italian Green Pass experience. *Expert review of vaccines, 21*(4), 423–425.

Staupe-Delgado, R. (2021). Life in Anticipation of the COVID-19 Pandemic 'Peak': Reflecting on 'Strategies' for and Variations in attempts at 'Flattening the Curve' and Managing the Crisis. *Journal of Extreme Events, 8*(01), 2150016.

Sætrevik, B., Bærøe, K., Carlsen, B., & Bjørkheim, S. B. (2021). Nordmenn stolte på myndighetenes informasjon og tiltak i starten av koronapandemien. *Tidsskrift for Velferdsforskning, 24*(2), 1–16.

Rippa, A., & Oakes, T. (2023). Infrastructural thinking in China: A research agenda. *The China Quarterly,* 1–13.

Rose, N. (1999) *Powers of freedom: reframing political thought. Cambridge.* Cambridge University Press.

Tazzioli, M. (2021). A "passport to freedom"? COVID-19 and the re-bordering of the world. *European Journal of Risk Regulation, 12*(2), 355–361.

Wollebæk, D., Fladmoe, A., & Steen-Johnsen, K. (2022). Tillit, følelser, normer og sosial distansering: En longitudinell studie av den norske befolkningen under Covid-19-pandemien. *Norsk statsvitenskapelig tidsskrift* (3), 63–80.

Empirical References: Chapter 4

FHI. (2020). Status covid-19 uke 34 Status covid-19 uke 34.

FHI. (2021a). Smittevernråd for befolkningen. https://www.fhi.no/nettpub/coronavirus/befolkningen/smittevernrad-for-befolkningen/

FHI. (2021b). Smittevernråd for religiøse feiringer. https://www.fhi.no/nettpub/coronavirus/rad-og-informasjon-til-andre-sektorer-og-yrkesgrupper/religiose-feiringer/

Helse-og omsorgsdepartementet. (2021). Rundskriv I-6/2021 om kommunale smitteverntiltak (I-6/2021) [Rundskriv]. https://www.regjeringen.no/contentassets/caaee441fe19451a9bad3333d98a7a7a/rundskriv-i-6-2021-om-kommunale-smitteverntiltak.pdf

Helsedirektoratet. (2020a). Vedtak etter lov mot smittsomme sykdommer § 4–1 andre ledd om møteforbud og stengning av virksomhet. https://www.helsedirektoratet.no/tema/beredskap-og-krisehandtering/koronavirus/anbefalinger-og-beslutninger/Vedtak%20etter%20lov%20om%20vern%20mot%20smittsomme%20sykdommer%20%C2%A74-1%20andre%20ledd%20om%20m%C3%B8teforbud%20og%20stenging%20av%20virksomhet.pdf/_/attachment/inline/5c6032e8-3d56-44f2-a18c-8829a9db7c97:7686689d095ad59bf30786a730632036a1f9c2d1/Vedtak%20etter%20lov%20om%20vern%20mot%20smittsomme%20sykdommer%20%C2%A7%204-1%20andre%20ledd%20om%20m%C3%B8teforbud%20og%20stenging%20av%20virksomhet.pdf

Helsedirektoratet. (2020b). Anbefaling til kommuner rundt Oslo om å vurdere kommunale tiltak mot Covid-19 iforbindelse med lettelser i nasjonale tiltak fra 12. oktober 2020. https://www.helsedirektoratet.no/tema/beredskap-og-krisehandtering/koronavirus/anbefalinger-og-beslutninger/Anbefaling%20til%20kommuner%20rundt%20Oslo%20om%20%C3%A5%20vurdere%20kommunale%20tiltak%20mot%20covid-19%20091020.pdf/_/attachment/inline/d830e715-9945-4db0-82af-714130a647fe:f1569e3016cdf7f2a983665b2f2165db17d50754/Anbefaling%20til%20kommuner%20rundt%20Oslo%20om%20%C3%A5%20vurdere%20kommunale%20tiltak%20mot%20covid-19%20091020.pdf

Helsedirektoratet. (2020c). Brukermanual TISK. https://www.helsedirektoratet.no/statistikk/dokumenter/Brukermanual-TISK.pdf/_/attachment/inline/6c0beb4d-9946-4ccd-bbbe-d54a9f508d86:cc9260f3baa2e3f40494fa40c1c20d896781bebd/Brukermanual%20TISK%202021-01.pdf

Helsedirektoratet. (2020d). Rammeverk for testsentre ved grenseoverganger. https://www.helsedirektoratet.no/tema/beredskap-og-krisehandtering/koronavirus/anbefalinger-og-beslutninger/Rammeverk%20for%20testsentre%20ved%20grenseoverganger.PDF/_/attachment/inline/77a03cdb-9435-47d3-8427-f1b0d68daf78:2945c5180d6fd11693058ba8cf8ddc236cf7d35c/Rammeverk%20for%20testsentre%20ved%20grenseoverganger.PDF

Helsedirektoratet. (2020e). Oppdrag nr. 76 - Endringer i covid-19-forskriften. https://www.helsedirektoratet.no/tema/koronavirus/faglig-grunnlag-til-helse-og-omsorgsdepartementet-covid-19/Oppdrag%2076%20-%20Endringer%20i%20covid-19-forskriften%20-%20vurdering%20om%20treningssentre%20og%20sv%C3%B8mming.PDF/_/attachment/inline/4e2084b6-058d-44c8-89ae-cd8634ec1b6d:a9f4c407ad7e787aa9b2005930f33dd68638c6ca/Oppdrag%2076%20-%20Endringer%20i%20covid-19-forskriften%20-%20vurdering%20om%20treningssentre%20og%20sv%C3%B8mming.PDF

Helsedirektoratet. (2021a). Svar på covid-19 oppdrag fra HOD 389 - til Helsedirektoratet om vurdering av smittevernveilederne i skoler og barnehager. https://www.helsedirektoratet.no/tema/koronavirus/faglig-grunnlag-til-helse-og-omsorgsdepartementet-covid-19/Oppdrag%20389%20-%20Vurdering%20av%20smitteveilederne%20i%20skoler%20og%20barnehager.pdf/_/attachment/inline/dfddfca3-217a-44f9-9754-041c1b504a5f:e26661e9daa55972b52e25ef712ba2fbc1299055/Oppdrag%20389%20-%20Vurdering%20av%20smitteveilederne%20i%20skoler%20og%20barnehager.pdf

Helsedirektoratet. (2021c). Oppretter nasjonalt kontrollsenter for oppfølging av innreisende. https://www.helsedirektoratet.no/nyheter/oppretter-nasjonalt-kontrollsenter-for-oppfolging-av-innreisende

Helsedirektoratet. (2021d). Endrer regler om karantenehotell og innreisekarantene ved alvorlig sykdom eller bisettelse og begravelse. https://www.helsedirektoratet.no/nyheter/endrer-reglene-om-karantenehotell-og-innreisekarantene-ved-alvorlig-sykdom-eller-bisettelse-og-begravelse

Helsedirektoratet. (2022). Covid-19 (koronavirus). https://www.helsedirektoratet.no/tema/beredskap-og-krisehandtering/koronavirus

Lovdata. (2020a). Forskrift om smitteverntiltak mv. ved koronautbruddet (covid-19-forskriften). https://lovdata.no/dokument/SF/forskrift/2020-03-27-470

Lovdata. (2020b). Riksadvokatens brev om straff ved smittevern-lovbrot. https://lovdata.no/artikkel/riksadvokatens_brev_om_straff_ved_smittevern-lovbrot/2675

Lovdata. (2022). Lov om vern mot smittsomme sykdommer [smittevernloven]. https://lovdata.no/dokument/NL/lov/1994-08-05-55

Myrvang, S. E. (2021). Guldvog om 12. mars-nedstengingen: Ville ha «sjokkeffekt». https://www.vg.no/nyheter/i/41koqG/guldvog-om-12-mars-nedstengingen-ville-ha-sjokkeffekt

Norsk koronamonitor. (2020a). Tiltakstrøttheten i Oslo sterkt overdrevet. https://opinion.no/2020/10/tiltakstrottheten-i-oslo-sterkt-overdrevet/
Norsk Koronamonitor. (2020b). Ja takk til munnbind og tøffere tiltak. https://opinion.no/2020/09/ja-takk-til-munnbind-og-toffere-tiltak/
Norsk Koronamonitor. (2020c). Lite tiltakstrøtthet tross nye tiltak. https://opinion.no/2021/01/lite-tiltakstrotthet-tross-nytt-koronaar/
Norsk koronamonitor. (2020d). Slik er nordmenns koronavaner. https://opinion.no/2020/03/slik-er-nordmenns-koronavaner/
Norsk koronamonitor. (2020e). FOLK DROPPER FLYREISER I NORGE UT ÅRET. https://opinion.no/2020/09/folk-dropper-flyreiser-i-norge-ut-aret/
Norsk koronamonitor. (2021a). Flertallet feirer 17. mai hjemme. https://opinion.no/2021/04/flertallet-feirer-17-mai-hjemme/
Norsk koronamonitor. (2021b). Mer enn fire av fem unngår nærkontakter. https://opinion.no/2021/04/mer-enn-fire-av-fem-unngar-naerkontakter/
NTB. (2020). Ni av ti støtter videreføring av koronatiltak. https://www.dn.no/helse/koronaviruset/meningsmalinger/ni-av-ti-stotter-videreforing-av-koronatiltak/2-1-780724
Stortinget. (2020). Skriftlig spørsmål fra Kjersti Toppe (Sp) til helse- og omsorgsministeren. https://www.stortinget.no/no/Saker-og-publikasjoner/Sporsmal/Skriftlige-sporsmal-og-svar/Skriftlig-sporsmal/?qid=79504
Regjeringen.no. (2020a). Dette er ikke tiden for "jeg". Dette er tiden for "vi". https://www.regjeringen.no/no/aktuelt/dette-er-ikke-tiden-for-jeg.-dette-er-tiden-for-vi/id2694026/
Regjeringen.no. (2020b). En felles kamp mot en usynlig fiende. https://www.regjeringen.no/no/aktuelt/en-felles-kamp-mot-en-usynlig-fiende/id2695024/
Regjeringen.no. (2020c). Holde fast og holde ut. https://www.regjeringen.no/no/aktuelt/holde-fast-og-holde-ut/id2702383/
Regjeringen.no. (2020d). Statsministerens innledning på pressekonferanse om tiltak knyttet til koronaviruset. https://www.regjeringen.no/no/aktuelt/statsministerens-innledning-pa-pressemote-om-korona-viruset/id2693618/
Regjeringen. (2020e). Koronavirus blir meldeplikt sykdom. https://www.regjeringen.no/no/aktuelt/koronavirus-blir-meldepliktig-sykdom/id2688415/
Regjeringen. (2020f). Statsministerens innledning på pressemøte om koronaviruset. https://www.regjeringen.no/no/dokumentarkiv/regjeringen-solberg/aktuelt-regjeringen-solberg/smk/taler-og-innlegg/statsministeren/talerogartikler/2020/statsministerens-innledning-pa-pressemote-om-korona-viruset/id2693618/
Regjeringen. (2020g). Gode nyheter. https://www.regjeringen.no/no/aktuelt/gode-nyheter/id2702326/

Regjeringen. (2020h). Statsministerens innledning på pressekonferansen om økonomiske tiltak. https://www.regjeringen.no/no/dokumentarkiv/regjeringen-solberg/aktuelt-regjeringen-solberg/smk/taler-og-innlegg/statsministeren/talerogartikler/2020/statsministerens-innledning-om-okonomiske-tiltak-i-korona-krisen/id2693477/

Regjeringen. (2020i). Justis- og beredskapsministerens orientering om koronasituasjonen 23. Mars. https://www.regjeringen.no/no/dokumentarkiv/regjeringen-solberg/aktuelt-regjeringen-solberg/jd/taler_og_innlegg/ministeren/taler-og-innlegg-av-justis--og-beredskapsminister-monica-maland/2020/justis--og-beredskapsministerens-orientering-om-koronasituasjonen-23.-mars/id2694611/

Regjeringen.no. (2020j). Redegjørelse om norske tiltak for koronavirusutbruddet. https://www.regjeringen.no/no/dokumentarkiv/regjeringen-solberg/aktuelt-regjeringen-solberg/hod/taler-og-innlegg/minister/taler-av-helse-og-omsorgsminister-bent-/2020/redegjorelse-om-norske-tiltak-for-a-mote-koronavirusutbruddet/id2693018/

Regjeringen. (2020k). Justis- og beredskapsministerens orientering 21. April. https://www.regjeringen.no/no/dokumentarkiv/regjeringen-solberg/aktuelt-regjeringen-solberg/jd/taler_og_innlegg/ministeren/taler-og-innlegg-av-justis--og-beredskapsminister-monica-maland/2020/justis--og-beredskapsministerens-orientering-21.-april/id2698492/

Regjeringen. (2020l). Frihet under stort ansvar. https://www.regjeringen.no/no/dokumentarkiv/regjeringen-solberg/aktuelt-regjeringen-solberg/jd/taler_og_innlegg/ministeren/taler-og-innlegg-av-justis--og-beredskapsminister-monica-maland/2020/frihet-under-stort-ansvar/id2698065/

Regjeringen. (2020m). Vil åpne samfunnet gradvis og kontrollert. https://www.regjeringen.no/no/aktuelt/Vil-apne-samfunnet-gradvis-og-kontrollert/id2697060/

Regjeringen. (2020n). Justis- og beredskapsministerens orientering. April. https://www.regjeringen.no/no/aktuelt/justis-og-beredskapsministerens-orientering-21-april/id2698492/

Regjeringen. (2020o). Hold dere hjemme, ha minst mulig sosial kontakt https://www.regjeringen.no/no/dokumentarkiv/regjeringen-solberg/aktuelt-regjeringen-solberg/smk/pressemeldinger/2020/-hold-dere-hjemme-ha-minst-mulig-sosial-kontakt/id2783763/

Regjeringen. (2020p). Redegjørelse om koronapandemien. https://www.regjeringen.no/no/aktuelt/redegjorelse-om-koronapandemien-i-stortinget/id2770148/

Regjeringen. (2020q). Statsministerens innlegg på pressekonferanse om smittesporing. https://www.regjeringen.no/no/aktuelt/statsministerens-innlegg-pa-pressekonferanseom-smittesporing/id2697826/

Regjeringen. (2020r). Minst en meter gjelder. https://www.regjeringen.no/no/aktuelt/tydeligere-rad-om-besok-hos-eldre/id2702502/
Regjeringen. (2020s). Gå varsomt ned fra toppen. https://www.regjeringen.no/no/dokumentarkiv/regjeringen-solberg/aktuelt-regjeringen-solberg/hod/taler-og-innlegg/minister/taler-av-helse-og-omsorgsminister-bent-/2020/turen-ned-er-den-tyngste/id2702442/
Regjeringen.no. (2020t). Prop. 62L (2020–2021). https://www.regjeringen.no/no/dokumenter/prop.-62-l-20202021/id2791046/?ch=5
Regjeringen. (2021a). Regjeringens plan for slå ned den nye virusvarianten. https://www.regjeringen.no/no/aktuelt/regjeringens-plan-for-sla-ned-den-nye-virusvarianten/id2830148/
Regjeringen. (2021b). Planen for å slå ned den nye virusvarianten. https://www.regjeringen.no/no/aktuelt/regjeringens-plan-for-a-sla-ned-den-nye-virusvarianten/id2830146/
Regjeringen.no. (2021c). Begrunnelse for endringer 28. april 2021 i covid-19-forskriften § 5 om oppholdssted for innreisekarantene. https://www.regjeringen.no/no/tema/Koronasituasjonen/begrunnelserfor-endringer-i-covid-19-forskriften/begrunnelse-for-endringer-28.-april-2021-i-covid-19-forskriften-5-om-oppholdssted-for-innreisekarantene/id2862154/
Regjeringen. (2021d). Prop. 103 L (2021–2022). https://www.regjeringen.no/no/dokumenter/prop.-103-l-20212022/id2909279/?ch=4
VG. (2020). Unnamed. https://akamai.vgc.no/v2/images/3055afac-bc68-4670-a346-6fa68fed473d?fit=crop&format=auto&h=1264&w=1900&s=3f308dba3fd6fef3e2cf49bbdd80ee2aea27afea

CHAPTER 5

A Soft Leviathan? Examining the Politics of COVID-19 in Sweden

5.1 Introduction

As discussed, the politics of COVID-19 represents a break with established, more moderate forms of pandemic policies, the predominant choice for dealing with diseases in recent centuries (Green, 2021). There are nonetheless apparent Western deviants, Sweden being the most infamous and heavily debate case. Yet, how different is Sweden really? The Minister of Health and Social Affairs Lena Hallengren claimed that there is 'no unique Swedish approach' (Government, 2020a). Similarly, the 'infection control commander-in-chief' Anders Tegnell (2021) asserted that the Swedish approach was highly similar to that of other countries. While my findings support other studies, which declare that the Swedish state indeed acted more moderately (i.e. Aucante, 2022; Giritli Nygren & Olofsson, 2020), the exceptionalism of the Swedish state appears overstated, as this and the next chapter will discuss. The Swedish strategy differed from the lockdown approach, but there are numerous similarities worthy of mention. However, the Swedish approach is not merely different. It is highly controversial (Girtli Nygren & Olofsson 2021; Grothe-Hammer & Roth, 2021; Hagström et al., 2023; Larsson, 2022). While death rates were infamously high during the initial stages, in the end, the Swedish approach *may* have achieved 'normal' results. The approach may have been superior, inferior or inconsequential, with

L. E. L. Gjerde, *Nordic Leviathans*, International Political Theory, https://doi.org/10.1007/978-3-032-00689-9_5

regard to infection control (cf. Wallace-Wells, 2023). This particular question, however, does not interest me. My concern lies with the issue of state power and control of the *population*, as in the less controversial Norwegian case.

While the Swedish case, due to its controversy, has been extensively studied (i.e. Aucante, 2022; Girtli Nygren & Olofsson, 2020; Kamerlin & Kasson, 2020; Larsson, 2022; Pierre, 2020; Winblad et al., 2022), my study addresses several gaps in the literature. The mobilization of society in Sweden has been studied through the lens of voluntarism, thereby overlooking the manner in which the state formally mobilized various social actors as infection control agents. Voluntarism has been granted a dominant position within the literature, at the expense of non-voluntaristic forms of governance, such as the mobilization of society, but also more limited instances of juridical-sovereign denial and the enforcement of a softer but still potent disciplinary regime. Because of the relative lack of attention to the Swedish state's formal governance, the way in which the Swedish politics of COVID-19 was two-tiered remains unexamined. Moreover, I shall seek to explore the link between the macro- and microphysics of power that has not been investigated, such as the state and its sources of power and autonomy, which like in Norway has been left relatively disregarded. As in the last chapter, I shall attempt to remedy these empirical and theoretical issues through the Weberian-Foucauldian theory of the state. Again, I shall analyse how the state's infrastructural, coercive and ideological powers manifest at the micro-level through mechanisms of power when the state enacts these sources through its actions.

As discussed, these theoretical and empirical objectives are grounded in a single research question: *how did the Swedish state govern its territory and population during the pandemic?* To answer this question, various public documents and 17 interviews, based on the interview guide (see Gjerde, 2024), serve as data. The public data sources can be found in the bibliography, under the heading 'empirical references: chapter 5', and more information on the methodology can be found in the digital appendix (Gjerde, 2025). Illustrative excerpts from the interviews will be referred to in the text. The data is explored through a Weberian-Foucauldian lens, facilitating further theory-building.

As in the chapter dedicated to Norway, I have structured the analysis around an exploration of the state's governmental actions by investigating the link between the macro- and microphysics of power. The Swedish state utilized voluntarism to a greater extent, hence the chapter is arranged somewhat differently to the corresponding chapter on Norway which was separated into two distinct parts with symbolic governance through the communication campaign and the use of voluntarism on the one hand, and an exploration of the state's use of its autonomous powers on the other. Such an analytical separation made sense as there was a clear distinction in Norway between how and when voluntarism was used vis-à-vis formal governance. This is not the case in Sweden, where formal and informal forms of government interweaved in a complex two-tier system, making the Swedish strategy elude such typologies. Voluntarism was used to a much greater extent, often within contexts where the autonomous sources of power were enacted, manifesting in mechanisms of juridical-sovereignty, control, discipline and self-regulation, in complex webs of power. Therefore, the analysis is divided as follows: I first explore the communication campaign of the state, before moving on to voluntarism. Then, I investigate the 'soft law' of Sweden, and how 'soft law' manifested in limited juridical-sovereign mechanisms. Thereafter, I discuss how the soft law-voluntarism dichotomy (i.e. Winblad et al., 2022) is a simplification, neglecting the core of the politics of public life in Sweden: the mobilization of society. These different tactics show that the Swedish strategy worked as a two-tier system. The remainder of the chapter is dedicated to further clarifying the logic of this system, by examining how control over (potentially) dangerous and vulnerable bodies, as well as the border control regime, worked through the Swedish state as it exploited different tactics.

5.1.1 Swedish Tactics

5.1.1.1 Exercising Ideological Power

As in Norway, the Swedish state had to convince citizens and residents about the dangers of COVID-19 and the importance of subordinating their interests to those of the national community. The state played upon the gravity of the situation to produce a sense of urgency, upon the moral necessity of complying, through communitarian rhetoric, and upon science, by referring to evidence-driven measures and dismissing novel measures as untested (cf. Bjørkdahl et al., 2021). The state represented the situation, socially constructing it in the process, as its vision was accepted and spread throughout society. This communication strategy also revolved around justifying the Swedish state's approach, as in other countries (Baekkeskov et al., 2021). While the rhetorical techniques have been addressed (i.e. Baekkeskov et al., 2021), we must examine how they worked at the micro-level and how they were enabled through enactment of sources of power.

The Swedish state largely played upon the same propaganda techniques as the Norwegian state. There is however one key difference. Whereas the Norwegian state had to legitimize the strictest forms of state coercion and the transgression of all state/non-state boundaries, the Swedish state had to influence the public to legitimize its softer approach. While both states sought to legitimize their approaches and convince citizens to comply, the Swedish state had a more complex task ahead of it, as it had to balance between justifying its comparatively soft stance on COVID-19 and producing compliance with recommendations, which entailed voluntary sacrifices for private individuals. Therefore, the Swedish state had to reduce its use of fear as an instrument. The Swedish state was *more* dependent upon political rhetoric for convincing citizens, due to the relative lack of state coercion, and yet it could not fully utilize the propaganda arsenal at its disposal without delegitimizing its own approach.

The Swedish communication campaign revolved around making private individuals take responsibility by participating in solving the crisis, i.e. voluntarism (Krisinformation, 2020a; see also Girtili Nygren & Olofsson, 2020; Larsson, 2022). Voluntarism in Sweden functions as a legal practice. The individual was therefore legally obliged to show consideration for fellow humans and limit the risk of spreading COVID-19 (Folkhälsomyndigheten, 2023a). There was no punishment for inconsideration, but this had symbolic effects. It formalized the moral obligation of compliance. The rhetorical politics of crisis in Sweden was both at the core of the communication strategy, as well as constituting a major point of contradiction. To solve this issue, the crisis rhetoric in Sweden had to be, and was, more muted than in Norway or other countries that depended more heavily on state coercion. The pandemic was described as a crisis (Government, 2020b) with 'negative consequences' that had to be reduced (Government, 2020c). Thus, 'there is no denying that this pandemic is a tragedy, affecting all countries and all levels of society', and individuals had to comply to protect lives and the healthcare system (The Local, 2020a). References to the situation as a crisis, a tragedy or in other ways a horrible situation were plentiful, but the very nature of these consequences of this crisis were often disregarded, and the language was less colourful than that used in Norway.

Beyond such explicit statements, various gestures carry the same symbolic meaning. For instance, the Swedish state declared COVID-19 to be a public health threat and a danger to society in February 2020 (Krisinformation, 2020b). Similarly, the measures implemented in March and April of 2020, and later tightened in November 2020, had symbolic potential, by indicating that the situation was dire. In a non-globalized world, these measures could have had a significant juridical-sovereign impact as a ritualistic and vigorous show of force. However, we live in a globalized world where the Swedish measures were, in particular at the beginning, *significantly* milder, and implemented at a slower pace, than in other countries. Therefore, they had a different form of symbolic impact. As stated by an informant: 'I haven't taken this [the pandemic] very seriously, which resonates somewhat with the politics chosen here' (Pensioner 11). The Swedish state's use of coercion was interpreted within an international context where Sweden was the 'liberal outlier' (Aucante, 2022). This carried symbolic meaning, indicating that the Swedish state did not consider the situation to be *that* abnormal. While meaning to not create too much fear, the Swedish state was incapable of preventing fears from emerging. As stated by an informant: 'I was very scared, and then the government couldn't even articulate clear commands… there was much fear' (Cafeteria/nurse 3). Those who were frightened were likely to comply with the state's moral reasoning, albeit without supporting the state's relatively soft approach.

The Swedish state's politics of community resembles the Norwegian state's rhetoric to a greater extent. As the head of the Public Health Agency of Sweden, Anders Tegnell, articulated, 'the responsibility for reducing the spread of infection primarily falls upon the individual' (Krisinformation, 2020c). This individual responsibility must be taken seriously 'for Sweden' (The Local, 2020a). The actions of the individual are connected to the whole, behind the mantra that personal responsibility entails 'protecting yourself and others' (Folkhälsomyndigheten, 2023b). As the Prime Minister Stefan Löfven puts it: the population must act 'as one country, where we continue to take responsibility for each other, for Sweden, for our society, where we continue to face hard times and good times together' (Government, 2020b). Based on such a communitarian logic, individuals must take personal responsibility, for themselves and for the (national) community (Folkhälsomyndigheten, 2020a).

The purpose of such statements, articulated throughout the pandemic in all kinds of speeches and documents, was to impose moral obligations upon the individual. The individual had to comply for the sake of Sweden, but also for loved ones and oneself. Personal responsibility and the importance of protecting one's fellow Swedes were common themes throughout the communication campaign. This was perhaps most of all made clear in the Prime Minister's address to the nation on 22 March 2020. This was a key date, as it was 10 days after neighbouring countries had began closing down their societies, and Sweden had remained committed to its more liberal approach. The Prime Minister stated that 'every person now needs to be mentally prepared for what is coming', that 'lives, health and jobs are at risk', and that 'more people will have to say a final farewell to a loved one'. Then, he added a communitarian dimension—'the only way to manage this crisis is to face it as a society, with everyone taking responsibility'. And while 'I know that many of you are worried', it was expressed that 'our society is strong', and 'we as a society are handling this crisis with our collective strength', through each individual taking 'personal responsibility', which also included a responsibility to 'avoid spreading panic' (Embassy of Sweden, 2020). This key speech built on typical themes of the Swedish communication strategy, legitimizing the Swedish state's aversion to coercion, while imposing upon the private individual a moral responsibility to act. One had to comply, for Sweden, for one's fellow humans. The state imposed moral obligations upon all. This worked on the basis of a similar logic to the Norwegian discourse on *dugnad*. Individuals had to comply with moral obligations for the greater good.

These were coupled with the language of science. As we shall discuss further in the next chapter, the Public Health Agency dismissed lockdowns and other measures as not based on evidence (Boden, 2020; Paterlini, 2020). This justified the stance of the state, which leaned heavily upon the technocratic knowledge and scientific authority of the Public Health Agency (Bylund & Packard 2021). The state based its measures and recommendations on science and hence, alternative ways of governing were implicitly unscientific, as we shall also discuss in the next chapter. This way, the Swedish state, like the Norwegian state, referred to the same legitimizing source—science—to make its power 'true'. The truth of science justified power being exercised in a softer manner (cf. Foucault, 2014: 9). Standing together with experts at press conferences, the Swedish state sought to impose its vision of reality by grounding this vision in both political and scientific authority. The combination of leading experts and leading government officials standing together with a united vision in such formal state settings imposed the political authority of the state, and the scientific authority of experts, leading the two forms of authority to become tightly interwoven (i.e. Bergstrøm, 2021).

However, the Swedish state could not monopolize the public information space like in Norway. As one informant stated: 'I had more trust in the Norwegian authorities!' (Works abroad 15). The political opposition demanded stricter measures than what the government implemented, as the Swedish approach was nationally contested (Girtli Nygren & Olofsson 2021; Nielsen & Lindvall, 2021), obviously in relation to the well-known fact that the Swedish state deviated from the 'COVID consensus' (cf. Green, 2021). Nevertheless, trust in the state's approach remained high, despite the Swedish state choosing a controversial pathway (see Nielsen & Lindvall, 2021; Almlund et al., 2023). As stated by an informant: 'I am typically Swedish, I trust the state' (Healthcare 4). The communication campaign, as in Norway, manifested at the level of hearts and minds. The Swedish state's legitimacy withstood initially high death rates, coupled with massive criticism, while implementing fewer restrictions than neighbouring countries.

This reveals the great meaning-making capacities and the legitimacy which the state's voice carries. The Swedish state declared that too coercive measures were problematic and not called for—and this was *largely* accepted—while people in culturally and politically similar neighbouring countries accepted state coercion readily when the state declared it necessary. Populations accepted the lockdown, or the lack of one, largely listening to the voice of state actors, insofar as a given state had the legitimacy and trust necessary to garner support, showing the autonomy of the Swedish state and consequently of the other states which chose different pathways. The Swedish state's communication campaign was, like that of Norway, enabled by the infrastructural power of a state with a coherent, rationalized bureaucracy, and technological and logistical resources related to the digital revolution combined with various technical instruments, making it possible to spread the state's message throughout all of society. Ideological sources of power were enacted through various instruments, manifesting at the micro-level when consumed by citizens reading digital media, watching television, listening to speakers on public sites or seeing posters spread around society, which all served as infrastructural resources (cf. Kristensen & Hartley 2023). For instance, posters would be placed around society: 'we had guidelines at the toilets [at work]' (Office 1) (cf. Folkhälsomyndigheten 2020b; Krisinformation, 2020d). The state's message was omnipresent, as the state ensured that nobody could avoid being informed about the state's resolve. Thereafter, communication manifested as individuals were inclined to accept their state's stance and vision, reproducing its understanding of the world, complying with its will. These microphysical effects only make sense when we contextualize these together with the ideological sources of power that brought about the acceptance of the state's narrative, and the infrastructural sources of power that enabled the state to spread its message in the first place.

Even the most critical would comply with the state's will, while problematizing the relative lack of formal restrictions and the behaviour of the Swedish population. In the words of one informant: 'many did not care about being careful, they would rather do nothing, and that's why one has to tell them [what to do]' (Cafeteria/office 3). Such criticism is supported by a study of the behaviour of populations in Sweden in comparison with the UK and Denmark, which found that the population of Sweden reduced its activities more slowly than the British and Danish populations (Mishra et al., 2021). The curtailed use of state coercion reduced the symbolic effects of propaganda along two lines: a) the state's approach sent a message that the situation was not that dire, and b) the state could not properly utilize fear as that would have delegitimized its relatively soft approach.

5.1.1.2 The Politics of Private Lives

While the communication strategy had many purposes, including justifying the Swedish approach (Baekkeskov et al., 2021), a key objective was *responsibilizing* citizens, the core of liberal governmentality (Foucault, 2008). The Prime Minister said that 'every person in Sweden needs to take individual responsibility' by following authorities' guidelines, which mostly meant reducing their movement and interactions, and staying at home if they had symptoms (Government, 2020a). The Minister for Health and Social Affairs stated that 'strong legal measures are not the only way of achieving behavioural change' as 'people mostly follow recommendations' issued by the government and its agencies (Government, 2020b). Instead of 'strong legal measures', the Prime Minister proclaimed that the crisis must be solved through individuals' responsible conduct (Government, 2020e). This is the core of the Swedish strategy as it has been represented, so it is unsurprising that this is also a core issue for scholars exploring the politics of COVID-19 in Sweden (i.e. Girtli Nygren & Olofsson, 2020; Kamerlin & Kasson, 2020; Pierre, 2020; Larsson, 2022).

The politics of private lives was organised around the principle of voluntarism, based on a liberal governmentality. Recommendations articulated towards autonomous actors, not state coercion, served as the political instrument for governing private lives. Even the ban on gatherings was voluntary in private settings. As the Prime Minister stated: 'No social situations involving more than eight people should take place, regardless of whether they are covered by the law in purely formal terms' (The Local, 2020b). The order was given, but it was of a moral nature within private homes. The individual was supposed to self-regulate to automatically behave in a manner that was consistent with infection control—the quintessence of discipline (Foucault, 1991)—but without disciplinary mechanisms imposed per se. The state acted through the communication campaign that was meant to constitute communitarian ethics, in order to foster voluntarism and self-regulation. The state tried to 'nudge' individuals towards behaving in the most appropriate way. This entailed mobilizing the private individual as an infection control agent, who had to voluntarily participate in the struggle against COVID-19 (see Girtli Nygren & Olofsson, 2020; Larsson, 2022; Pierre, 2020), reflecting the voluntarism that was manifest in Norway.

Through its guidelines, the government recommended new forms of conduct for individuals. These guidelines were to change how individuals lived their lives, from morning to evening, from their meetings with friends to going to work. These recommendations revolved around handwashing, reduced interaction and other measures meant to reduce the spread of COVID-19 (see Folkhälsomyndigheten, 2023c). The state told individuals how to wash their hands properly, how to cough to minimize the spread of pathogens and how distancing and hygiene in general should be practised to reduce the likelihood of catching and/or spreading COVID-19. The state also refrained from placing restrictions on travelling abroad, preferring instead to advise against non-essential travel (Government, 2020d, 2020e). Individuals were also supposed to behave responsibly, for instance, planning when to go to stores to avoid crowds (Munkfors kommun, 2020), while wearing facemasks was recommended in crowds or other places where distancing could not be practised (Folkhälsomyndigheten, 2023d). The most important recommendation was however to keep at a physical distance from others (Folkhälsomyndigheten, 2021a). While extensive advice was shared with the general population, those belonging to groups at risk received increased and specialized recommendations to protect themselves (Government, 2020f).

The body of the individual, together with all social interaction, was to be tightly regulated by the individual him- or herself. As in Norway, mundane bodily activities and social life in general were transformed into objects of self-regulation, as the individual became morally obliged to self-govern, based on the state's will. Self-regulation worked through a diverse series of mechanisms of power where individuals altered their own conduct based on recommendations and moral obligations. Thus, self-regulation became an instrument of state power where individuals used their personal freedom for the state's biopolitical objectives, embracing these objectives as their own.

The Swedes generally accepted their moral responsibilities, as seen in the high levels of compliance with recommendations (Berman et al., 2022; Gustavsson & Beckman, 2020). Therefore, physical contact was avoided, and distancing practised: 'I always hugged people… it has been hard, saying things like "no, I don't want a hug!" I have several adult children, and we stopped hugging… we stopped touching each other' (Office 6).

Moreover, many went beyond not touching one another: 'We kept more to ourselves' (Local politician 14). Others would still arrange gatherings, but change the manner they interacted outside the household. For instance, 'we only met friends outside' (Therapist 16). This later led to the coining of a new expression—'outdoorification'–which applied to leisure in Sweden, as activities were generally moved outside when this was possible (see Hansen et al., 2023; Hedenborg et al., 2022). Self-regulation manifested in numerous activities being altered by the individual, as a mechanism of power working through, rather than against, individual freedom.

This turned the individual's private life into an object of *self*-governance, in a self-disciplinary manner, depending upon the individual already being a disciplined subject. The body and social interaction had to be regulated on the basis of numerous prescriptions and proscriptions related to self-restraining behaviour. Bodies were supposed to be keep spatially apart and practice hygiene. Individuals had to preferably self-isolate or at least avoid meeting in 'dangerous' contexts, such as private homes. The state told individuals that it was in their self-interest to comply, the essence of liberal governmentality. Therefore, 'obedience was about self-preservation' (Office 5). The state actively worked to make it easier for individuals to comply with recommendations. A good example was the state altering incentives, for instance by removing restrictions on sick leave, so to grant individuals no economic incentive to work if sick (Government, 2020f). Creating conditions of interest convergence along practical dimensions enhanced freedom as a political instrument.

Nevertheless, self-interest was not at the core of the Swedish state's attempt to foster self-regulation, as the core of the politics of private lives revolve around 'ethical self-governance' (see Dean, 2007: 61). Self-interest was to be accomplished through the aforementioned communitarian ethics which the state sought to impose, on the grounds of this ethical position: 'I wanted to protect myself and others' (Cafeteria/Office 3). The state sought to translate its symbolic resources into action by demanding that individuals take personal responsibility—which manifested in ethical self-regulation based on moral obligations. One had to act, and if one was not deterred by the virus, then one had to act for Sweden, for one's fellow Swedes. The mobilization of the private individual was formally voluntary, but morally compulsory (cf. Sandset & Villadsen, 2023). Thus, ideological power did not only manifest at the micro-level through opinions. Changed opinions manifested in self-governance, as the individual was morally tasked with taking responsibility for practising infection control. This is the link between the ideological sources of power, the communication campaign and the voluntarism which the state depends upon in relation to private lives.

My interviews and Weberian-Foucauldian analysis largely reproduce insights from Girtli Nygren and Olofsson (2020), which cover the microphysics of voluntarism in Sweden through governmental documents. This voluntarism was grounded in the ideological sources of power fostering and enabling self-governance to occur on a societal scale. This depended upon the already-high levels of trust Swedes have in the state (cf. Brandebo, 2021; Helsingen et al., 2020; Norberg et al., 2022), the state's high legitimacy (Girtli Nygren & Olofsson 2021) and rhetorical techniques (see Baekkeskov et al., 2021; Almlund et al., 2023). Similarly, the various recommendations the state shared as it attempted to impose self-regulation were based on the Public Health Agency's expertise, and knowledge which they based on their analyses of contagion trends (Glaser, 2021). Models created based on contemporary data were seen as useful for predicting the development of the pandemic (Folkhälsomyndigheten, 2021b). These models, biopolitical forms of infrastructural power contained within the state bureaucracy and expert institutes, were utilized to articulate recommendations and legitimize them by virtue of the authority of science (cf. Sandset & Villadsen, 2023). This expertise served as ideological sources of power, justifying the Swedish state's approach and the necessity of complying with recommendations, which obtained a scientific aura.

During the pandemic the state was the centre which made individuals take care of themselves and others, and if necessary, supervise others by reminding them of their responsibilities: 'if people stand to close to me, then I tell them they're standing too close to me, and that I think they should step back' (Office 6). The state successfully garnered and harvested trust and legitimacy through an effective use of propaganda, as compliance remained high (see Helsingen et al., 2020), even if compliance dropped with time, as in Norway. In the words of an informant: 'people were very good [at complying] during the spring of 2020, but then people became less and less so' (Nurse 2). As in Norway, the ideological power of the state imposed the state's narrative, which fostered self-governance, in a manner that was likely to drop as time passed. Nonetheless, we should not underestimate the power of persuasion, which allowed the state to remodel individuals into infection control agents, through the forces of morality, obedience and trust. A good citizen henceforth had to comply and govern his/her own life according to the state's vision and the moral obligations this vision brought forth. After all, these social changes, such as '*outdoorification*' or the reduction in social interaction and movement, were achieved by the state, acting through the individual. Hence, the microphysics of power, observed in voluntary isolation, which changed people's behaviour, as with 'outdoorification', etc., resulted from the macrophysics of the state's ideological power and the moral authority which its legitimacy constitutes, through a subtle and yet pyramidical exercise of ideological state power. Power radiated from the centre of the state, manifesting at the level of minds and hearts, making individuals self-govern in practice.

5.1.1.3 Lest You Forget the Power of Law

The claim that the Swedish response was exceptional is based on an accurate assessment that voluntarism was *declared* to be the central principle of governance. Many scholars also proclaim that voluntarism was the core of the Swedish strategy (i.e. Girtli Nygren & Olofsson, 2020; Larsson, 2022; Pierre, 2020). While voluntarism was the guiding principle of governance which the Swedish state depended upon in *private* homes, the Swedish response combined voluntarism with 'soft law' (i.e. Winblad et al., 2022). The mechanisms of power emerging as a result of this 'soft law' have thus far remained untouched.

As covered before, law is central because it allocates responsibilities and rights to the state and its citizens, meaning that law functions as a coercive source of power. Yet, many claim that Swedish law *hindered* the Swedish state from intervening in social life in a manner similar to that which we have seen in other European countries (i.e. Bylund & Packard 2021; Larsson, 2022; Paterlini, 2020; Tegnell, 2021). However, the Swedish government can through parliament intervene and alter courses, regardless of experts and their opinions (Aucante, 2022; Winblad et al., 2022). In fact, the Swedish state altered its legal conditions in April 2020, illustrating how legal restraints are *self-restraints* and thus something the state technically can ignore. A temporary law based on the Epidemic Law in April 2020 was implemented, allowing the state to enforce various restrictions on gatherings and events in general (Government, 2020d). While this law was never actually utilized (Larsson, 2022; Saunes et al., 2022), its implementation revealed the state's coercive capacities. Swedish institutional and legal norms can be suspended if the state decides that the situation is abnormal to a degree justifying such suspensions. The state thus has the legal capacities, i.e. the coercive sources of legal power, necessary to act with severity, even if it refrained from utilizing its capacities. On a similar note, the Swedish parliament passed a new Pandemic Act for more effectively handling COVID-19 in January 2021. The Pandemic Act allowed the government to 'introduce legally binding rules for gyms and sport centres, swimming baths, shops, shopping centres and places for private gatherings' (Government, 2021; Krisinformation, 2021a; Folkhälsomyndigheten, 2021c). The situation became increasingly viewed as abnormal as time passed, justifying increased levels of state coercion, despite the state's open and clear aversion to strict measures.

While the state restrained itself, it also formalized restrictions in law. Restrictions were imposed, for instance through the closed border or the ban on visiting medical facilities, which we shall discuss below. Similarly, the state imposed various restrictions on the businesses allowed to remain open. The core restriction was the ban on gatherings, as this also underpinned other restrictions. This ban took a moral and legal form, working as in Norway, albeit more moderate. Initially, the ban allowed gatherings of up to 500 to take place before the limit was reduced to 50, and then finally, to 8. These limits were only compulsory in public settings. As in Norway, there were exemptions from the strictest limits on numbers, for instance at funerals, where the limits were less severe, as 20–50 could gather in such contexts. This ban was *legally* enforced. The state declared that 'the penalty for violating the prohibition [against holding public gatherings and events] is a fine or imprisonment for at most six months', rooting this in the infection control law (Covidlawlab, 2020a). The police would disperse crowds and punish those responsible for organizing such events (Krisinformation, 2020e, 2020f).

This led to various juridical-sovereign mechanisms of power. For instance, it gave rise to limited close-downs of amusement parks (The Local, 2020b). Similarly, some sports and activities were closed down at times in a juridical-sovereign fashion: 'it [my dance classes] closed down' (Nurse 1), and 'there was no training [for my children] for a while' (Teacher 8). The state similarly asserted juridical-sovereign power as it closed down educational facilities for those *above* the 7th grade. Within these educational facilities, pupils and students were at times forced to pursue 'home studies' via Zoom and other digital instruments, as in Norway. The state used its power *over* society to forcefully close down educational facilities for the older pupils and students (Krisinformation, 2020g, 2020h, 2020i).

We can see similar juridical-sovereign mechanisms at work when looking at how the state handled commerce. Visiting customers and clients, a common practice in many organizations and businesses, was prohibited. In the words of an informant: 'from the spring of 2020, our office stopped accepting visitors… we were not allowed to visit [other businesses] anymore (Office 5). The state allowed businesses and other workplaces to remain open as long as the businesses complied with conditions decided upon by the state, which seized various pre-pandemic rights, suspending them for the time being. Home working was used as a technique for keeping people apart without closing down organizations, manifesting in individuals being sent home. Yet, in private businesses, *some* of these measures were implemented *formally on a voluntary level*. Employers made decisions based on recommendations to send people home, with exemptions potentially given to employees desiring it: 'it was said that one should work from home, but one could come to the office if one wanted to, it was voluntary' (Office 1). In the public sector owned by the state, home office was more strictly enforced. In the words of an informant: 'We had home office; we weren't even permitted to come to the office' (Office 6). Thus, the state varied the extent to which it formalized restrictions in law. Some of these orders were open to exemptions, for instance, regarding home office in certain cases as employers retained a certain level of decision-making, which we shall discuss below. As in Norway, this ban worked primarily as a juridical-sovereign mechanism as the state seized liberties by denying the possibility of or changing the conditions under which various activities could take place. Power was exercised negatively, and punishment, i.e. imprisonment and fines, worked as juridical-sovereign punishments (cf. Stenson 2005).

The unused laws as well as these juridical-sovereign mechanisms reveal how the Swedish state cages the coercive sources of power needed to restructure society and impose restrictions. The Swedish state imposed and enforced prescriptions and proscriptions upon society, even as it reduced the severity of its measures. The Swedish state made it clear to organizers of public events and activities that disobedience would be punished with fines or even imprisonment. These coercive resources allowed the Swedish state to enact various restrictions and formalize infection control responsibilities, in a similar way to that observed in Norway beyond the lockdown. Following Dean (2007: 163), we see the workings of the exception-normal spectrum in this use of law. The situation was not understood to be fully exceptional, as it appeared to be in Norway, but neither was it fully normal. Sovereignty operated in a different manner in Sweden compared to beyond its borders. The Swedish state—sovereign and thus the 'monopolist of the decision' (Schmitt, 1996)—defined the situation as too normal for the kinds of measures seen in Norway, Denmark, Italy, China, etc. The state decided that that the level of abnormality of the situation warranted some extraordinary measures, without breaking away completely from established political and institutional norms. Nevertheless, the state rooted its response in its sovereignty, and thus in its authority to enforce its will through coercion.

This was made possible by the state's coercive sources of power, which enabled the state to exercise power in such a top-down manner. On the basis of its claim to monopoly over the legitimate means of violence, institutionalized in the police and the penal system and Swedish law, the state cages coercive capacities. These sources were unleashed to enforce numerous restrictions, punishing dissidents with fines or imprisonments rooted in law. The state made decisions, which were binding due to the coercive sources of power the state enacted to produce the negative mechanisms of power studied above. As in Norway, the coercive sources of power used to subjugate society depended upon a rationalized bureaucracy and surveillance technology, i.e. infrastructural sources of power, and ideological sources of power related to its legitimacy and capacity to convince citizens, which rendered the state coercion in hand legitimate and thus largely accepted (cf. Almlund et al., 2023; Nielsen & Lindvall, 2021). Ideological and infrastructural sources of power thus supported and enhanced the use of coercive power.

5.1.1.4 Conscription and Mobilization

Although voluntarism *was* combined with 'soft law' (Winblad et al., 2022), this dichotomy is a simplification. While the studies operating with such a dichotomy elude the 'juridical model' reducing state power to law—an issue some Foucauldians identify as widespread among the mainstream governmentality literature (see Bröckling et al., 2011; Dean, 2007; Opitz, 2011)—the picture thus far is nevertheless incomplete. Voluntarism and law operated together with the formal mobilization of society. As in Norway, the mobilization of society entailed governing at a distance (Miller & Rose, 2008), through conscription. This conscription, being an indirect and non-linear form of government, cannot be reduced to voluntarism or law, and it has not been studied in Sweden to date.

Conscription as a mechanism worked by the state imposing infection control obligations upon abstract roles, such as those of funeral organizers or teachers. Those undertaking such roles were endowed with formal responsibilities as state agents. The individual had to comply with these responsibilities imposed upon the role conscripted, or refrain from taking such roles that had infection control responsibilities, namely, employers, teachers, etc. Similarly to Norway, the state used the conscript as a medium to govern at a distance, as power radiated from the state and *through* the conscript, who exercised power excluding, denying and disciplining on the state's behalf.

Conscription can be studied in various contexts, where it manifests in the state governing through the conscript. For instance, children were generally allowed to 'come [to training] with all equipment and fully dressed [while] we [parents etc.] could not enter' (Teacher 8). Similarly, some gyms were allowed to remain open, under restrictions: 'one could continue [training at my gym] with restrictions on how many could enter at a given time' (Doctor 16). Conditions were thereby imposed, under which the gym could remain open or sports could be practised. The state limited its use of juridical-sovereign powers, so to govern *through* non-state actors, here the organizers of sports. They could organize sports insofar as precautions were followed, such as stopping parents from entering sport facilities, or by controlling the number of people entering a gym.

The school is another telling example, even if most schools, contrary to sport clubs, are public institutions and the personnel are therefore public employees. Schools usually remained open and no classes below the 8th grade were sent home. Within those contexts, teachers and other personnel were allocated infection control responsibilities throughout the pandemic:

> Instead of the pupils sitting next to one another, they sat at the ends of the table... we also tried to move desks around the classroom, but there were limits to what we could do, as the classrooms are small. But we tried making more space in between the desks.... We also distributed books and equipment to the children while they sat still at their chairs. The children washed their hands, every time they entered.... (Teacher 8).

The teacher became a formal infection control agent, mobilized to minimize the likelihood of infection propagating within the confines of the school. This was generally the case for all educational personnel, except when schools were closed down (Krisinformation, 2020g, 2020h, 2020i). Making the pupils sit in specific places—at a distance from each other—transformed pupils' bodies into objects of governance in a disciplinary manner. The distribution of equipment, so as to keep the children still, and the control over their bodily activities, i.e. washing, also functioned in a disciplinary manner, making pupils' bodies objects to regulate according to infection control requirements. Another technique, where distancing could not be ensured within the confines of the facility, was to reduce the number of pupils: 'the pupils were at school every second day' (Pedagogue/nurse 9). This was an ad hoc distancing technique, which lowered the number of pupils at the school so as to facilitate social distancing in areas where it could not be achieved due to lack of space. While teachers had the formal responsibility of disciplining children, school leaders were charged with ensuring that the school was organized appropriately, which included guiding and reassuring staff and parents (see Ahlström et al., 2020; cf. A. Harris & Jones, 2020, 2022; Sahlin et al., 2023).

The teacher became responsible for imposing the state's will, as educational facilities were placed under heavy infection control regulations, transforming them into infection control institutions. Pupils were to be disciplined, so that their bodies were regulated according to the infection control necessities identified by the state. Thus, 'if a child was sick, we placed the child out in the hallway and called their parents, who had to come and pick them up' (Pedagogue/nurse 9). The teachers became responsible for ensuring that the classroom remained safe from the virological threat of COVID-19. This entailed disciplining bodies and controlling their movements, positioning and hygiene. It also entailed monitoring the health statuses of pupils, and acting if sickness was suspected. The supervision of the teacher had to identify both behavioural risks and somatic dangers. However, while the state thereby imposed a certain form of infection control responsibility related to surveilling in order to exclude potentially dangerous bodies from the classroom, tracing infection would only be undertaken in an ad hoc manner:

> we called the school and told them my child had tested positively and had been at school.. they wouldn't call anyone else because my child had no symptoms while at school... I decided to personally call my child's classmates [to inform them about the positive test] (Teacher 8).

The lack of clear guidelines was not an *educational* issue per se, as it was based on the state prioritizing tracing within the medical sector, as we shall discuss further on. As an informant states: '[the contagion tracing] was not much to brag about, it was up to the individual to report and take responsibility... to pass the message on' (Local politician 14). The Commission charged with evaluating the Swedish testing regime labelled it a 'failure' (SOU, 2022: 18). This relates to the overall lack of a formalized framework for identifying whom to test, and, in contrast with methods adopted in Norway, there was no formalized manner of tracing (potentially) dangerous bodies throughout society, partly because these bodies were not formally quarantined in either case, hence thwarting the utility of tracing in the first place.

The state also expanded into non-state spaces of a more sensitive nature, in a more formal and less liberal manner. Funerals were the most obvious example. The funeral was defined as a public ritual rather than a private event. Therefore, the funeral was to be governed according to infection control criteria, which included distancing measures and restrictions on the number of people allowed to attend (cf. Jarnkvist, 2023). The responsibility of fulfilling these tasks fell upon the organizer. Funerals were allowed, but the organizer had to discipline guests, ensuring that they kept their distance, avoided hugging, etc. Moreover, the organizer had to exclude some from attending. Even close relatives were excluded from participation:

> There was a funeral of a close relative of my partner, and I couldn't go. Then a second close relative of my partner died, and even my partner could not go, because this relative had children and grandchildren who had to be prioritized. It was a surreal situation; my partner was so close to this relative (Teacher 17).

As in Norway, the organizer of the funeral was conscripted. This entailed the funeral becoming part of the infection control regime, with power manifesting in control (over access) in terms of the number of guests allowed and disciplinary measures undertaken within the context of the funeral itself. Even close relatives could be denied access to the funeral.

Those organizing different establishments and events were obliged to supervise these social contexts according to infection control regulations. For instance, establishments where people tended to meet, such as cafeterias, bars, etc., were legally obliged to impose social distancing at their locales, keep track of the number of people entering, ensure that eating and drinking occurred only at tables, position tables far enough from one another, restrict the number of individuals sitting at individual tables, limiting the periods in which alcohol could be sold and close early (Krisinformation, 2021b, 2021c, 2021d, 2021e). Thus, some resturants would ensure that people sat at least one metre away from one another. Most restaurants moved their tables around and they removed a few tables (Nurse 13). The employer would be conscripted, and made responsible for ensuring that employees disciplined guests and customers. Much of the mobilization of society was formalized to make it compulsory.

Nevertheless, the state's aversion to coercion meant that the mobilization of society worked in a more liberal manner than in Norway, where it was more hierarchical and formalized. The Swedish mode of power was both voluntary and coercive, being premised upon local actors' relative autonomy:Not many guests entered the cafeteria. They called, and we went out when customers arrived, and we worked with facemasks.

The employer implemented these rules to protect us [the employees]. (Cafeteria/office 3)

The Swedish state governed through active non-state actors who, taking their cue from the moral obligations and *recommendations* from the state, could make their own decisions. This partly worked in line with liberal governmentality and the relative autonomy this grants non-state actors. The state conscripted both public servants and non-state actors such as employers and employees in private businesses, remodelling them as infection control agents. The overall system of conscription, i.e. the mobilization of society, was a form of state power manifesting in a series of mechanisms of power where the conscript exercised power over employees, guests, clients, etc., on the basis of formal criteria and in certain cases even beyond these formal requirements. Power was exerted towards bodies, relations and spaces, for infection control purposes within schools, bars, offices and other spaces. It mattered not whether conscripted agents were formally part of the state or not prior to conscription. The individual became a state agent in any case, mobilized for biopolitical purposes. The actions undertaken by conscripted agents belonged to the state, coordinating, controlling and regulating society *through* society. To a greater extent than in Norway, this occurred through the typical liberal manner of governing through non-state actors, as formally non-state actors tended to retain more autonomy than that observed in Norway (cf. Arts, 2014; Miller & Rose, 2008; Sending & Neumann, 2006). The relative softness of the state's mobilization can be seen as a regulatory form of government. The state regulated outcomes at the macro-level without seeking to micro-manage every single context as the approach adopted in Norway, where the state acted more formally and coercively towards more social spheres. Despite working in a somewhat liberal manner, conscription functioned pyramidically. Power was exercised from the centre of the state, from where it diffused throughout numerous joints, within and beyond the state, so as to allow the state to govern indirectly at a distance, through the hands of the conscript.

Thinking macrophysically, the mobilization of society demanded administrative and coercive resources, as the state subjugated the conscript, transforming him/her into a state agent with formal infection control responsibilities and obligations. Infrastructural sources of power were key to this governmental operation. Embeddedness, a known characteristic of the Swedish state (Jacobsson et al., 2015), enabled the state to conscript individuals into the infection control regime, which thereafter manifested in various mechanisms of power at the micro-level where the conscript enforced the state's will. By formalizing less, the state depended more upon embeddedness and semi-voluntary compliance with infection control regulations compared to the Norwegian state. Due to the relatively soft mobilization of society, the Swedish state's embeddedness depended heavily upon ideological sources of power. Thus, the mobilization was partly enabled by the communication campaign enacted to produce communitarian obligations. That this power—working partly 'beyond the state' (Miller & Rose, 2008)—was state power—shows that studies of power 'beyond the state' should beware of dismissing the potential presence of the state beyond its formal apparatus.

While embeddedness was key, we should be careful not to underestimate how the Swedish state depended upon a rationalized administration and bureaucracy (Petridou, 2020), known for its efficacy (see Hall, 2016). Through its administrative organs, the state monitored society and ensured that its orders were carried out (Krisinformation, 2020e). This made it possible for the state to demand that all 'take special measures' to ensure that infection control was practised at social sites (Krisinformation, 2020f). Non-compliance would in many cases be illegal, and punishable (Krisinformation, 2020e). The sources of coercive power were therefore central, enabling conscription and the mobilization of society, underpinning the power *through* society that we see in practice with power *over* society as a threat to ensure conscripts' compliance. Like in Norway, infrastructural and coercive sources of power were interwoven as they were combined together in a complex governmental operation, where tens or even hundreds of thousands of individuals became state agents with formalized responsibilities, obliged to govern on the state's behalf.

To fully understand the Swedish strategy, we must however look beyond singular tactics of rule. The state based its rule on voluntarism, primarily supported by ideological sources of power, 'soft law', primarily supported by coercive sources of power, and mobilization, primarily supported by infrastructural sources of power. Obviously, all of these tactics were underpinned by complex combinations of these sources of power. To fully understand the Swedish strategy, we have to explore how these tactics operate together within the two-tier system of the Swedish state, where coercive and infrastructural sources of power are enacted for formal government and ideological sources of power are enacted for informal government, contingent upon whether an issue is rendered governable as private or public.

5.1.2 The Swedish Two-Tier Strategy

5.1.2.1 Two Styles of Control

While all bodies were regulated, both formally and morally, some, i.e. the (potentially) dangerous and the vulnerable, were handled in more elaborate ways. The (potentially) dangerous body was governed through voluntarism and moral obligations, while shielding occurred morally *and* formally. This reveals the logic of the public–private dichotomy guiding the Swedish approach. The Swedish state remained committed to governing private individuals in their private lives through symbolic forms of governance. Therefore, quarantine and isolation were not *formally* imposed. However, medical facilities were treated as public spaces, and therefore formally governed. The moral government of the (potentially) dangerous has not been analysed. While the experiences of the vulnerable have been touched upon (Nilsson et al., 2021), the mechanisms of power they experienced through shielding has not, and these mechanisms must be examined.

We shall first examine how the Swedish state handled (potentially) dangerous bodies. In Norway, those suspected of being infectious were quarantined, those diagnosed were isolated. These techniques were enforced by the state. In Sweden, isolation and quarantine were synonymous. There was no distinction between being quarantined and isolated. Both the sick and the potentially sick were told to avoid workplaces and other social sites. *Hypothetically*, quarantine could be enforced. Yet, such a command occurred at an individual rather than general level. Thus, unless an individual was specifically ordered to quarantine, he or she had no legal obligations to comply (Krisinformation, 2020j; ST, 2020). If this occurred, 'the rules may include that you are not allowed to go to work for seven days' (Krisinformation, 2020m). In practice, there was a lack of a general system for monitoring and tracing (SOU, 2022). Instead, tracing of contagion was prioritized within the healthcare system, to prevent medical personnel from bringing disease into medical facilities (Vasterviks kommun, 2020; Folkhälsomyndigheten 2023e). While quarantine was labelled a *duty* imposed upon the individual by the Epidemic law (Krisinformation, 2020k), this duty was moral rather than legal, as seen by (a) *recommendations* that COVID-19-positive individuals and travellers from 'dangerous' countries pass a period in quarantine (Krisinformation, 2020l), and by (b) the lack of any legal order that one must quarantine/isolate if (potentially) sick.

The state sought to impose moral obligations so to create ethical self-regulation: 'There was no obligatory quarantine... but I and a friend I live with had to stay home... it was like a strong cold, but one had to stay home until one got well and then for a few more days' (Nurse 2). Hence, the ideological sources of power caged by the Swedish state and exercised through the communication campaign manifested in individuals voluntarily quarantining. Personal autonomy served as a political instrument, as with regard to the politics of private lives more generally. Yet, the lack of formal rules had consequences. For instance, '[while sick with COVID-19] we went a bit outside, but we mostly stayed in isolation.... We could go to the store. I wore a mask [when I went to the store while ill]' (Nurse 13). The individual's private life remained a private affair. The state acted ideologically upon this private life, so to make the individual morally obliged to comply, but the individual could 'stretch' the moral rules. The individual had to self-regulate in the same manner that individuals were externally and forcefully governed in other countries, like Norway. The individual was essentially tasked with controlling his/her own movements, and was thus obliged to withdraw from social and spatial spaces if sick. The state sought to foster communitarian and moral sentiments, leaning upon its ideological sources of power, which manifested in the self-regulation of the willing and free individual. Thus, the state refused to 'purify' society from contagion by forcefully isolating dangerous bodies (cf. Foucault, 1994b:146).

Shielding was on the other hand enforced in medical facilities. Shielding worked by the state excluding bodies from certain spatial and social sites, considered to be vulnerable, to protect the vulnerable from potentially dangerous outsiders. Shielding of a formal nature occurred in all medical facilities, which were placed under tight restrictions. This could be and was perceived as traumatic, and it was also resisted. As an informant notes:

> Some brought ladders and climbed into the window of their parent's room [in medical facilities] to visit them! Others brought their parents home because they were concerned with their wellbeing ... (Pedagogue/nurse 9)

The state imposed a visitation ban to keep those living or briefly staying in medical facilities isolated and thus shielded from society at large. This manifested at the micro-level in their isolation from the outside world, leading some to bypass the state. The state lifted the visitation ban on 1 October 2020 (The Local, 2020c). The Swedish state shielded medical facilities by denying outsiders access. This made the elderly and sickly individuals objects of protection by suspending their rights to receive visitors. In hospitals, this also entailed denying final farewells when individuals were infected with COVID-19: 'The most difficult part (of the job) was that we could not allow close ones to enter the hospital when someone was dying' (Nurse 13). Dying patients and their loved ones experienced the same mechanism of exclusion, manifesting in the isolation of the dying person.

While isolation was not formally imposed upon individuals in their private lives, it *was* formally implemented within all medical facilities. The rooms and homes of the vulnerable were sealed off from visits and all social contact from the outside world. Individuals were kept apart, and would-be guests were denied entry. In a similar manner, would-be patients could be excluded from entering the hospital for treatment, if their conditions were considered non-critical, as 'we had to call patients and ask, for instance, if they had trouble breathing. We'd have to decide whether they could come to the medical centre or not' (Doctor 7). Thus, getting treatment became contingent upon perceived necessity, as a result of the closure of medical spaces. This closure manifested in the exclusion of patients' family and loved ones, as well as exclusion of would-be patients determined by stricter criteria for becoming a patient in the first place. Thus, the Swedish regime of shielding was stricter and lasted longer than in Norway, revolving around the state suspending the autonomy and rights of perceived vulnerable individuals for a long period of time (see also Nilsson et al., 2021).

Restrictions, such as mandatory equipment, which included facemasks and face-shields combined with gloves and special suits, were also implemented within medical facilities. This imposed strict guidelines on the medical worker, while having symbolic effects when patients saw healthcare workers wearing protective gear: 'Most became very uneasy when they saw us in this outfit, I don't think I had to tell a single patient that they had to keep their distance!' (Nurse 13). Imposing infection control requirements was both a way of supervising and regulating the bodies of medical personnel, and a symbolic act signalling the danger of the situation to patients. Moreover, the state demanded that spatial sites were reorganized so to as facilitate infection control behaviour. For instance:

> There were major changes, we are many employees and we don't have the biggest locales, so there were many restrictions on how many could enter when we had lunch.... We tried to distribute [ourselves] in different rooms [when eating], people sat in smaller groups within the rooms. (Therapist 16)

The medical facility was tightly regulated so as to limit the probability of COVID-19 entering the facility, and if it entered, to limit it spreading within the facility (Socialstyrelsen, 2020). Moreover, as already mentioned, the state tried to ensure that medical personnel respected their quarantine duty, ***at least*** by not entering their workplaces (Vasterviks kommun, 2020; Folkhälsomyndigheten 2023e). This entailed granting medical staff increased infection control duties, consisting of the restructuring of spatial and social spaces.

However, the state returned to voluntarism and its moral authority when governing those who were vulnerable living ***outside*** medical facilities. The state recommended that these individuals fully isolate. This also included warning families, who were told to refrain from visiting their relatives. The length of time for which the elderly were isolated varied according to the extent to which they (and their relatives) voluntarily complied with these moral obligations: 'I met my grandchild... but I know grandparents who didn't see their grandchildren. It was full stop' (Pensioner 12). The state imposed moral responsibilities upon the elderly and their close ones, while refraining from imposing formal restrictions if they resided outside medical institutions, thereby letting private individuals make these private decisions.

The two-tier logic is unveiled as we study how (potentially) dangerous and vulnerable bodies were handled in radically different ways, through different tactics of rule. This division between the coercive approach in medical facilities, rooted in the conscription of medical personnel, that manifested in exclusion and seizures of rights, and the voluntaristic approach rooted in morals towards private lives, was not naturally demarcated by some natural law. The state socially constructed a private–public binary through these political actions. Some places were beyond the state's formal reach, such as private homes, where only liberal governance through individuals' freedom was appropriate. Other places were turned into formal affairs of the state, such as the nursing home, which de facto is the home of many residents. These processes of statification were undertaken by the state, as an autonomous actor, determining how its boundaries with society should look, based on the liberal notion that one should 'avoid governing too much… or too little' (Rose 1999: 70). To avoid governing 'too much', the state tended to govern *through* rather than *against* the autonomy of the individuals in question—except with regard to medical facilities—where even the homes of individuals became formal affairs of the state.

This was all enabled by the sources of power which the state cages. Through ideological sources of power, the state acted to influence the feelings and thoughts of individuals, regarding the politics of private lives more generally, in order to make individuals voluntarily quarantine/isolate, and voluntarily isolate their elderly and sickly relatives and friends. The moral sentiments the state imposed worked in this context, as in private life more generally. Furthermore, the state mobilized the private and public workers of these facilities as state agents, as in Norway, formalizing its orders and turning the entire medical sector into an apparatus for controlling contagion. This was enabled by the state's embeddedness within the medical sector more generally, and by a state bureaucracy capable of quickly mobilizing huge numbers of people for new purposes. The state's administrative capacities, grounded in its bureaucracy, enabled the formalized redirection of medical personnel to impose mechanisms of exclusion upon family members and would-be patients. The state's infrastructural sources of power allowed the state to govern through medical facilities.

As the state mobilized the personnel of these sites and imposed numerous prescriptions and proscriptions through its infrastructural sources of power, naturally underpinned by the power of law and thus coercive sources of power, so power pyramidically moved from the top of the state and through various institutions, until it finally reached the elderly or the sick and their close ones, keeping them separated. In medical facilities, these exclusions were formal, as the state conscripted medical personnel to shield medical facilities from outsiders. Technically they may have been nurses or doctors denying individuals the possibility to enter or preventing the elderly from receiving visitors, but they did not conduct this administrating of their own accord. The state's hands reached these individuals at the micro-level, through the conscripted medical personnel in private and public establishments. Power flowed from the centre of the state towards the micro-level, through the state bureaucracy and down to the local level of bodies, minds and feelings.

The state's governance over the elderly and vulnerable can be seen as a series of 'dividing practices', creating divisions between patients and the elderly and 'others': both in nursing homes where they were formally separated from 'outsiders', and in private lives, where the state requested that individuals should voluntarily create such divisions (cf. Foucault, 1994a: 326). The state acted more harshly towards medical facilities and patients living there than towards private businesses and establishments of a non-medical nature; only ideological power was exercised towards private individuals residing outside medical facilities. This control over bodies and their access to social contact was based on the private–public binary around which the Swedish approach revolved, manifesting in the state governing in heterogenous ways, with heterogenous sources of power, based on criteria related to liberal governmentality (cf. Villadsen, 2016).

5.1.2.2 A Closed or an Open Border?

The two-tier system at work in relation to the control over (potentially) dangerous and vulnerable bodies also operated at the border. Most states closed their borders during the pandemic. In Sweden, as in Norway, as more generally, this proved the continued importance of territoriality, as controlling the border meant controlling access to the interior, a key instrument of power. This transformed the Swedish border into a political instrument, delimiting territories so as to define 'inside' and 'outside' and 'address different types of threats and problems' (Dean, 2007: 39). Some studies of the Nordic border control regimes (i.e. Gustavsson, 2022; Heinikoski & Hyttinen, 2022) have been carried out. Nevertheless, my particular intention is to examine the border regime as a series of mechanisms of power and to show how these emerged, revealing how the two-tier logic manifested in the Swedish border being both closed *and* fully open. The status of the border depended on the status of the traveller. Contrary to Norway or most other countries, where all faced restrictions, and entry became conditional upon submission to punitive sanctions and restrictions like testing and quarantine, the Swedish state operated with a two-tier system.

The Swedish state banned entry into Sweden for non-residents and non-citizens for 'non-essential' reasons, and crossing through Sweden as a transit country to other EU or EEA-countries, except for residents/citizens of the destination, meaning that for a while only Swedish nationals, residents and those with 'valid reasons', (death in the family) could enter Sweden (Covidlawlab, 2020b). The Swedish state denied entry to those without an appropriate reason, such as the death of a relative or to those without citizenship/residency, enacting its coercive sources of powers to refuse access. The border was also, *in principle*, closed fully to people from the UK, Norway and Denmark—during late 2020 and early 2021—due to the so-called 'British' variant (Region Vasterbotten, 2021). As in Norway, this meant demanding proof of travellers' 'safe' status, as well as proof of some valid reason to enter Sweden in general. Individuals were granted entry only if they fulfilled these various conditions, and if not, entry was denied. While the border control was perceived to have been softer than the border control towards neighbouring Norway—'I called it [Norway] "Little North Korea!"... the border to Sweden, on the other hand, was fully open' (Nurse 13), the Swedish border control was also characterized by patrolling and policing, including examination of travellers' papers: 'they wanted proof that one lived in Sweden. They demanded proof even after I showed my driving license, even though one only gets a Swedish licence if one lives in Sweden' (Works abroad 15).

The state channelled the strength rooted in its territorial integrity, as power flowed from the centre of the state towards the border, where individuals not granted entry would feel the coercive powers of the state through exclusion, potentially manifesting in deportation. Whether one was granted or denied access was determined by the logic of control—was the passport (or other documents) 'red' or 'green'? Was the traveller a resident, citizen, or at the very least, someone able to document that their entry into Sweden served a 'legitimate' purpose? If the traveller was not a resident/citizen, did he/she have a green code in the 'corona passport'? The Swedish state placed conditions for entering Sweden, but only for non-residents and non-citizens. This manifested in disciplinary examinations, as individuals and their papers were closely inspected. Those lacking permission were subject to juridical-sovereign power denying them entry.

Thus, the state controlled access to Sweden, acting through its institutional capacities, underpinned by a professional state bureaucracy, and the coercive resources of a professional police force and border control agents, in order to monitor those who entered. The interweaving of coercive sources of power, related to the organization of violence and repression, and infrastructural sources of power, related to technological infrastructure like surveillance instruments, social infrastructure determined by the bureaucracy and organizational techniques for facilitating potent border management, all enabled the state to control the frontier. This way, the state could deny access to those lacking the right documents, as well as punish those disobeying the state's orders, and monitor those seeking to enter, ensuring that those crossing into Sweden had their papers in order.

These disciplinary conditions related to proving the safe status of the body, but there were no mechanisms of discipline imposed upon the traveller *after* entering Sweden. One simply had to possess the right documents to cross the border, by submitting to testing requirements and obtaining documentation of a valid reason for travel. Thus, the Swedish border was governed on the basis of a two-tier logic. On the one hand, the border was closed, with exemptions under certain conditions. To those lacking the right to enter, the border was fully closed, it was not possible to cross over, and people would be deported if they tried. On the other hand, the border was fully open. In Norway, the state excluded those it could exclude, and imposed conditions which had to be satisfied for access to be granted to the rest. The border was not fully open to anyone—even citizens and residents *had to* satisfy certain conditions and accept sanctions for entering. The Swedish state refused to impose conditions for entry upon citizens and residents, instead seeking to nudge would-be travellers in the right direction—i.e. to stay put—by *recommending* that individuals refrained from travelling.

Thus, the border was governed on the basis of the principle of voluntarism, as a private issue beyond formal state control. Travel was defined as a risky affair due to both COVID-19 and potential restrictions in the countries of destination (Government, 2020g). The recommendation to not travel was supplemented by recommendations to travel safely. People had to avoid travelling with symptoms. Similarly, they had to keep a safe distance and behave according to the rules and recommendations more generally. While it was necessary to take care, there were no quarantine obligations imposed on travellers. Quarantines were morally, but not legally, imposed. Individuals were *recommended* to isolate after travelling (Krisinformation 2020n). Quarantine remained a moral rather than a formal obligation throughout the period—even for those entering from the UK, Denmark or Norway, during the period when nobody was supposed to enter Sweden from these countries, due to fears of mutated variants of COVID-19. Similarly, while testing requirements were mandatory for non-citizens and non-residents exempted from the entry ban, enabled by infrastructural surveillance capacities as border control personnel had to both monitor who entered and their status, by investigating their papers and keep control over checkpoints, as in Norway, residents and citizens were exempt from such conditions. Citizens and residents were granted unconditional access, albeit under moral obligations, as they were recommended to test themselves if they had to travel (Region Vasterbotten, 2021). The state imposed moral obligations upon the traveller, while refusing to politicize the border for those living within Sweden. Leaving or entering Sweden was rendered a private matter, as the state exclusively depended upon ideological sources of power as leverage to sway the hearts and minds of the population.

Thus, while the Swedish state did close the border, the border simultaneously remained open. By refusing to impose conditions upon residents and citizens, the border control regime was two-tiered. Infrastructural and coercive power was exploited to close and tightly control the border in principle, closing it to (most) foreigners not residing in Sweden. However, the Swedish state's use of the border differed from what emerged in the previous chapter. The Swedish state partly followed the 'normal' COVID-19 response, by closing the border. Simultaneously, crossing the border became a purely private and thus moral question for citizens and residents. The Swedish state refused to use its formal sources of power and control over the border to create conditions, which would have meant crossing into a private context. Instead, it enacted ideological sources of power, through the communication campaign. The Swedish state governed the border as a two-tier system, where infrastructural, coercive and ideological sources of power were executed in different ways, manifesting in different mechanisms of power, based on the private–public binary on which the Swedish strategy was hinged.

5.1.2.3 The Logic of the Two-Tier Strategy

On the one hand, the Swedish response to COVID-19 resembles the Norwegian post-lockdown approach which dominated between lockdowns. On the other hand, the Swedish state strongly demarcated the line between private and public spheres. Some public spheres during the pandemic would have been considered private prior to the state formally moving into them, thereby *making* them public. There was nothing essentially public about hospital rooms, funerals or nursing homes. The Swedish state made private–public distinctions through its choices to formally intervene or abstain from such interventions. The state balanced between voluntarism and coercion, operating with contradictory approaches to COVID-19 because certain spheres were formally left untouched, even if the state acted symbolically towards these spheres as well.

The two-tier system was created by virtue of the state operating with contradictory principles of governance, acting differently at different levels of society. On the one hand, certain areas were handled formally. The formal governance of the public was rooted in a mixture of infrastructural and coercive sources of power, underpinned and supported by ideological sources of power such as trust, legitimacy, etc. Businesses and state-owned facilities, cultural centres and religious organizations, as well as those living in state-owned facilities such as nursing homes, were placed under strict restrictions. Medical facilities were even isolated from the outside world. This included public sites, but also the homes of many private individuals, who lived out their final days in such facilities, thereby being isolated from their close ones when these facilities were segregated. Moreover, business and commerce were placed under the tight grip of the state, even if the state sought to avoid close-downs. Similarly, the border was closed. The Swedish state's implementation of coercive sources of power was to be sure soft in a *comparative* perspective, but such sources were undeniably a central part of the Swedish politics of COVID-19. The state formally expanded into various non-state spheres, and the infrastructural power it depended upon to govern public life was underpinned by coercion. The Swedish state governed numerous sites, which became public affairs of the state, in a similar manner to that in which the Norwegian state governed when the lockdowns were lifted. Society was mostly governed through society, albeit in a softer manner than in Norway. Whereas the Norwegian state tended to place non-state actors firmly at its mercy, the Swedish state was more likely to grant non-state actors a combination of moral and formal obligations, thus granting them increased leeway.

On the other hand, the Swedish state governed the private lives of individuals in an exclusively liberal manner, through voluntarism, as the literature on Sweden posits (i.e. Girtli Nygren & Olofsson, 2020; Kamerlin & Kasson, 2020; Larsson, 2022). Private lives were governed through ideological sources of power, which were enacted to motivate individuals to practise their autonomy in an ethical way. Therefore, the border remained fully open to Swedish residents and citizens, while private homes remained free of restrictions. Even those diagnosed with COVID-19 could organize parties at home, from a legal point of view. The state decided to keep a major part of life beyond its formal reach, instilling communitarian sentiments into the individual rather than imposing formal prescriptions and proscriptions. The state varied between a firm and soft, formal and moral, grip. This depended upon the social site in question, and partly upon the status of the individual in question. As stated by an informant: 'there were strict rules within the healthcare system… but when we came home from work there were no masks, we experienced it as if COVID-19 existed at the workplace but not outside of it' (Nurse 13). There was a huge contrast between the hospital where the informant worked and society at large: from the most severe restrictions in the former, to the borderline-normal everyday life of the latter. The two tiers were governed according to different principles of rule, contrary to the totalizing lockdown strategy implemented in Norway.

The Swedish two-tier system shows the importance of the public–private division. Critics of the agential definition of the state will claim correctly that this is a social construct (i.e. Foucault, 2009; Jessop 2001; Mitchell, 1991). Indeed, the state's colonization of final farewells in hospitals, in old people's homes or nursing homes, or again, in the case of funerals, entailed statification, given that formerly private spheres were placed under the state's control, thus becoming (temporarily) affairs of the state through their inclusion into the formal infection control regime. These processes were underpinned by governmentalization processes where spheres were placed within or outside the state's domain. However, the state as an actor created these statification processes, by acting and intervening. In line with Foucauldian views, this shows that 'civil society' is only partially exterior to the state. The state operated with demarcations, yet where and how power could be exercised was determined according to whether spheres were defined as formally state spheres, or as spheres beyond the state, i.e. civil society. The state operated with this demarcation to determine how power should be exercised towards different parts of society, and the implicit private realm worked as a principle of restraint, which the state itself decided to comply with (cf. Villadsen, 2016). During the pandemic, the Swedish state identified a 'domain outside "politics"', following the liberal rationality of the pre-pandemic period (see Miller & Rose, 2008: 60). The Swedish state chose to do its utmost to respect this domain during the pandemic. Thus, the interventionism of the Swedish state existed within a space of liberal governmentality in practice, as the boundaries between the state and civil society was never crossed.

While this would be harder to notice in Norway, where the state formally made *every* sphere *formally* political, the Swedish state showed how this process of boundary making works, by operating with two tiers, thereby leaving some spheres of life *formally* untouched. This also shows that, while the Norwegian state did indeed retain certain liberal characteristics during the pandemic (cf. Gjerde, 2021b; Sandset & Villadsen, 2023), the suspension of civil society as a site beyond formal state power in Norway means that such past findings are *somewhat* misleading. The Norwegian state suspended the principles of rule characterizing liberal governmentality in numerous ways, not just because it became increasingly interventionist, but also because it temporarily suspended the state-civil society division.

Besides showing how liberal governmentality was never fully subordinated to interventionist biopolitics in Sweden—unlike in Norway—the two-tier system illustrates how liberal governmentality can work with and alongside authoritarian governmentality and thus non-liberal methods of government. Other Foucauldians have reflected upon the potentiality of liberal governmentality to 'un-limit' state power (i.e. Dean, 2007; Opitz, 2011). In Norway, liberal governmentality was primarily suspended as the Norwegian state chose a suppressive technique, demanding state interventions and coercion everywhere, to 'crush' the virus (cf. Christensen & Lægreid, 2020a; Staupe-Delgado, 2021). However, the Swedish state's softer approach worked with liberal methods throughout huge segments of society, while biopolitical concerns led to coercive interventions in a more limited number of social sites. The state acted coercively, for instance with regard to massive gatherings or in medical facilities. Moreover, numerous formal prescriptions and proscriptions were imposed upon businesses and others organizing social events and spaces. Where the Norwegian state largely suspended liberal governmentality, the Swedish state remained committed to liberal governmentality. Therefore, the indirect governing at a distance of the Swedish state, through the actions of the conscripted agents, was less formal and less compulsory than in Norway. The Swedish state reduced the strength of its grip. The same self-restraints were visible with regard to the power of law. Thus, the Swedish state demonstrates how we should beware of speaking about the capacities of liberal governmentality for 'unlimited' government (i.e. Opitz, 2011). Liberal states may perhaps become unlimited if liberal governmentality is suspended, although this does not work through liberal governmentalizations. As in the Swedish case, state power remained restrained by liberal governmentality, manifesting in the two-tier system. The two-tier system paved the way for severe state intervention by suspending liberal governmentality in reference to the public sphere, while still restraining the state vis-à-vis civil society.

5.1.3 *Reflections on the 'Soft' Leviathan*

Using the Weberian-Foucauldian framework, I have examined the Swedish politics of COVID-19 by exploring how the state, as an autonomous actor, acted during the pandemic. The state used the sources at its disposal—the macrophysics of power—to exercise power in a manner leading to numerous mechanisms of power—the microphysics of power. As in the chapter on Norway, my intention was to study the link between the two, so to explain how the state could act in a manner leading to these mechanisms of power. I studied the Swedish state's approach through a Foucauldian lens, supplementing the work of Girtli Nygren and Olofsson (2020) in two ways.

I explored the formal manner in which the Swedish state governed, with the same microphysical lens, albeit in a somewhat broader manner due to the Swedish state utilizing more tools as time went on. While voluntarism is at the core of the Swedish approach, the Swedish state formally governed its society as well, as shown by its mobilization of society as well as various juridical-sovereign denials, including limited close-downs, the ban on gatherings, and how the border was closed. The Swedish strategy was two-tiered, and thus heterogenous, even contradictory. This indicates that the Swedish approach was less exceptional than the literature implies—even though the lack of a lockdown and the existence of a private realm beyond formal state intervention made the Swedish state deviate from the 'global norm' (cf. Green, 2021). This two-tier system demands attention, so as to offer nuanced analyses of the Swedish strategy, which is less exceptional than the literature implies (i.e. Andersson & Aylott, 2020; Claeson & Hanson, 2021; Holmström, 2021; Jonung, 2020).

Moreover, the state is as an autonomous actor, which served as the centre of power during the pandemic in Sweden. Like the aforementioned Foucauldian studies, I take the mechanisms of power seriously, but I also seek to move beyond the level of microphysics by exploring how this relates to the sources of power, here understood as the macrophysics of power. We have seen how the Swedish state, albeit to a much more moderate extent than the Norwegian state, used similar tactics, as it enacted the same sources of power, even if to different degrees, creating similar mechanisms of power, again even if to different extents. The pyramidical nature of power is harder to spot in Sweden than in Norway, because power was less forcefully exercised. This gives power a horizontal *appearance*. The Swedish state governed in a more liberal manner through various formally non-state actors (cf. Arts, 2014; Sending & Neumann, 2006). While the Swedish pyramid of power was more horizontal, we are still looking at a pyramid, whose vertical nature is undeniable. The Swedish state stood vertically above other actors within its territory, like the Norwegian state did in Norway. The difference is that the Swedish state preferred to act *through* rather than *over* society, and it preferred to depend as much as possible on voluntarism and liberal methods of rule. Therefore, even the usage of infrastructural sources of power took a less compulsory form, as the conscription of individuals as infection control agents was less formalized than in Norway. As the analysis shows, the Swedish state preferred to grant more leeway to these mobilized infection control agents. Similarly, the Swedish state created barriers for itself, and it sought to respect these self-imposed restrictions. Thus, like in Norway, the Swedish state functioned as a centre of power, showing how understanding mechanisms of power without taking (state) agency and (state) sources of power into account leaves an analysis with important unanswered questions. How could power be exercised in such a manner? Under what conditions can a regime of power, such as the mobilization of society in Sweden, or the disciplinary society Foucault (1991) analysed, come into being? Without discussing state agency, such an analysis can never fully explain how society is structured, not when society itself is structured within the context of the state apparatus, which encompasses it, and acts in order to shape society.

While breaking with the Norwegian state—which preferred acting in a more vertical manner—the Swedish state similarly proves the importance of taking the state's agency seriously whenever one seeks to study how the state positions itself vis-à-vis non-state boundaries, and how the state's actions themselves produce the boundaries which we consider sacred—but which the state itself may transgress whenever a situation is found to demand it. The Swedish state reproduced the boundaries which most states transgressed, even if the Swedish state also crossed numerous pre-pandemic boundaries. Studying the Swedish politics of COVID-19 in isolation, disregarding the fact that it deviated from the global norm and the 'universal' lockdown (cf. Cheibub et al., 2020; Green, 2021), one can hardly deny that this was a massive, and coercive, political operation. The state imposed a multitude of prescriptions and proscriptions of a formal and moral nature upon all of society. This massive political operation included the state expanding into numerous spaces previously considered non-state, such as the offices of businesses, funerals or nursing homes.

Thus, the Swedish state used its agency and autonomy to regulate society, and especially business and commerce, with a firm hand, even if this firm grip was moderate *compared* to that of the Norwegian, Italian or Chinese states. While seemingly moderate, we should beware forgetting how extraordinary the Swedish measures analysed above would have seemed in the pre-pandemic years. To understand the state, we must take its agency seriously, and we must beware of assuming falsely that the state acts only in violent or formal ways. These theoretical and ontological lessons are important for analytical reasons, as the ways which the state governs, also when soft instruments and techniques are preferred, become hard to grasp without this agential lens. After all, while the Swedish state respected its boundaries more than the Norwegian state, the two-tier strategy is the result of the actions of the state, including its voluntary relative passivity vis-à-vis society. Without an agential definition of the state, we can hardly explain how these boundaries came to be reproduced in Sweden during the pandemic. Consequently, soft Leviathan of Sweden reveals how state/non-state boundaries exist due to the state respecting these boundaries, something likely to be voluntary in developed states such as the Norwegian or Swedish states, which proves that they possess the coercive, infrastructural and ideological capacities to transgress these boundaries if this is found to be necessary.

References

Ahlström B, Leo U, Norqvist L and Isling PP. (2020). School leadership as (Un)usual. Insights from principals in Sweden during a pandemic. *International Studies in Educational Administration* (Commonwealth Council for Educational Administration & Management

Almlund, P., E Kjeldsen, J., & Mølster, R. (2023). Expressions of governance, risk, and responsibility: Public campaigns in the crisis and risk management of Covid-19 in Denmark, Norway, and Sweden. In B. Johansson, Ø. Ihlen, J. Lindholm, & M. Blach-Ørsten (Eds.), *Communicating a pandemic:*

Crisis management and Covid-19 in the Nordic countries. University of Gothenburg.pp. 121–149

Andersson, S., & Aylott, N. (2020). Sweden and coronavirus: Unexceptional exceptionalism. *Social Sciences, 9*(12), 232.

Arts, B. (2014). Assessing forest governance from a 'Triple G'perspective: Government, governance, governmentality. *Forest Policy and Economics, 49*, 17–22.

Aucante, Y. (2022). *The Swedish Experiment. The COVID-19 resposne and its controversies.* Bristol Bristol University Press

Baekkeskov, E., Rubin, O., & Öberg, P. (2021). Monotonous or pluralistic public discourse? Reason-giving and dissent in Denmark's and Sweden's early 2020 COVID-19 responses. *Journal of European Public Policy, 28*(8), 1321–1343.

Berman, A. H., Bendtsen, M., Molander, O., Lindfors, P., Lindner, P., Granlund, L., ..., & Andersson, C. (2022). Compliance with recommendations limiting COVID-19 contagion among university students in Sweden: associations with self-reported symptoms, mental health and academic self-efficacy. *Scandinavian Journal of Public Health, 50*(1), 70-84.

Brandebo, M. F. (2021). Sweden's Covid-19 strategy from a leadership perspective: Importance of trust and role models. In T. Fang, & J. Hassler (Eds.), *Globalization, political economy, business and society in pandemic times* (International Business and Management, Vol. 36, pp. pp. 143–156). Emerald Publishing Limited. https://doi.org/10.1108/S1876-066X20220000036013

Bröckling, U., Krasmann, S., & Lemke, T. (2011). From Foucault's lectures at the College de France to studies of governmentality: An introduction. In Bröckling, S. Krasmann, & T. Lemke, *Governmentality: Current issues and future challenges.* Routledge.

Bjørkdahl, K., Kjeldsen, J. E., Villadsen, L., & Vigsø, O. (2021). Argumentum ad solidaritatem: Rhetorical leadership strategies in Scandinavia during COVID-19. Communicating COVID-19: *Interdisciplinary Perspectives*, 163–184.

Bylund, P. L., & Packard, M. D. (2021). Separation of power and expertise: evidence of the tyranny of experts in Sweden's COVID-19 responses. *Southern Economic Journal, 87*(4), 1300–1319.

Cheibub, J. A., Hong, J. Y. J., & Przeworski, A. (2020). Rights and deaths: Government reactions to the pandemic. Working paper. https://doi.org/10.2139/ssrn.3645410

Christensen, T., & Lægreid, P. (2020a). Balancing governance capacity and legitimacy: How the Norwegian Government handled the COVID–19 crisis as a high performer. *Public Administration Review, 80*(5), 774–779. https://doi.org/10.1111/puar.13241

Christensen, T., & Lægreid, P. (2020b). The coronavirus crisis—Crisis communication, meaning-making, and reputation management. *International Public Management Journal, 23*(5), 713–729.

Claeson, M., & Hanson, S. (2021). COVID-19 and the Swedish enigma. *The Lancet, 397*(10271), 259–261.

Dean, M. (2007). *Governing societies. Political perspectives on domestic and international rule*. Open University Press.

Foucault, M. (1991). *Discipline and punish: The birth of the prison*. Penguin books.

Foucault, M. (1994a). Subject and power. In F. D. Faubion & M. Foucault (Eds.), *Power. Essential works of Foucault 1954–1984 Volume 3* (pp. 326–349). The New Press.

Foucault, M. (1994b). The birth of social medicine. In F. D. Faubion & M. Foucault (Eds.), *Power. Essential works of Foucault 1954–1984 Volume 3* (pp. 134–156). The New Press.

Foucault, M. (2008). *The birth of biopolitics - Lectures at the Collège de France, 1978–1979*. Palgrave Macmillan.

Foucault, M. (2009). *Security, territory, population: Lectures at Collège De France, 1977–1978*. Palgrave Macmillan.

Foucault, M. (2014). *The government of the living*. Picador.

Giritli Nygren, K., & Olofsson, A. (2020). Managing the COVID-19 pandemic through individual responsibility: the consequences of a world risk society and enhanced ethopolitics. *Journal of Risk Research*.

Giritli Nygren, K., & Olofsson, A. (2021). Swedish exceptionalism, herd immunity and the welfare state: A media analysis of struggles over the nature and legitimacy of the COVID-19 pandemic strategy in Sweden. *Current Sociology, 69*(4), 529–546.

Gjerde, L. E. L. (2021b). Governing humans and 'things': Power and rule in Norway during the Covid-19 pandemic. *Journal of Political Power, 14*(3), 472–492. https://doi.org/10.1080/2158379X.2020.1870264

Gjerde, L. E. L. (2024). Interview guide: Online appendix. https://doi.org/10.13140/RG.2.2.24808.69126

Gjerde, L. E. L. (2025). Methodology: Digital appendix. *Research Gate*. https://www.researchgate.net/publication/387958773_Methodology_Digital_Appendix

Gustavsson, J., & Beckman, L. (2020). Compliance to recommendations and mental health consequences among elderly in Sweden during the initial phase of the COVID-19 pandemic—A cross sectional online survey. *International Journal of Environmental Research and Public Health, 17*(15), 5380.

Gustavsson, A. K. G. (2022). The consequences of the Covid-19 pandemic on the Norwegian/Swedish national border. *Arv. Nordic Yearbook of Folklore, 78*, 111–155.

Green, T. (2021). *The Covid consensus: The new politics of global inequality*. Hurst.

Grothe-Hammer, M., & Roth, S. (2021). Dying is normal, dying with the coronavirus is not: A sociological analysis of the implicit norms behind the criticism of Swedish 'exceptionalism.' *European Societies, 23*(sup1), S332–S347.

Hagström, L., Wagnsson, C., & Lundström, M. (2023). Logics of othering: Sweden as other in the time of COVID-19. *Cooperation and Conflict, 58*(3), 315–334.

Hall, P. (2016). The Swedish administrative model. In J. Pierre (Ed.), *The Oxford handbook of Swedish politics* (pp. 299–314). OUP.

Harris, A., & Jones, M. (2020). COVID 19 – School leadership in disruptive times. *School Leadership & Management, 40*(4), 243–247.

Harris, A., & Jones, M. (2022). Leading during a pandemic – What the evidence tells us. *School Leadership & Management, 42*(2), 105–109.

Hansen, A. S., Beery, T., Fredman, P., & Wolf-Watz, D. (2023). Outdoor recreation in Sweden during and after the Covid-19 pandemic–management and policy implications. *Journal of Environmental Planning and Management, 66*(7), 1472–1493.

Heinikoski, S., & Hyttinen, T. (2022). The impact of Covid-19 on the free movement regime in the north: Analysis of border closures in Denmark, Finland, Norway and Sweden. *Nordic Journal of International Law, 91*(1), 80–100.

Helsingen, L. M., Refsum, E., Gjøstein, D. K., Løberg, M., Bretthauer, M., Kalager, M., & Emilsson, L. (2020). The COVID-19 pandemic in Norway and Sweden–threats, trust, and impact on daily life: A comparative survey. *BMC Public Health, 20*(1), 1–10.

Holmström, M. (2021). Sverige sämst i Norden: Långsam och otillräcklig krishantering ledde till högsta andelen döda i covid-19. *Statsvetenskaplig tidskrift, 123*(5).

Hedenborg, S., Fredman, P., Hansen, A. S., & Wolf-Watz, D. (2022). Outdoorification of sports and recreation:A leisure transformation under the COVID-19 pandemic in Sweden. *Annals of Leisure Research*, 1–19.

Jacobsson, B., Pierre, J., & Sundström, G. (2015). *Governing the embedded state: The organizational dimension of governance*. OUP Oxford.

Jarnkvist, K. (2023). Articulations of 'Funeral'in Swedish newspapers during the Covid-19 pandemic. *OMEGA-Journal of Death and Dying*, 00302228231174601.

Jessop, B. (2001). Bringing the state back in (yet again): Reviews, revisions, rejections, and redirections. *International Review of Sociology/Revue internationale de sociologie, 11*(2), 149–173.

Jonung, L. (2020). Sweden's constitution decides its COVID-19 exceptionalism. *SSRN*. https://doi.org/10.2139/ssrn.3796848

Kamerlin, S. C., & Kasson, P. M. (2020). Managing coronavirus disease 2019 spread with voluntary public health measures: Sweden as a case study for pandemic control. *Clinical Infectious Diseases, 71*(12), 3174–3181.

Kristensen, L. M., & Hartley, J. M. (2023). The infrastructure of news: Negotiating infrastructural capture and autonomy in data-driven news distribution. *Media and Communication, 11*(2), 307–318.

Larsson, O. L. (2022). The Swedish Covid-19 strategy and voluntary compliance: Failed securitisation or constitutional security management? *European Journal of International Security, 7*(2), 226–247.

Miller, P., & Rose, N. (2008). *Governing the present: Administering economic, social and political life*. Polity Press.

Mitchell, T. (1991). The limits of the state: Beyond statist approaches and their critics. *The American Political Science Review, 85*(1), 77–96.

Mishra, S., Scott, J. A., Laydon, D. J., Flaxman, S., Gandy, A., Mellan, T. A., …, & Bhatt, S. (2021). Comparing the responses of the UK, Sweden and Denmark to COVID-19 using counterfactual modelling. *Scientific Reports, 11*(1), 1–9.

Nielsen, J. H., & Lindvall, J. (2021). Trust in government in Sweden and Denmark during the COVID-19 epidemic. *West European Politics, 44*(5–6), 1180–1204.

Nilsson, G., Ekstam, L., Axmon, A., & Andersson, J. (2021). Old overnight: Experiences of age-based recommendations in response to the COVID-19 pandemic in Sweden. *Journal of Aging & Social Policy, 33*(4–5), 359–379.

Norberg, J. R., Andersson, K., & Hedenborg, S. (2022). Fighting a pandemic by recommendations and trust – Sports in Sweden during Covid-19. In J. Krieger, A. Henning, & L. Parks Pieper (Eds.), *Restart. – Sport after the Covid-19 lockdown* (pp. 167–182). Common Ground.

Opitz, S. (2011). Government unlimited. The security Dospositif of illiberal governmentality. In Bröckling, S. Krasmann, & T. Lemke (Eds.), *Governmentality: Current issues and future challenges* (pp. 93–114).

Petridou, E. (2020). Politics and administration in times of crisis: Explaining the Swedish response to the COVID-19 crisis. *European Policy Analysis, 6*(2), 147–158.

Pierre, J. (2020). Nudges against pandemics: Sweden's COVID-19 containment strategy in perspective. *Policy and Society, 39*(3), 478–493.

Rose, N. (1999). *Powers of freedom: reframing political thought*. Cambridge University Press.

Sahlin, S., Sjöstrand, M., Styf, M., & Lund, S. (2023). Novice principals coping strategies during the Covid-19 pandemic in Sweden. *Educational Management Administration & Leadership*, 17411432231208789.

Sandset, T., & Villadsen, K. (2023). Pandemic modelling and model citizens: Governing COVID-19 through predictive models, sovereignty and discipline. *The Sociological Review*, 00380261221102023.

Saunes, I. S., Vrangbæk, K., Byrkjeflot, H., Jervelund, S. S., Birk, H. O., Tynkkynen, L. K., …, & Karanikolos, M. (2022). Nordic responses to Covid-19: Governance and policy measures in the early phases of the pandemic. *Health Policy, 126*(5), 418–426.

Schmitt, C. (1996). *The concept of the political*. University of Chicago Press.

Sending, O. J., & Neumann, I. B. (2006). Governance to governmentality: Analyzing NGOs, states, and power. *International Studies Quarterly, 50*(3), 651–672.

SOU. (2008). *Krisberedskapen i grundlagen: Översyn och internationell utblick*. Fritzes Offentliga Publikationer.

Staupe-Delgado, R. (2021). Life in anticipation of the COVID-19 pandemic 'peak': reflecting on 'strategies' for and variations in attempts at 'flattening the curve' and managing the crisis. *Journal of Extreme Events, 8*(01), 2150016, 27–470.

Stenson, K. (2005). Sovereignty, biopolitics and the local government of crime in Britain. *Theoretical criminology, 9*(3), 265–287.

Villadsen, K. (2016). Michel Foucault and the forces of civil society. *Theory, Culture & Society, 33*(3), 3–26.

Wallace-Wells, D. (2023). How did no-mandate Sweden end up with such an average pandemic? *New York Times*. https://www.nytimes.com/2023/03/30/opinion/sweden-pandemic-coronavirus.html

Winblad, U., Swenning, A. K., & Spangler, D. (2022). Soft law and individual responsibility: A review of the Swedish policy response to COVID-19. *Health Economics, Policy and Law, 17*(1), 48–61.

Empirical References: Chapter 5

Bergstrøm, I. I. (2021). Fewer people than expected died in Norway last year. The opposite is true in Sweden. https://www.sciencenorway.no/covid19/fewer-people-than-expected-died-in-norway-last-year-the-opposite-is-true-in-sweden/1878720

Boden. (2020). Information om det nya Coronaviruset SARS-CoV-2 (som kan leda till sjukdomen Covid-19) - uppdaterat 2020-03-11. https://www.boden.se/nyheter/2020/information-om-det-nya-coronaviruset-sars-cov-2-som-kan-leda-till-sjukdomen-covid-19-uppdaterat-2020-03-11

Covidlawlab. (2020a). Maximum of eight people permitted Maximum of eight people permitted at public gatherings and events at public gatherings and events. https://www.covidlawlab.org/item/maximum-of-eight-people-permitted-at-public-gatherings-and-events/

Covidlawlab. (2020b). Questions and answers about the entry ban to Sweden. https://www.covidlawlab.org/wp-content/uploads/2022/07/Sweden-Entry-Ban-Removed.pdf

Embassy of Sweden. (2020, March 22). Prime Minister's address to the nation. https://www.swedenabroad.se/es/embajada/mozambique-maputo/current/news/prime-ministers-address-to-the-nation-22-march-2020/

Folkhälsomyndigheten. (2020a). Gemensamma författningssamlingen avseende hälso- och sjukvård, socialtjänst, läkemedel, folkhälsa m.m. https://www.folkhalsomyndigheten.se/contentassets/0ac7c7d33c124428baa198728f813151/hslf-fs-2020-12u.pdf

Folkhalsomyndigheten. (2020b). Undvik att bli smittad och att smitta andra. https://www.folkhalsomyndigheten.se/contentassets/db046108bf2b4b3b833d2b501370ac0c/undvik-att-bli-smittad-och-att-smitta-andra-affisch.pdf

Folkhälsomyndigheten. (2021a). Förslag om anpassade smittskyddsåtgärder. https://www.folkhalsomyndigheten.se/nyheter-och-press/nyhetsarkiv/2021/maj/forslag-om-anpassade-smittskyddsatgarder/

Folkhälsomyndigheten. (2021b). Modeller för smittspridning bidrog till att förstå pandemins utveckling. https://www.folkhalsomyndigheten.se/nyheter-och-press/nyhetsarkiv/2021/maj/modeller-for-smittspridning-bidrog-till-att-forsta-pandemins-utveckling/

Folkhälsomyndigheten. (2021c). Beslut om fortsatta åtgärder mot covid-19 i handeln och på serveringsställen. https://www.folkhalsomyndigheten.se/nyheter-och-press/nyhetsarkiv/2021/april/beslut-om-fortsatta-atgarder-mot-covid-19-i-handeln-och-pa-serveringsstallen/

Folkhälsomyndigheten. (2023a). Upphävda föreskrifter och allmänna råd. https://www.folkhalsomyndigheten.se/publikationer-och-material/foreskrifter-och-allmanna-rad/upphavda-foreskrifter/

Folkhälsomyndigheten. (2023b). Skydda dig själv och andra – rekommendationer om covid-19. https://www.folkhalsomyndigheten.se/smittskydd-beredskap/utbrott/aktuella-utbrott/covid-19/skydda-dig-sjalv-och-andra-rekommendationer-om-covid-19/

Folkhälsomyndigheten. (2023c). Upphävda föreskrifter och allmänna råd https://www.folkhalsomyndigheten.se/publikationer-och-material/foreskrifter-och-allmanna-rad/upphavda-foreskrifter/

Folkhälsomyndigheten. (2023d). Användning av munskydd. https://www.folkhalsomyndigheten.se/smittskydd-beredskap/utbrott/aktuella-utbrott/covid-19/om-sjukdomen-och-smittspridning/smittspridning/munskydd/

Folkhälsomyndigheten. (2023e). Personal inom vård och omsorg angående covid-19. https://www.folkhalsomyndigheten.se/smittskydd-beredskap/utbrott/aktuella-utbrott/covid-19/information-till-varden/personal-inom-halso--och-sjukvard/?pub=78165

Glaser, M., (2021). Tegnell: Tredje vågen är i värsta fall här om veckor. https://omni.se/tegnell-tredje-vagen-ar-i-varsta-fall-har-om-veckor/a/JJlVe4
Government. (2020a). Speech by Minister for Health and Social Affairs Lena Hallengren at WHO Briefing 23 April. https://www.government.se/contentassets/0550da61a00f4fcda2e600fdb0fbd79e/lena-hallengren-speeches-2018-2022.pdf
Government. (2020b, September 8). Statement of government policy. https://government.se/speeches/2020/09/statement-of-government-policy/)
Government. (2020c). The Government presents the 2020 Spring Fiscal Policy Bill. https://www.government.se/press-releases/2020/04/the-government-presents-the-2020-spring-fiscal-policy-bill/
Government. (2020d). Tillfälliga bemyndiganden i smittskyddslagen med anledning av det virus som orsakar covid-19. https://www.regeringen.se/rattsliga-dokument/proposition/2020/04/prop.-201920155
Government. (2020e). Swedish experiences during the COVID-19 pandemic. https://government.se/articles/2020/07/swedish-experiences-during-the-covid-19-pandemic/
Government. (2020f). Further extension of business emergency package 'Företagsakuten'. https://www.government.se/contentassets/74f1b9be65c84c4987a47fdf3a4bdff1/minister-for-financial-markets-and-housing-deputy-minister-for-finance-per-bolund-press-releases-2014-2021.pdf
Government. (2020g). Great uncertainty surrounding travel abroad. https://www.government.se/press-releases/2020/03/great-uncertainty-surrounding-travel-abroad/
Government. (2021). En tillfällig covid-19-lag. https://www.regeringen.se/rattsliga-dokument/proposition/2021/01/prop.-20202179
Krisinformation. (2020a). Vecka 7 2020. https://www.krisinformation.se/om-krisinformation/for-myndigheter-och-andra-aktorer/omvarldsbevakning/omvarldsbevakning-2020/vecka-7-2020
Krisinformation. (2020b). The Swedish government classifies the coronavirus as an illness that is dangerous to society. https://www.krisinformation.se/en/news/2020/february/the-swedish-government-classifies-the-coronavirus-as-an-illness-that-is-dangerous-to-society
Krisinformation. (2020c). Detailed recommendations for shops, shopping centres and training facilities. https://www.krisinformation.se/en/news/2020/december/advice-to-businesses
Krisinformation. (2020d). Text message with information about Covid-19. https://www.krisinformation.se/en/news/2020/december/sms-with-information-about-covid-19
Krisinformation. (2020e). Prohibition of public gatherings with more than 50 people. https://www.krisinformation.se/en/news/2020/march/further-restriction-of-gatherings

Krisinformation. (2020f). Public Health Agency of Sweden: Ban on crowding in restaurants, cafés and bars. https://www.krisinformation.se/en/news/2020/march/public-health-agency-of-sweden-ban-on-crowding-in-restaurants-cafes-and-bars

Krisinformation. (2020g). The Public Health Agency of Sweden recommends remote learning. https://www.krisinformation.se/en/news/2020/march/remote-learning

Krisinformation. (2020h). The Government: Upper secondary schools can reopen. https://www.krisinformation.se/en/news/2020/may/upper-secondary-schools-can-reopen

Krisinformation. (2020i). Children and adolescents with symptoms of covid-19 are recommended testing. https://www.krisinformation.se/en/news/2020/august/barn-och-unga-med-covidsymtom

Krisinformaiton. (2020j). Vecka 6 2020. https://www.krisinformation.se/om-krisinformation/for-myndigheter-och-andra-aktorer/omvarldsbevakning/omvarldsbevakning-2020/vecka-6-2020

Krisinformation. (2020k). The Public Health Agency of Sweden recommends testing of patients who have been to the Tyrol. https://www.krisinformation.se/en/news/2020/march/the-public-health-agency-of-sweden-recommends-testing-of-patients-who-have-been-to-the-tyrol

Krisinformation. (2020l). No entry from the UK and Denmark. https://www.krisinformation.se/en/news/2020/december/entry-ban-from-uk-and-denmark

Krisinformation. (2020m). Stay at home if anyone in the household has covid-19 https://www.krisinformation.se/en/news/2020/october/stay-at-home-if-anyone-in-the-household-has-covid-19

Krisinformation. (2020n). No entry from the UK and Denmark. https://www.krisinformation.se/en/news/2020/december/entry-ban-from-uk-and-denmark

Krisinformation. (2021a). Parliament says yes to new pandemic law. https://www.krisinformation.se/en/news/2021/january/parliament-says-yes-to-new-pandemic-law

Krisinformation. (2021b) The Government: Ban on serving alcohol after 20 pm extends. https://www.krisinformation.se/en/news/2021/january/the-government-ban-on-serving-alcohol-after-20-pm-extends

Krisinformation. (2021c). Extension of several Covid-19 restrictions. https://www.krisinformation.se/en/news/2021/january/extension-of-several-covid-19-restrictions

Krisinformation. (2021d). Vaccination against Covid-19. https://www.krisinformation.se/en/hazards-and-risks/disasters-and-incidents/2020/official-information-on-the-new-coronavirus/vaccination-against-covid-19

Krisinformation. (2021e). New restrictions for shops and gyms. https://www.krisinformation.se/en/news/2021/january/new-restrictions-for-shops-and-gyms

Munkfors kommun. (2020). Senaste nytt om coronaviruset. https://www.munkfors.se/print-info.php?print=15495

Paterlini, M. (2020). Closing borders is ridiculous': the epidemiologist behind Sweden's controversial coronavirus strategy. https://www.nature.com/articles/d41586-020-01098-x

Region Vasterbotten. (2021). Nya rekommendationer till personer som varit i Norge. https://www.regionvasterbotten.se/nya-rekommendationer-till-personer-som-varit-i-norge

Tegnell, A. (2021). The Swedish public health response to COVID-19. *APMIS, 129*(7), 320–323.

The Local. (2020a). In English: Prime Minister Stefan Löfven's televised speech to the nation. https://www.thelocal.se/20201122/in-english-prime-minister-stefan-lfvens-televised-speech-to-the-nation

The Local. (2020b). Sweden bans public events with more than 8 people. https://www.thelocal.se/20201116/breaking-sweden-introduces-limit-of-eight-coronavirus/

The Local. (2020c). Sweden to lift ban on visits to elderly care homes. https://www.thelocal.se/20200915/sweden-to-lift-ban-on-visits-to-elderly-care-homes

Socialstyrelsen. (2020) Basal hygien i vård och omsorg. https://www.socialstyrelsen.se/globalassets/sharepoint-dokument/artikelkatalog/foreskrifter-och-allmanna-rad/2015-5-10.pdf

SOU. (2022). Sverige under pandemin. (Sweden under the Pandemic) Andre delrapport fra coronakommisjonen. Statens Offentlige Utredningar.

ST. (2020). Folkhälsomyndighetens uppmaning till de som bor med smittade av covid-19: "Stanna hemma". https://www.st.nu/2020-10-01/folkhalsomyndighetens-uppmaning-till-de-som-bor-med-smittade-av-covid-19-stanna-hemma

Vasterviks kommun. (2020). Pressmeddelande: Medarbetare på äldreboende i Edsbruk smittad av coronaviruset, smittspårning och testning inleds av alla på boendet. https://www.vastervik.se/Kommun-och-politik/Pressmaterial-och-extern-kommunikation/Pressmeddelanden/pressmeddelande-medarbetare-pa-aldreboende-i-edsbruk-smittad-av-coronaviruset-smittsparning-och-testning-inleds-av-alla-pa-boendet

CHAPTER 6

Seeing Like Two States? The Political Reasoning of Hobbesian Norway and Crypto-Hobbesian Sweden

6.1 Introduction

I have so far analysed the politics of COVID-19 in Norway and Sweden, prioritizing the exercise of power, the sources enabling such enactment of power and the mechanisms of power such enactments produced. Clearly, there are differences between the Swedish and Norwegian approaches, as seen in the Swedish state's *relative* aversion to state coercion. This has however merely been explored at a superficial level, in passing. I shall now scrutinize this more closely, investigating why these states acted as they did, and the similarities between their reasonings and actions.

As established above, states act. While states' actions are always important (Nordlinger, 1981), political choices are especially important during crises (Weiss & Thurbon, 2022). States are, as I have maintained throughout this book, political organizations possessing agency. But actions are not mere reactions or reflexes. As Foucauldians assert, governmental practices—the government of individuals, populations, territories—are always based on political reasoning (Dean, 1999; Foucault, 1985, 1991, 2008; C. Gordon, 1994; Miller & Rose, 2008). The administration, fostering and protection of biological life is one of the core objectives of the contemporary state (Buchanan 2022; Rose, 2009). The relevance of biopolitics is shown by the massive political operations of most states at the global level, as they tried to stop COVID-19 and limit its death tolls and adverse health effects. On the basis of these reflections,

L. E. L. Gjerde, *Nordic Leviathans*, International Political Theory,
https://doi.org/10.1007/978-3-032-00689-9_6

this chapter is guided by the second research question of my book—*how do the Norwegian and Swedish states render reality governable?*—as I study the rationalizations and problematizations underpinning the Swedish and Norwegian response. To answer this question, I review public sources, referred to in the section 'empirical references: chapter 6', located under the bibliography, and explained in detail in the digital appendix (Gjerde, 2025).

Answering this question fills an empirical gap, insofar as the political rationality of the Swedish state, while analysed at a theoretical level through explorations of the politics of COVID-19 in Sweden (i.e. Larsson, 2022; Nygren & Olofsson, 2020), has not been discussed empirically in consideration of a systematic analysis of the Swedish state actors' articulations. Therefore, the biopolitical and socio-political discourses of the Swedish state and their internal contradictions have been left aside until now. In Norway, the break between liberalism and biopolitics in early March 2020 has been studied (i.e. Gjerde, 2021a), but no study thus far has handled how the Norwegian state's discourses underpin the political responses beyond references to biopolitics' primacy. Therefore, the Norwegian case would benefit from a richer general study of how problematizations and rationalizations render reality governable, especially when this is done comparatively by discussing how these two states' discourses relate to one another at the end of the chapter.

This is also useful as it allows me to explore the relationship between liberal governmentality and non-liberal rationalizations (Dean, 2007; Opitz, 2011). As we shall see, both the Norwegian and Swedish states define the situation as a great crisis, calling for unprecedented measures. The Norwegian state prioritized the pandemic as a pathological, biopolitical event—which may bring society down. The Swedish state *partly* shared this biopolitical Hobbesian understanding with the Norwegian state. However, only the Norwegian state based its governing action on a principle of caution, as also found in another study on the Norwegian lockdown (see Askim & Christensen, 2022). The lack of a principle of caution in Sweden means that state coercion was more slowly implemented, although it *was* still implemented if and when a need was identified. Whereas the lockdown was the result of the Norwegian state granting primacy to a Hobbesian biopolitical rationality, the Swedish two-tier response to COVID-19 was the result of a mix of Hobbesian *and* Anti-Hobbesian reasoning, leading the Swedish state to a Crypto-Hobbesian position. I speak of Sweden as Crypto-Hobbesian because the

Swedish state has Hobbesian characteristics related to its prioritization of *security*, but this priority is concealed by the Swedish two-tier system as well as the Swedish state's own statements. The Leviathans in question do not automatically emerge, but grow out of society, among other things based on the Hobbesian reasoning of its representatives, which define the situation as too grave for 'normal' politics. The reference to Hobbesian is meant to complement my understanding of these states as Nordic Leviathans. The Hobbesian element is discursive, related to the reasoning underpinning Leviathan, whereas Leviathan refers to the model of the state I operate with. These discourses, I will argue, largely explain the political outcomes we have seen in the last two chapters, as they are structuring, showing the possible room for political action (Dean, 2007; Miller & Rose, 2008). Theoretically, this approach is useful, as it shows how reasoning motivates state agency. The cultural, institutional and political similarities of Norway and Sweden are rendered largely irrelevant by the two states perceiving the situation differently, as these ways of seeing motivate different political approaches.

To illustrate these points, I refer to numerous state sources, prioritizing key texts, such as those articulated during the initial stages of COVID-19 and during the periods when measures were tightened, and when the state had to make decisions, such as March and April 2020, or November 2020. I cover speeches, comments, action plans and legal documents. The excepts I refer to are meant to illustrate the logic underpinning the problematizations and rationalizations that buttress these states' political strategies during the pandemic. Using an intertextual lens, I demonstrate how the logics I have identified are relevant beyond the singular texts, so that the reader can observe how a multitude of texts are connected through a shared logic, hence fixating the meaning of these texts around certain problems, leading to a structured set of rationalizations. The texts I refer to are meant to be general, chosen so as to reveal not just concrete articulations, but the logic underpinning these and similar statements, to illustrate the discursive regularities in hand (cf. Foucault, 1972). Analytically, I prioritize the study of signs and discursive logic for mapping problematizations, while following the Foucauldian ideal of describing how rationalizations enable specific political actions in the second part of the discourse analysis. For more insights on the discourse analytical approach taken, see the appendix (Gjerde, 2025).

Before scrutinizing the Norwegian and Swedish states' discursive processes of governmentalization, I must put forward some reflections on the two states' similar and dissimilar political actions. Thereafter, I shall explore the Norwegian and Swedish discourses separately, probing the problematizations and the manner in which the two states rendered reality governable, before conducting an analysis of the similarities and differences between the two states and how these represent the situation.

6.1.1 Biopolitical Strategies and Tactics

Some comparisons should be drawn prior to looking into the political rationalities of the Norwegian and Swedish states, and commenting on the discursive underpinnings of their responses. Essentially, what are the core differences and similarities between the two states? Most importantly, the states had a common biopolitical objective. They sought to contain and reduce the spread of COVID-19, by coercing people into physically and socially maintaining their distance and limiting the number of people they interacted with. Second, both states depended upon voluntarism. However, there are major differences. Their strategies, while related, are different.

6.1.1.1 The Coercion/Voluntarism Spectrum

The Swedish state deviated from standard COVID-19 practice by refraining from empowering the executive to deal with this crisis (Larsson, 2022). Sovereignty enables states to suspend norms valid under normal times. While the Norwegian state's rule during the pandemic naturally calls for reflections on Schmitt's state of exception (see Graver, 2020a, 2020b), this is not the case in Sweden, where political power clearly 'remained within constitutional boundaries' (Larsson, 2022: 242). Instead, the Swedish state sought to control and regulate the pathogen, limiting its impact, whereas the Norwegian state acted to eradicate it, to control all of society with a tight grip. These are two different approaches to the pandemic—based on different rationalizations—as we shall discuss below.

The exercise of sovereignty, dependent upon subjective interpretations of necessity (Agamben, 2008: 30), shapes political possibilities. The Swedish state refrained from delving deeply into this political resource, thereby reducing the forcefulness of its political response. However, sovereignty is a meta-mechanism of power, thereby being abstract. In order to better clarify the differences, I will reflect upon the sources and mechanisms of power. There are qualitative and quantitative differences.

First, a qualitative difference: the Swedish state operated with a two-tier system. The Norwegian state operated with the lockdown, a totalizing approach. The Swedish state's two-tier system revolved around creating barriers that the state refrained from crossing. The Norwegian state knew few such barriers. Second, a series of quantitative differences: the Swedish state sought to restrict its use of formal commands when intervening in society, trying to both reduce the force of its coercion and the strength of its commands. These differences in the use of coercion relate to significant dissimilarities in how these two states used their infrastructural, ideological and coercive sources of power, thereafter manifesting in voluntarism, juridical-sovereignty, control (over access) and discipline being imposed at the micro-level in different ways, and to different extents.

The main difference between these two states can be found in their relative use of state coercion, and their relative dependency upon voluntarism. The less formally and coercively a state governs, the more it depends upon regulating society through voluntarism. Both states mobilized private individuals to engage actively in the infection control campaign, imposing moral obligations to comply with recommendations. These were articulated to teach individuals about their moral obligations and how to deal with the situation, and the recommendations were highly similar in both countries. They revolved around limiting social contact, avoiding crowds and staying at home, on the one hand, as well as how to practise proper hygiene by washing and sanitizing hands, coughing/sneezing properly, using facemasks, etc.

The Norwegian state imposed numerous moral obligations—reduce the number of people you meet, do not travel abroad or within the country unnecessarily, do not gather in crowds, stay at home if possible, wash your hands, etc. The Swedish state also sought to responsibilize citizens by imposing moral obligations in such cases. However, the Swedish state went beyond the Norwegian state. It recommended individuals to limit the size of gatherings in their private homes and isolate/quarantine if sick. This reduced the verticality of the politics of COVID-19 in Sweden, as the state refused to utilize its hierarchical position vis-à-vis society to the same extent as other countries, including but not limited to, Norway. The Swedish state tried to regulate bodies as well as social and spatial spaces, while limiting social circles and interaction, in a manner similar to the Norwegian approach. Both states sought to govern in a liberal manner by making individuals take responsibility (Gjerde, 2021b; Nygren &

Olofsson, 2020; Sandset & Villadsen, 2023), but the Norwegian state depended less upon these liberal methods.

This brings us to the question of ideological power, as voluntarism was fostered, enabled and affected by communication campaigns through which the two states enacted their ideological sources of power. These sources were centred around legitimacy, trust, rhetorical techniques and communicational instruments. Unsurprisingly, their communication campaigns were highly similar, and they were based on similar sources of power. Yet, there were differences worthy of attention regarding how these sources could be and were enacted. The main difference relates to the use of fear. The Swedish state was forced to refrain from implementing this political resource, which would have rendered the relative lack of coercion illegitimate. This weakened the symbolic effects of calls to communitarian responsibility—as fear was not taken advantage of. This is not merely the case because of the more muted crisis discourse. The lack of lockdowns and similar forms of state coercion also implied that the situation was under control. Thus, the Norwegian state had a stronger potential for symbolic impact, despite the Swedish state depending more upon ideological sources of power than the Norwegian state. Self-regulation within the context of the pandemic heavily depended upon citizens accepting a moral responsibility to self-restraint, and the more urgent the situation, the higher levels of compliance a state would be likely to achieve. The Swedish and Norwegian states use ideological sources of power in similar ways, despite the difference of degree enabled by the Norwegian state being less dependent upon voluntarism, as a result of its increased use of coercion.

6.1.1.2 Mobilizing Tactics

Both the Norwegian and Swedish states acted to mobilize society and conscript individuals in a formal manner, through infrastructural power. Both states mobilized society through conscription, imposing responsibilities upon individuals at the local level. In Norway as in Sweden, conscripts had to reorganize their spaces so as to ensure that individuals could keep their distance when eating at a cafeteria or while sitting in the office. Infrastructural power was enacted so that conscripts would be tasked with imposing discipline on the state's behalf. Interestingly, while formalizing such conscriptions to a lesser extent, the Swedish state depended upon infrastructural power to a greater extent than its Norwegian counterpart, due to its reduced use of coercion. This supports findings that the Swedish state governed more through networks, and in a less hierarchical manner, than its neighbours (Christensen et al. 2023). Yet the Swedish state did also formally conscript individuals by allocating numerous infection control responsibilities. The Norwegian state depended less upon infrastructural sources of power, because it frequently exercised power in a negative fashion through close-downs. However, the Norwegian state formalized its use of infrastructural power to a greater extent *when* it acted through its institutional capacities, and it used these capacities to create numerous political organs for the purpose of controlling the population, i.e. quarantine hotels or systems for monitoring travellers as well as the quarantined in general. This stands in contrast to the Swedish state, which largely depended upon pre-existing institutional capacities, barely instituting any infection control organs. Moreover, the Swedish state mobilized in a more liberal manner, allowing local actors more autonomy when it came to how infection control was to be practised. The Norwegian state, through a more hierarchical model, commanded and formalized its mobilizations to a greater extent. Thus, while Mann (1984, 1993, 2012, 2013) operates with a binary between infrastructural and coercive sources of power, in reality, they interweave in ways in which coercive sources of power enhance infrastructural power and vice-versa. A state may move from coercive to infrastructural priorities, but infrastructural power can be exercised more efficiently whenever a state is willing to back up power through society with power over society.

The mobilization of society revolved chiefly around constituting disciplinary and exclusionary mechanisms of power. First, on discipline. Both states rendered the individual's location in spatial space governable, as well as bodily conduct and functions such as coughing or washing hands. In both Norway and Sweden, all of society was to be restructured so that individuals could strictly regulate their own bodies, keep at a distance from one another, reduce the sizes of private gatherings and behave in such a way as to limit the risk of contagion when touching doors, washing hands, etc. Discipline was to be imposed by, and supervised under the watchful gaze of, the state, mostly through agents conscripted into the state's controlling machinery. These state agents were granted infection control responsibilities, and they may originally have been civil servants or working in the private sector. Here, there are quantitative and qualitative differences. Both states imposed disciplinary obligations on mobilized individuals, who had to discipline employees, guests, clients and others by enforcing distancing rules in cafeterias, churches, classrooms, etc. In Norway, discipline was enforced almost universally, besides in private homes where there were mostly moral obligations regarding discipline, as bodies could legally be close to one another. In Sweden, discipline was formally enforced in places such as cafeterias, classrooms and hospitals, but not throughout society in general. Moreover, the enforcement of discipline in Sweden was laxer, because the state sought to curtail the severity of its own interventions in society, thereby only imposing discipline in some contexts. The Norwegian state thus imposed discipline in a harsher manner, and in social contexts the Swedish state only governed informally and morally, such as against travellers and the (potentially) sick. Here, the state again mobilized society, including employees at hotels, to monitor and police the (potentially) dangerous.

Second, on control (over access) and the mechanisms of exclusion. Both states controlled access, and they both used exclusion as a mechanism to control access to medical facilities. However, there are major differences, especially as only the Norwegian state *formally* controlled access for the (potentially) dangerous bodies. Only the Norwegian state formalized quarantine and isolation, backed up by a disciplinary tracing and surveillance system where individuals were closely monitored, disciplined and thereafter forced to comply if an individual was unconvinced by moral obligations. The Swedish state used its ideological powers to act towards the (potentially) dangerous, thereby deviating from the 'norm' in this regard. Only medical personnel were likely to experience an explicit order to not enter their workplaces, if sick.

However, the Swedish state also used control (over access) in a coercive manner, in medical facilities. The Swedish state acted in a harsher manner towards medical facilities than the Norwegian state, as the Norwegian state already in May 2020 took steps to formalize and safeguard the right of the elderly and the sick to receive visitors (Regjeringen, 2020a). In Sweden, this ban continued until the autumn of 2020, and strict rules were in place throughout the entire period. The Swedish state's use of control was paradoxically both more lenient and harsher, depending upon the sphere of life examined, as its two-tier system created major contradictions between the private sphere where the state was formally absent, and the public sphere where the state was formally present.

The relative severity of the imposed discipline and control relates to a significant difference—the two states' attitude towards coercion. The coercive powers of these states were utilized, but to different extents. The

Swedish state refrained from formally touching upon numerous spheres where other states, such as Norway, used its monopoly over the legitimate means of violence to enforce its will. This relates to juridical-sovereign mechanisms of power. The Norwegians relied heavily upon this form of rule. On the one hand, the Norwegian lockdowns were soft compared to those enforced in Italy or in China, mostly because individuals were always allowed to move freely outside their private homes, unless classified as (potentially) dangerous (cf. Cheibub et al., 2020). On the other hand, this was nevertheless a totalizing juridical-sovereign tactic of unprecedented intensity and extensiveness. This stands in contrast to the Swedish state, which refrained from closing down society, choosing to depend less upon law. The main difference at the micro-level can be seen in the relative aversion of the Swedish state to seizing, repressing and denying liberties. However, the close-downs of spheres, such as educational facilities for those above the 7th grade, or the ban on gatherings, signal a reluctant willingness to act in a juridical-sovereign manner. While the initial Swedish ban on gatherings was lenient by international standards, at a limit of 500 people, it quickly dropped to 50, and when the ban was reduced to 8, it was comparable to those of the other Scandinavian countries, despite the state refusing to make this prohibition valid in private homes. While more permissive than the Norwegian state, other states such as Denmark also refrained from transgressing such state-private boundaries, refusing to impose the ban *legally* on gatherings in private homes (Regeringen, 2020).

6.1.1.3 Hobbesian Politics

It is easy to categorize Norway and Sweden as radically different due to the softness of the Swedish state, which explains the discourse on Swedish exceptionalism in the literature (i.e. Andersson & Aylott, 2020; Giritli Nygren & Olofsson, 2021; Jonung, 2020). However, scholars must beware of overstating these differences. Aversion towards state coercion and scepticism towards intervening into society in a formal manner limited the Swedish state's implementation of state coercion. This manifested in the two-tier system which made Sweden differ from the 'COVID consensus' (i.e. Green, 2021), which broke with the general totalizing strategies related to the lockdown, as in Norway. Nevertheless, a common biopolitical, Hobbesian understanding of the state's responsibilities manifested in shared objectives. While the Swedish state governed in a more liberal manner, its approach during the pandemic should be considered Crypto-Hobbesian, meaning that it had *hidden* Hobbesian tendencies, concealed by problematizations of coercive and top-down state governance, the heavy use of voluntarism, and the narrative of Swedish 'exceptionalism' within public and scientific discourse. While Norway was more clearly part of the 'global consensus' than Sweden, due to its use of lockdowns, the Norwegian state governed in a relatively moderate manner, as seen in the absence of curfews (Cheibub et al., 2020).

Both the Norwegian and Swedish states depended upon coercive, infrastructural and ideological sources of power, which were enacted in a complex manner, resulting in juridical-sovereign, disciplinary, exclusionary and self-regulatory mechanisms of power manifesting in complex and sometimes contradictory ways at the micro-level, with the Swedish state's strategy underpinned by the idea of security and thus regulating and mitigating, whereas the Norwegian strategy was centred more around the notion of suppressing the virus and thus of controlling the entirety of the social body. Moreover, the Norwegian state governed all of society in a coherent manner. It mixed different forms of governing at different sites. The Swedish state, on the other hand, created a two-tier approach, to implement according to different principles of governance. This made Sweden an interesting outlier, but we should beware of overstating the differences. The Swedish strategy revolved around a dual set of goals—related to both biopolitical and socio-political objectives—whereas the Norwegian state clearly prioritized the former (Christensen & Lægreid, 2020; Gjerde, 2022). The Norwegian and Swedish states' strategies both differ significantly, and have obvious similarities, as both states exercised power in a pyramidical manner to control their respective populations for the purposes of infection control. These differences do however warrant an explanation.

6.1.2 Hobbesian Norway

Biopolitical considerations making the administration of life a core state concern are central in Norway. Interestingly, a *liberal* understanding of how pandemics should be dealt with had been the political norm for decades prior to COVID-19. For instance, the 2014 'National readiness plan for pandemic influenza' prioritized solutions that did not violate personal freedom and rights, or the open market (FHI, 2014: 60). Thus, biopolitical objectives must be accomplished while being subordinated to liberal considerations, meaning that voluntarism is defined as necessary, and that state coercion shall be limited to a bare minimum. This is in line liberal governmentality replacing interventionist biopolitics, leading to liberal biopolitics as the norm (Rose, 2009). However, liberal considerations were subordinated to biopolitics within a few days after the situation was declared exceptional in mid-March 2020 (Gjerde, 2021a).

To explore the political reasoning underpinning the Norwegian state's approach to COVID-19, I separated the analysis into two parts. First, I examined how COVID-19 was problematized from a biopolitical standpoint. This meant probing how the problems were represented (Bacchi, 2009). To study this issue, I also analysed the logic underpinning problematizations, or in other words, mapping discursive regularities. Analysing state documents, a coherent biopolitical discourse can be identified. COVID-19 and its somatic capabilities were prioritized, and other issues (including those created by state intervention), were seen as sad necessities to mitigate within the infection control framework. Second, I investigated how these problematizations manifested in rationalization, which entailed rendering reality governable, considering (a) reflections on the utility of voluntary participation, in line with liberal governmentality, and (b) a principle of caution based on Hobbesian reasoning, which subordinates liberal governmentality to biopolitical interventionism, leading the state to find coercion to be necessary. Excerpts are provided, showing the logic of the discourse, and describing the intertextual chains between different texts that articulate meaning in a similar manner, as they are fixated by a common logic, framing the situation coherently. Note that the initial analysis prioritizing problematizations is more interpretive, as I explore the signs and how statements are regulated around a cogent, biopolitical logic, whereas the second analysis of rationalizations revolves around a more descriptive review of how reality is rendered governable, building on the initial analysis of problematizations.

6.1.2.1 *Biopolitical Crisis*

COVID-19 was problematized due to its pathological capacities and what these entailed for the individual and society. While initially dismissed as something citizens had to manage through self-regulation in late February and early March 2020 (Gjerde, 2021a), by March 5, the tune had changed. The government distributed an operational readiness document proclaiming that state coercion *may* be needed 'to handle a crisis created by a dangerous epidemic which may spread in the population and overload health- and care services' (Regjeringen, 2020b). On March 13, a day after the lockdown was implemented, and with the closing of the border now a reality, it was stated that the pandemic 'is of such a character that it may threaten public health' (Regjeringen, 2020c). In the words of the Prime Minister, 'we put life and health first', as this is a life-or-death situation where the state 'must…limit the [spread of] infections' (Regjeringen, 2020e; see also Regjeringen, 2020f).

Through this his biopolitical lens, the state construes its main objective as 'limiting contagion and deaths' from the coronavirus as well as other illnesses (Regjeringen, 2020g). Importantly, protecting life itself is portrayed as an end. As the Minister of Health and Care Services articulated in mid-March 2020, 'the values of the healthcare services stand firm in the coming period', as it was asserted that everybody should get equal treatment, and the healthcare system could not 'choose' whom to treat in the case of emergency (Regjeringen, 2020d). All life was defined as equally valuable, and all life had to be protected. This became the normative core of the Norwegian politics of COVID-19, based on an explicitly biopolitical discursive logic.

Directing our attention away from the specific assertions and towards the signs comprising them, we can observe the *logic* of these articulations, and how they belonged to a biopolitical crisis discourse. Articulations are not free-floating, but fixated by discursive logics which regulate the meaning of specific statements (Foucault, 1972; Laclau & Mouffe, 1985). In our case, these statements were framed in a biopolitical manner around the situation being a public health crisis where the core problem was in the pathological effects of COVID-19 upon public and individual health. This is seen in the key signs allocating meaning to the situation within these statements. Signs such as *life*, *protection*, *contagion*, *death* and *(public) health* serve as dominant signifiers, fixating the meaning of these statements around biopolitical concerns. In other words, these signs fixate texts and thus their meaning-making around COVID-19's virulence and the implications of this for individual and public health.

Looking intertextually at these texts, we see a shared discursive logic of a biopolitical nature. This manifested in biopolitical problematizations using the signs of life, death, health and infection to make the situation primarily about the problem of COVID-19 causing death, and the state's objective therefore became, first and foremost, to curb the risk COVID-19 posed to individual and public health, both directly by killing individuals and indirectly by (potentially) sabotaging the health-care system. Hence, we can observe a biopolitical *signifying chain,* where the same meaning was generated through different articulations referring to COVID-19 as a biopolitical threat.

This frames the issue of the pandemic as a public health problem, the core of biopolitics (Foucault, 2008; Rose, 2009). COVID-19 was represented as being especially dangerous to the 'vulnerable', a category that comprehended the elderly, those with serious diseases such as cancer, and various chronic diseases, i.e. those who were at increased risk from somatic complications if infected (Stortinget, 2020). The abstract sign 'vulnerable' pertained to 1/3 or 33% of the Norwegian population, and the state declared that it had to act to defend them (Regjeringen, 2020e, 2020f, 2020g).

This biopolitical discourse—pivoting on the notion that public health was under threat and had to be defended—defined the situation as a *crisis.* More specifically, the situation constituted 'a health crisis and national crisis which affects every single sector of society' (Regjeringen, 2020h; see also Regjeringen, 2020i, 2020j). Such articulations represented the biopolitical crisis as a more general emergency affecting all of society. The situation was depicted as being so extraordinary that the state had to impose 'the strictest.... measures ever implemented [in Norway] during peace time' (Regjeringen, 2020l). Using definitions such as the most dangerous 'peace time' situation Norway had experienced, ministers, including the Prime Minister, described the situation as the severest since WW2 (Regjeringen, 2020a, 2020k). Equating the circumstances with the greatest crisis most Norwegians can imagine goes to show just how serious it was considered to be. This defines the crisis as an unprecedented life-and-death situation.

COVID-19 was portrayed as perilous along various lines. It was not only a biological danger to the individual—the situation was also problematized according to its potential to undermine 'critical societal functions'. The authorities spent much time discussing how these functions had to be protected (Regjeringen, 2020e, 2020i). The Prime Minister, together with the Minister of Health and Care Services, as well as the Minister of Finance, made this point clear. As they wrote:

> We must avoid too many becoming ill simultaneously. So that societal critical functions will not be risked. To ensure that we have the capacity to save those in need of life-saving treatment (Regjeringen, 2020e)

This explicitly answers the question 'what's the problem represented to be?' (Bacchi, 2009). The problem was a combination of (a) biological lives being directly threatened by COVID-19's pathological capacities, and (b) wide-scale contagion with COVID-19 causing individual harm which could damage societal critical functions. COVID-19 was not only harmful for individual and public health, but for society at large. The sign '*critical functions*' revolved around numerous concerns considered necessary for society to work, and comprehended healthcare, law and order, energy, food and other essential logistics (Regjeringen, 2020e). The references to COVID-19 threatening to undermine those 'critical functions' which society depends upon to operate *implied* that the society was at risk of collapsing if the state failed to get COVID-19 under control. The situation was not merely abnormal, but exceptional to an unprecedented degree, thereby demanding action. Of these critical functions, healthcare services are especially discussed frequently. The state articulated fears that COVID-19 could bring the healthcare system to a halt, with unknown consequences for patients (Regjeringen, 2020k; see also Regjeringen, 2020c). The possibility of this occurring was made explicit with comparisons to other countries. The state referred to 'terrible images [of a situation where] healthcare capacity was long gone. Norway must not reach this point', (alluding to Spain and Italy) (Regjeringen, 2020e, 2020l). By threatening individuals' health, the virus threatened public health and the healthcare system. Jeopardizing the healthcare services and the lives of the many vulnerable, the pandemic assumed the proportions of a macro-problem, based on an explicitly biopolitical reasoning.

These texts were intertextually connected by their common view of the situation as exceptional, on account of COVID-19's somatic capacities and how these would impact society in the absence of state intervention. The Norwegian state's articulations were regulated by a coherent biopolitical logic, pivoting on the virological capacities of COVID-19, which were construed as a more general societal problem. The key signs comprehended biopolitical signs related to *life and death*, *public and individual health*. These signs fixated meaning around biopolitical themes, manifesting in biopolitical problematizations. The state's discourse triggered an unprecedented crisis by coupling micro-level signs, such as *individual health*, *death and life*, with macro-level signs, such as *societally critical functions*, *public health*, *healthcare collapse*, not to mention comparisons with WW2. Infection control began to be the focal point of all discussion, whereas other concerns, such as law, economy or mental health, were relatively subordinated to this issue (cf. Christensen & Lægreid 2020; Graver, 2020b).

In essence the state problematized how the micro-effects of COVID-19 would create macro-effects, leaning upon a coherent biopolitical discourse. The situation became increasingly dire and urgent. Surely, the state could not remain passive and inert after comparing the situation to WW2 or warning about the risk of societal collapse and mass mortality.

6.1.2.2 Biopolitical raison d'être

On the grounds of the aforementioned biopolitical problematizations, the objective of the Norwegian state became, in the words of the Minister of Justice and Security Mæland, 'to limit contagion [and] deaths, both for those infected with COVID-19 and those with other life-threatening illnesses or injuries' (Regjeringen, 2020g). Mæland summarizes this objective as: 'the authorities... always have a responsibility to protect the population' (Regjeringen, 2020n). This hints at a biopolitical *raison d'être*—protecting life was represented as the core mission of the Norwegian state—in line with Hobbesian mentalities (cf. Hobbes, 1996; Schmitt, 2008).

These security objectives, while having priority, were combined with liberal rationalizations. In the words of Mæland, in the same speech: 'it is the sum of everybody's contribution which has allowed Norway to thus far do better than basically all countries we may compare ourselves with', and 'this is behaviour most of us now live by voluntarily' (Regjeringen, 2020n). Such a statement referred to the utility of individuals' participation as subjects rather than objects of government. The Norwegian state rationalized much of its governance in a liberal manner, thus imparting a liberal flavour to its biopolitics (cf. Gjerde, 2021b; Sandset & Villadsen, 2023). This is the case despite security having primacy over liberal concerns, and even with the suspension of liberalism as a governmentality, as discussed in Chapter 5.

Let us now explore how the entirety of the population became both object and subject of governance, to understand the very mobilization of society, in its formal and moral forms. As the state declared, 'all must participate in a infection control dugnad', to limit the spread of COVID-19 (Regjeringen, 2020o, 2020p). All had to participate because 'the only way to avoid COVID-19 spreading is by reducing contact with other people to the bare minimum' (Regjeringen, 2020q). Such articulations were common, as the state declared that every person had to participate in preventing the spread of COVID-19. Since COVID-19 was spread through interaction and contact, so social situations were rendered governable as objects of infection control. Such statements transformed the social lives of citizens into biopolitical affairs of the state. The collective aspect of this is clear, as the population had to, and did, solve the crisis 'together' (Regjeringen, 2020o), and 'voluntarily' (Regjeringen, 2020n). This was not merely a rhetorical strategy imposing communitarian responsibility, but also a political rationalization. These articulations rendered the private individual governable as a infection control agent, who was constrained to join the dugnad against COVID-19. This was partly liberal governmentalization. The state considered the contributions of individuals a core aspect of its strategy. This had to occur through the dugnad which by default is formally voluntary, even if morally obligatory. The autonomy of the individual was to be channelled against the virus, making voluntarism central. From such a position, the document 'Long-term strategy for handling the COVID-19 pandemic' from 2020 discloses how voluntarism was interpreted vis-à-vis formal measures:

> prescriptions and proscriptions are preferred when measures must have quick effects or high compliance... but recommendations and voluntarism should be tried before proscriptions, coercion and punishment are utilized. (Regjeringen, 2020r)

Voluntarism and formal measures, which included prescriptions of proscriptions related to close-downs as well as demands to restructure social spaces to ensure infection control, were discussed in a manner that granted the former *ethical* primacy, while the latter was granted *practical* primacy as a more efficient form of governance (see also Regjeringen, 2020e, 2020s).

Furthermore, while emphasizing voluntarism, the state nevertheless depended heavily on coercion. How did coercion become necessary? The state saw the situation as demanding *pre-emptive action*: 'the Directorate of Health decided to close down the schools to be on the safe side' (Regjeringen, 2020s). One of the most controversial measures in the Norwegian lockdown—it was not repeated in the later lockdowns—was justified through the idea that acting too much was better than acting too little, in open contradiction of the liberal governmentality positing that states should search for a balance between the two (i.e. Foucault, 2008; Rose, 1999). This related to problematizations of the rapidity with which the situation changed. On numerous occasions, the situation was represented as fluid, as changing from not just day to day, but from hour to hour (Regjeringen, 2020t). Due to the perceived ambiguity of this quickly changing and exceptional situation, a corona law was represented as necessary to ensure that the government could go beyond normal laws without deliberation in parliament, when necessary (Regjeringen, 2020u). Restrictions, also of a pre-emptive nature, became necessary, as 'an uncontrolled pandemic will leave hundreds of thousands ill, tens of thousands hospitalized, and many will die too early' (Regjeringen, 2020v). Such articulations were based on a principle of caution (cf. Askim & Christensen, 2022). This idea functioned as a governing principle in Norway, explaining why the Norwegian state acted with severity in the face of uncertainty (cf. Regjeringen, 2020e). The principle of caution is a Hobbesian form of rationalization, prioritizing security to render reality governable in a proactive rather than reactive manner. Thus, the state could not depend upon voluntarism, as it had to act too strongly as opposed to too softly, too swiftly rather than too slowly.

As the entirety of society had already been rendered governable, and as coercion had been represented as more efficient than voluntarism, so the state had to act pre-emptively within various social contexts to ensure the safety of the population, on the grounds of its biopolitical objectives. While the state, in a liberal manner, posited that coercion should be limited as far as possible, and that voluntarism had to be tried first, if possible, the reality is that the principle of caution made it problematic to experiment with voluntarism. The situation was simply so dangerous and abnormal that state coercion came to be necessary. The Prime Minister, in a joint statement with the Minister of Health and the Minister of Finance, wrote:

> Intervening in people's everyday lives in such a manner is an experience we wish we could do without. We do this because we must. We must limit contagion as much as possible. (Regjeringen, 2020e; see also Regjeringen, 2020u)

Hence, the gravity of the situation and the dangers that this comprised could *only* be handled with severity. The state did not want to but had to act decisively, even if this entailed colonizing private contexts previously considered non-state spaces and using state coercion. The state was forced to use its macrophysical powers to impose restrictions and protect society from COVID-19, because the situation was so extraordinary that normal politics simply was unable to solve the crisis. Hence the state was guided by an explicitly stated principle of caution, as perceived through the Hobbesian lens regarding the state's responsibility to protect lives, and pursuing Schmittian considerations regarding the necessity of suspending everyday life due to the exceptionality of the situation.

While this manifests in Hobbesian, biopolitical considerations clearly having primacy, the state nevertheless perceived limits to the necessity of coercion. The Norwegian government and the Directorate of Health contemplated altering the legal framework in early 2021, so as to juridically enabled the implementation of curfews (Regjeringen, 2021c). However, Parliament, the Institute of Public Health and others participating in the process opposed such a political move. They labelled such juridical changes extreme, a breach of human rights, inefficient and problematic for numerous other reasons (Regjeringen, 2021d). The Norwegian minority government found itself isolated as its right-wing partner and the left-wing opposition united against it, making such legal alterations impossible. Attempts to tighten the state's grip were delegitimized and dismissed by the state itself. The Norwegian state remained committed to liberal ideals and indeed the liberal governmentality predominating before the lockdown throughout the pandemic, partially in regard to voluntarism, and fully in regard to the idea that state interventions in society should be limited if possible (Sandset & Villadsen, 2023). The principle of pre-emptive action and the primacy of Hobbesian considerations nevertheless implicated the subordination of liberal governmentality to the necessity of decisive action.

Foucauldians ask how liberal governmentality can give way to authoritarian measures, and ponder the relationship between liberal and authoritarian methods of rule (Dean, 2007; Opitz, 2011). In Norway, the relationship can be seen as follows: liberal governmentality invites the state to place limits upon itself and use indirect methods of government, if possible, while Hobbesian considerations are superordinate to liberal ones, meaning that liberal governmentality can be suspended if a great crisis, such as the pandemic, calls for it. Thus, basing our reflections on Schmitt's writings (1996, 2014) pertaining to sovereignty and exceptions, liberal governmentality can be defined as a *contemporary government of the normal situation*, a governmentality likely to be suspended either *partially or fully*, should the perceived security of the state or population demand it. While partially suspended, liberal governmentality remained relevant throughout the pandemic in Norway, as seen in both the use of voluntarism and the relative aversion to state coercion, which among other things thwarted the implementation of the curfew. Nevertheless, the rationalizations in hand abolish all boundaries separating state from society, rendering all of society an object to administer, with any means *necessary*, thereby demoting liberal governmentality to a supporting role.

6.1.3 Crypto-Hobbesian Sweden

The Swedish strategy was comparatively mild, as the Swedish state refrained from closing down society, and was thus conspicuous as an outlier (i.e. Aucante, 2022; Pierre, 2020). The relative lack of coercion along numerous axes must be explained—why did the Swedish state refrain from closing down? And equally importantly, why did the Swedish state use coercion to a more limited extent? Why did the Swedish state opt for a two-tier system? The two-tier system was based on contradictory problematizations and rationalizations, indeed on contradictory ends. Harsh measures were both called for *and* discredited. Precisely in the way that the US state's foreign policy is 'schizophrenic' as it embraces American exceptionalism and unilateralism while subscribing to multilateralism and universalism (Mann 2005), so the Swedish state was schizophrenic as it embraced both Hobbesian and anti-Hobbesian thought *and* politics with regard to COVID-19. This 'political schizophrenia' does not imply irrationality, but rather the existence of contradictory logics operating side-by-side within the state.

To explore this, I shall separate the analysis into two parts, first examining how the situation becomes problematic, including the discursive logic underpinning and fixating statements around the creation of problems. Through investigation of state documents, two contradictory discourses become apparent, manifesting in contradictory problematizations and thereby also rationalizations. From this study it emerges that the Swedish state both problematized the pathological potential of COVID-19, and then intervened to mitigate this potential. Hence a contradictory set of objectives comes to light, related to protecting two different sets of individuals categorized as vulnerable. While biopolitical problematizations retained primacy, there was overt antagonism with mutually exclusive discourses articulated by the state itself. Second, after exploring this issue by analysing the signs of the discourses and how they are regulated by specific logics fixating meaning, I shall proceed with the issue of rationalizations. As in the Norwegian case, I prioritize a descriptive study where the objective is to show how different modes of reasoning rendered reality governable in mutually exclusive ways, based upon the two discourses and their contradictory meaning-making. I identified two types of rationalization—one biopolitical and one liberal—with roots in different discourses. As in the Norwegian case, the initial discourse analysis is more interpretive, whereas the second part moves beyond the issue of interpretation so as to describe how reality is rendered governable, in line with governmentality scholars' recommendations (cf. Rose, 1999).

6.1.3.1 *Biopolitical Versus Liberal Problems*

The Swedish state governed in a comparably liberal manner during the pandemic, but it nevertheless imposed numerous proscriptions and prescriptions upon the population. To understand why the Swedish state acted as it did, we must look at the problems the state identifies, thereby allowing us to explore the discourse regulating these statements' meaning-making and the logic of the Swedish response. The Swedish state's main objective is construed as reducing the spread of COVID-19 and controlling the virus. However, while COVID-19 is problematized through a biopolitical discourse, the state interventions characterizing the politics of COVID-19 are problematized, too. Thus, biopolitical considerations are both made and contested.

My starting point is the biopolitical discourse of the Swedish state which resembles that of the Norwegian state. In February 2020, the state declared that it 'classifies the coronavirus as an illness that is dangerous to society', thereby making COVID-19 a public health threat (Krisinformation, 2020a, 2020b). Similarly, the state justified the legal alterations made in the spring of 2020, which entailed comparatively mild and nevertheless severe interventions in society, by referring to 'the urgent nature that normally characterizes a crisis' (Government, 2020a). This is a biopolitical framing, fixated around clinical and somatic signs. Therefore, when justifying restrictions on cafeterias, bars and similar facilities, the state declared that 'COVID-19 is a serious disease which in the worst cases will lead to death' (Government, 2020b). In the Prime Minister's words during November 2020, as the Swedish state tightened restrictions: 'people's health and lives are still at risk. And the danger is increasing. More and more people are being infected' (The Local, 2020a). COVID-19 is defined as an 'unprecedented threat' (Government, 2020c), demanding 'unprecedented measures' (The Local, 2020b).

Thus, COVID-19 was portrayed as an 'unprecedented' biological danger demanding 'unprecedented measures'. Biopolitical considerations related to the issue of life and death were central. As the Prime Minister expressed in his address to the nation in mid-March 2020:

> The COVID-19 virus is testing our country, our society and all of us as fellow human beings. Every person now needs to mentally prepare for what is coming. In Sweden, the COVID-19 virus is now spreading in the community. Lives, health and jobs are at risk. More people will get the disease, more people will have to say a final farewell to a loved one. (Embassy of Sweden, 2020a)

As we can see, like in Norway, these statements are fixated in a biopolitical manner. This is evident in the signs used to allocate meaning to the situation. The situation is represented as a crisis, through biopolitical signs, such as '*lives*', '*health*', '*death*', '*danger*', '*(public health) threat*' and '*unprecedented*'. These signs produce meaning by painting a biopolitical picture of the situation as extraordinary and dangerous, due to the virulence of COVID-19 and what it could mean for (public) health. Here a general logic is disclosed, related to the Swedish state's vision being fixated around a common idea that the situation is primarily about the dangers that COVID-19 as a virus can bring to both individual and public health. This creates a signifying chain, fixated by a biopolitical logic, which underpins how the Swedish state represented COVID-19 and its impact upon society, revealing an intertextual link between these different statements.

However, in the same way that the Swedish state cannot act upon fear as the Norwegian state did—otherwise the relatively soft measures would be discredited by the state itself—so the crisis discourse is softer. The discourse can perhaps be labelled more 'informative' (see Almlund et al., 2023). In relation to the crisis discourse being more muted, biopolitical problematizations are often supplemented with non-biopolitical considerations, as in the aforementioned speech where threatened jobs were problematized alongside biopolitical issues. After all, 'the COVID-19 pandemic is a serious threat to people's lives and health. Serious economic consequences will follow in its wake' (Embassy of Sweden, 2020b).

Biopolitical concerns are raised, along with other problematizations, such as economic ones. The issue of the economy is frequently raised in Swedish texts, and the Swedish debate in general (Giritli Nygren & Olofsson, 2021). While the economy and various social concerns are relevant in all countries, such non-biopolitical problematizations challenged the primacy of biopolitics in Sweden, unlike in other countries, such as Norway, where the biopolitics of COVID-19 remained uncontested.

This means that multiple discourses operated within the Swedish state, in contrast with Norway, where a biopolitical discourse on infection control was of prime importance. Discursive regularities come to light, fixating meaning around alternative issues, unrelated to the somatic and medical aspects of COVID-19 as a virological threat. This is best illustrated by looking at the concept of 'vulnerable' in Sweden. The sign 'vulnerable' contains the clinically vulnerable, as in Norway. This includes the elderly and those with chronic or serious diseases, as they are under threat from the pandemic (Embassy of Sweden, 2020a; Government, 2020c). This made the vulnerable a biopolitical category, comprising individuals threatened by the pathogen, who required protection. This version of the 'vulnerable' was created and underpinned by the aforementioned biopolitical regularities: being vulnerable was determined by vulnerability to the potentially life-threatening capacities of COVID-19.

However, the category 'vulnerable' was *two*-dimensional in Sweden, compared with the single dimension discerned in Norway. The Swedish state supplemented the clinically vulnerable with groups represented as *socially* vulnerable. For instance, children, (young) women, those with disabilities and LGBTI people were represented as (socially) 'vulnerable':

> The coronavirus crisis threatens to exacerbate the vulnerability of children and young people at risk in their home environment. The same applies to victims of domestic violence and 'honour'-based violence and oppression, including women, children, young women, older people, LGBTI people and people with disabilities. Greater isolation can increase the incidence of violence and control. Those who are vulnerable might also find it more difficult to receive information and seek support. (Nordic Africa News, 2020)

Thus, the Swedish state problematizes the social impact of state coercion and measures which facilitate isolation. Quarantine and isolation, lockdowns and curfews turned into problems due to their perceived impact upon the socially vulnerable. Such socio-political problematizations are rooted in a typical liberal critique of state interventions and their dangers (see Foucault, 2008; Miller & Rose, 2008). The state similarly problematized that 'the virus outbreak can exacerbate the situation of people subjected to domestic violence or to honour-related violence and oppression' (Government, 2020d), thereby making isolation itself a problem, unlike in countries such as Norway, where isolation was a political instrument. Thus, by investing the sign '*vulnerable*' with meaning through a biopolitical *and* a socio-political discourse, the Swedish state operated with two mutually exclusive discourses. From the socio-political liberal discourse, the vulnerable became those perceived to be marginalized, those perceived to be at risk if society closed down. These individuals were at risk of being threatened by social practices—honour-related violence or 'generic' forms of domestic violence or social control—making political interventions facilitating their isolation problematic. This notion of 'socially vulnerable' enlarged the category 'vulnerable', turning it into a contradictory concept. Some were clinically vulnerable, threatened by the virus (and thus could implicitly need the state to enforce coercive measures), but others, i.e. the socially vulnerable, were threatened by such measures. The vulnerable as a category was thus created by two *contradictory* discursive logics.

State interventions were not only problematized due to their effects upon the socially vulnerable, but also due to their socio-economic and political impact. For instance, the Swedish government problematized how the economy and liberal democracy—i.e. the open society—would be damaged by state interventions. Sweden positions itself as a beacon of liberal democracy and liberal capitalism. In the words of the Minister for International Development Cooperation:

> The free world and open society, as we know it, has partly and temporarily been shut down for many citizens. Factories have had to close as global value chains have been severely interrupted. People have lost their jobs (Government, 2020e)

The *politics* of the pandemic was thus problematized as the contemporary free and open world shut down. In the same speech, it was proclaimed that 'a pandemic will not last for ever, but its effects will be felt for years to come. This is a time for reflection on what is fundamentally important to human life' (Government, 2020e). This challenges the primacy of biopolitics, asking whether closing down society is worth the high economic *and* socio-political costs, based on a liberal capitalist rationale. The government also feared a recession caused by the politics of the pandemic (Government, 2020f). These economic concerns were mixed with more general democratic problematizations, for instance:

> We are in the midst of a pandemic which has brought devastating human costs, new strains on open society, and disruption to economic activity around the world.... Democracy, respect for human rights and economic development have suffered during the pandemic, in Europe and elsewhere. (Government, 2021)

Thus, the state saw the pandemic as a multilayered crisis, in which COVID-19 led to numerous problems beyond the biopolitical issues of health and life itself. Problems related to democracy and human rights were perceived as political, not pathological, and one might argue that the economic troubles too were primarily the results of political choices. Thus, the Swedish state problematized measures against COVID-19 as potentially harming democracy and economic development—a problem the Swedish state identified in Europe as well as beyond. These problematizations were all underpinned by the liberal distrust and critique of state intervention—which posited that state interventions carry significant risks (see Foucault, 2008; Miller & Rose, 2008).

Looking beyond the specific statements, at the signs in use, a contradictory discursive logic appears, based on a different form of signs. Signs such as *open society*, *human rights*, *democracy* or *socially vulnerable* (LGBT people, young women, children, etc.) are connected because they are all understood to be threatened by the *politics* of COVID-19. This socio-political discourse is fixated by a *liberal* logic in which state interventions are perceived to be problematic, based on the liberal idea that one always risks governing 'too much' (Foucault, 2008; Rose, 1999). This meaning-making is fixated by a socio-political logic, shifting the focus from the dangers of COVID-19 to the dangers of state intervention, and thus from Hobbesian to liberal considerations, where interventions are found to produce problematic secondary effects, such as violence within the home as a result of isolation.

And so we come to 'what's the problem represented to be?' (Bacchi, 2009) In Sweden, this question was answered in two *contradictory* ways. On the one hand, the pathological properties of COVID-19 were frequently problematized, and coercion was effectively called for. The problem was biopolitical, relating to the issue of public health and COVID-19's pathological potential. On the other hand, state interventions were found to be the problem. The socio-political discourse, with liberal characteristics, challenged the Hobbesian and biopolitical problematizations of COVID-19 as a public health danger that had to be dealt with decisively. Problematizing state coercion due to its potential effects on vulnerable populations, the economy, democracy and civil rights meant delegitimizing attempts to stop COVID-19 with such measures. Therefore, the state had to protect society not just from COVID-19, but also from its own state interventions.

6.1.3.2 Two Styles of Rationalization

The identification of COVID-19 as a major threat to public health and the politics of COVID-19 as a principal socio-political problem make the situation complex and contradictory. From one angle, the Swedish state, like the Norwegian state, embraced a biopolitical, Hobbesian *raison d'être.* The state had to protect biological lives and public health, due to security objectives at least partially grounded in the protection-obedience axiom (Hobbes, 1996; Schmitt, 2008). Many statements problematized the potentiality of COVID-19 and emphasized the importance of protecting life. The Swedish state defined itself in a Hobbesian manner by granting security and life primacy. This is why the state governed beyond its normal liberal boundaries in the first place. Something about the situation was 'unprecedented'. However, there was no principle of caution, as also demonstrated by the relatively slow implementation of measures vis-à-vis comparable cases.

Like in Norway, every person was rendered governable as a subject of government, through voluntarism. In the words of the Prime Minister, 'we all have a great personal responsibility', and '[y]oung, old, rich, poor – it doesn't matter, everyone must play their part'. This did not merely make compliance an obligation. Such statements *defined* every single Swede as a participant in a political campaign to prevent the spread of COVID-19, rendering them objects *and* subjects of governance (Swedish Embassy 2020a; see also Folkhälsomyndigheten, 2020a). The entirety of society had to play a role, as in Norway, because distancing and therefore the regulation of social interaction had become an object of governance. Thus, the state called for collective action (The Government, 2020g; Local, 2020a, 2020b). This is justified historically, as Swedish infection control measures 'are built on a strong tradition of voluntarism placing emphasis on individual responsibility' (Foretagshalsor, 2020), where 'the responsibility for reducing the spread of infection primarily falls upon the individual' (Krisinformation, 2020c). These statements are liberal governmentalizations, where every individual is rendered governable as an autonomous, responsible subject willing and capable to act in accordance with ethical and rational obligations related to infection control. This makes responsibilization a key objective of the state, manifesting in communication campaigns that emphasize personal responsibility and communitarian ethics.

However, this is only part of the picture, as shown by the Swedish state clearly moving beyond voluntarism. Why was voluntarism defined as insufficient? Justifying the 'very intrusive measures with no parallel in modern times', such as the tightened ban on gatherings, the state declared 'we don't take it lightly to limit people's rights… but we see it as necessary' (The Local, 2020b). State coercion was defined as *necessary*. Physical distancing had to be imposed, even enforced, as the infection rates and the situation in the healthcare services made restrictions *necessary* (Folkhälsomyndigheten, 2021). This makes sense as the Swedish state posited the vulnerable as in need of protection—something especially urgent in the healthcare facilities where many of those particularly vulnerable were located. In the context of the healthcare sector, the Swedish state could even be said, as mentioned, to have been stricter than the Norwegian state. However, other restrictions had to be imposed besides the healthcare facilities accommodating the vulnerable. For instance, restrictions within gyms, malls and similar establishments were found to be necessary, as this 'facilitates distancing among people' (Folkhälsomyndigheten 2021a). Moreover, as the Public Health Agency document recommending alterations and a tightening on the ban on gatherings make clear:

> situations where many people gather [such as concerts] have shown to cause widespread contagion… the ban [on gatherings] is [a] far-reaching restriction of the Constitution's right to gather and protest, but it has been and remains effective for reducing the spread of COVID-19. (Folkhälsomyndigheten, 2020b)

This reasoning rendered the situation governable in a manner similar to that observed in Norway. Coercion was represented as necessary because of the severity of the situation: the efficacy of a coercive approach delineating restrictions to facilitate distancing and reduce gatherings has been amply corroborated. Moreover, as the Minister for Health and Social Affairs noted during November 2020, when measures were to be tightened:

> Over recent weeks, the recommendations have been sharpened and strong measures have been taken. Despite this, behaviour has not yet changed enough to turn the direction of the development. The curves are still going in the wrong direction. (The Local, 2020b)

This is an explicit problematization of voluntarism, which describes liberal governmentality and moderate restrictions as insufficient, thereby making state interventions necessary.

These arguments effectively suspended voluntarism as a guiding principle of government, inviting the state to intervene in society. Importantly, the failure of a mode of government opens 'opportunities for the formulation of another' (Miller & Rose, 2008: 17). Therefore, due to the perceived limitations of liberal governmentality during an 'unprecedented' crisis, the state called for transcending voluntarism, declaring that 'we are always prepared to implement stricter measures if necessary', because 'our measures aim to save lives and slow down the outbreak' (Government, 2020g). Indeed, 'the overarching goal is to safeguard people's lives and health and secure the healthcare capacity' (Government, 2020h). To achieve this 'overarching goal', the state had to 'slow down the outbreak' (Government, 2020i). The state hence granted primacy to the biopolitics of COVID-19, meaning that, in the absence of sufficient effective results through voluntarism, the state had to act with increased severity. This rationalized the need for state intervention, especially as voluntarism was identified as lacklustre. From such a position, the Prime Minister stated that the government:

> will take every decision that is necessary to protect the lives, health and jobs of as many people as we possibly can… the aim of the Government's work is to limit the spread of infection, to prevent too many people becoming seriously ill at the same time. But also to secure health care resources…. (Embassy of Sweden, 2020a)

These and similar statements *explicitly* granted biopolitics primacy over socio-political objectives, subordinating liberalism to a Hobbesian governmentality, where the state declared itself willing to 'take every decision' necessary. The Swedish state may have sought to limit its interventions in society, but such articulations nonetheless compelled the state to act. The aforementioned statements show how only coercion can fulfil the Hobbesian and biopolitical objectives of protecting (public) health and society. As in Norway, Hobbesian considerations ended up having primacy over liberal ones. However, unlike in Norway, there was no principle of caution, meaning that voluntarism was tried prior to the use of state coercion, especially as the Swedish state challenged the necessity of state intervention, while also calling for it. When voluntarism seemingly failed, the state was driven to increase the severity of restrictions.

State coercion was thereby called for. Yet, the Swedish state acted relatively moderately, despite these explicit calls for state intervention. Whereas liberal governmentality in Norway was subordinated to a principle of caution, such a principle was lacking in Sweden, with the Swedish state explicitly problematizing the utility of the coercion it simultaneously called for. For instance, the Public Health Agency reported at the time that voluntarism was 'more useful, as through coercion one risks imposing fear[, stopping people] from seeking protection [from healthcare services]', despite there being 'legal possibilities' for coercive measures (Krisinformation, 2020b). Enforcing quarantine or isolation, punitive techniques of governance which could be interpreted as sanctions, were problematized as potentially stopping individuals from voluntarily seeking out healthcare services. This is a typical liberal critique of state intervention, problematizing its adverse secondary effects, rendering reality governable through voluntaristic rather than compulsory methods (cf. Rose, 1999). The (potentially) dangerous are thereby only rendered governable in a voluntaristic manner, dismissing the formal use of isolation and quarantine. Moreover, lockdowns were amply criticized and various other coercive measures were described as lacking in scientific foundation, and were frequently the object of serious debate (Boden, 2020).

The state rationalizes in a liberal manner, making coercion problematic, counterproductive and potentially harmful for the infection control regime. This renders reality governable in a liberal manner, through voluntarism, according to the idea that 'strong legal measures are not the only way of achieving behavioural change', because 'people mostly follow recommendations' (Government, 2020i). However, while liberal governmentality remained imperative in Sweden throughout the pandemic (Larsson, 2022; Nygren & Olofsson, 2020), it was weakened by the increasingly rigorous position taken by the state, and by the dismissal of voluntarism as a guiding principle, especially during November 2020 (The Local, 2020b).

Whereas the rationalization of coercion has Hobbesian characteristics, this series of rationalizations can be seen as liberal biopolitics with anti-Hobbesian characteristics. These statements define voluntarism as pragmatically superior, in line with liberal governmentality, a reasoning which correlates with the aforementioned ethical problematizations of state coercion, dismissing the state's right to intervene in the private sphere, even for the sake of protecting lives. The state asserts that it is both pragmatically useless and, as covered earlier, socio-politically costly. Yet, such dismissals were articulated within a context where the state also posited coercion to be necessary, and within a context where the state declared the situation to be exceptionally dangerous to individual and public health. A biopolitical, Hobbesian rationalization demanding state coercion competed for primacy with a liberal governmentality dismissing state coercion and requesting that the state should restrain itself, reducing the severity of the restrictions and the strength with which it reached out towards the social body.

Hobbesian biopolitics eventually did obtain primacy, as shown practically by the state acting in an 'unprecedented' manner, and by the state defining the protection of (public) health as the 'overarching goal'. However, the Swedish state never discarded its two-tier strategy, as several parts of society remained formally beyond state intervention throughout the pandemic. The two-tier system was the political manifestation of the contradictions between different discourses, and the different problematizations and rationalizations grounded in these discourses. The state's strategy revolved around a two-sided objective, to (a) protect the clinically vulnerable and society at large from COVID-19, and (b) safeguard the socially vulnerable and society from state coercion and its effects by reducing state interventions in society. This compelled the state to act with severity at specific local sites, like nursing homes, as well as towards public spaces, such as offices or bars, while refraining from imposing measures defined as dangerous to the socially vulnerable in a more universal, general manner. These processes of governmentalization were what characterized the two-tier system, which was the result of these contradictory and antagonistic forms of political reasoning.

The two-tier system reveals how liberal governmentality can be supplemented by non-liberal governmentalities. While some discuss the authoritarian potential of liberal governmentality (i.e. Dean, 2007; Opitz, 2011), the two-tier system shows a different and potentially more useful approach to this question. Liberal governmentality cannot 'become' authoritarian per se, as it is based on a critique of state interventions which essentially make it anti-authoritarian. However, liberal governmentality can be suspended or replaced, partially or fully. While liberal governmentality operated in a subordinate position in Norway, to the extent that we can speak about its suspension and thus the suspension of civil society as a sphere beyond formal government, it nonetheless remained active in Sweden throughout the pandemic. This produced anti-interventionist sentiments that manifested in the state respecting the private sphere, never suspending public–private or state-non-state distinctions to the extent seen in Norway. Instead of liberal governmentality 'turning authoritarian' (i.e. Dean, 2007; Opitz, 2011), liberal governmentality can be more or less replaced and supplemented by alternative reasonings. This occurs through contestation and negotiation, as seen in Sweden, where internal contestation arose within the state. We can see this in Norway too, for instance in the case of the Directorate of Health and the Government being denied the legal right to impose curfews by Parliament and the Institute of Public Health. Liberal governmentality does not turn coercive and authoritarian, but it exists in a complex relationship with other political reasonings. Thus, even the extraordinary measures seen during the pandemic do not prove any 'unlimited' potential within liberalism (cf. Opitz, 2011). In Sweden, rather than 'un-limiting' the state, liberal governmentality limited the state quantitatively and qualitatively, reducing the use of coercion while creating a private sphere beyond state intervention for the duration of the pandemic. Liberal democracies can act in numerous interventionist ways, but this is likely to occur through non-liberal governmentalities suspending liberal governmentality, as during the pandemic.

6.1.4 Hobbesian and Crypto-Hobbesian Governmentalization

Having explored the Hobbesian biopolitics of the Norwegian state, with its coherent problematizations and rationalizations rooted in a coherent discourse, as well as the Crypto-Hobbesian position of the Swedish state, with its contradictory problematizations and rationalizations rooted in biopolitical and liberal discourses, I now move on to these discursive continuities and discontinuities, including the relationship between these discourses.

A clear correlation can be seen between the Norwegian and Swedish states' actions and their reasoning. Based on this correlation, we can make inferences on the causal roles of reasons, which structure the possible room for action (cf. Fairclough, 2010). The Swedish state's contradictory problematizations and rationalizations created conditions within which a two-tier system became a logical possibility, as the state both called for and discredited state interventions. Imposing severe action at certain sites, primarily where the clinically vulnerable were concentrated, such as hospitals and nursing homes, and more moderately in general, as the socially vulnerable are and were disseminated throughout society, makes perfect sense from a perspective where clinically and socially vulnerable individuals must be protected from COVID-19 *and* the politics of COVID-19, respectively. A contradictory discourse, constituting contradictory objectives related to protecting radically different groups threatened by the solutions of each other, invites the state to act contradictorily. The Norwegian state, reasoning in a more coherent biopolitical manner, acted in a manner that was compatible with this reasoning. Norwegian biopolitics faced restraints due to liberal considerations, but the primacy of a Hobbesian form of biopolitics ensured that no contradictions emerged. Thereafter, these processes of governmentalization manifested politically in statification as the two states expanded into new spheres, and in the Swedish case, by the state allowing various spheres to remain free of formal political control.

6.1.4.1 Agreement and Conflict

While the two states represent the situation differently, and acted in different, albeit related, ways, intertextual links between these different entities can be found. This intertextual link manifests in the construing of COVID-19 as a great public health threat. COVID-19 was defined as an object of danger from which society had to be protected. Signs related to *(public) health, life, death, infection, contagion, danger, healthcare services, the vulnerable* were fixated by a biopolitical logic (i.e. Government, 2020a, 2020b, 2020c; Regjeringen, 2020b, 2020c, 2020d). The reasonings of the two states were regulated by a shared biopolitical logic. At the micro-level, the vulnerable individual was threatened. At the macro-level, society was. From this biopolitical Hobbesian perspective, the state had to intervene in society to protect society itself.

Notwithstanding the intertextual chain linking the Norwegian and Swedish state's visions to one another, fundamental differences still persist. As addressed above, the Swedish state's biopolitical assertions were more muted, while the levels of abnormality and exceptionality articulated through discourse were moderate and partial. The Norwegian crisis was a great crisis of extraordinary proportions, legitimizing *almost* any kind of political measures. However, these differences are quantitative, not qualitative. They do not constitute a major discursive rupture. After all, the situation pivots on the pathological hazards that COVID-19 brought forth, and what this entailed and still could entail for society and the individual.

The main rupture between the two states' discourses relates to the Swedish state's socio-political problematizations, rooted in a liberal discourse, fixated around explicit criticism of state interventions (i.e. Government, 2020e, 2020f, 2021). This led the Swedish state to operate in a contradictory way, as the state had to, but could not, act coercively. The contradictions of the Swedish discourse are not merely an internal affair. They also mean that the Swedish state stands antagonistically and contradictorily vis-à-vis the 'global norm'. Discourses do not exist in a vacuum, but in discursive and political contexts where their very existence contradicts and struggles against other discourses and other political positions (Laclau & Mouffe, 1985). Naturally, the politics of COVID-19 is a central issue for the contestation of truth—where discourses are used as means in the struggle to determine what strategies political actors can and cannot legitimately impose (cf. Gjerde, 2023). This partly explains why the Swedish approach is so controversial. By problematizing coercion, and partly contradicting the 'COVID consensus', the Swedish state *delegitimized* the lockdown approach. Even when not openly targeting other states, the Swedish discourse on the dangers of state intervention by default problematized state coercion. The Swedish critique of state interventions was manifestly antagonistic towards its biopolitical discourse, but even more so towards those of other states (cf. Hagström et al., 2023; Idevall Hagren & Bellander, 2023). This is fundamentally at the core of the internationally controversial nature of the Swedish approach. The

Swedish politics and the discourses underpinning it contradict the interventionist policies and suspensions of democratic and liberal rights of various kinds.

Naturally, no conflict is one-sided. The discursive rupture is more complex than overt problematizations. The Norwegian state's biopolitical discourse and definition of the situation as so abnormal as to warrant lockdowns, and even the temporary suspension of civil society as a site beyond formal state interventions, constitutes a rupture with the Swedish state as a consequence of this socio-political discourse. The Swedish state explicitly delegitimized lockdowns and other equally severe measures, while the Norwegian biopolitical discourse implicitly delegitimized softer approaches, such as that of neighbouring Sweden. The situation was after all defined to be so abnormal that it demanded the most severe restrictions (i.e. Regjeringen, 2020g, 2020n). Any failure to apply coercion to save society became by default morally dubious. Indeed, most states, and even the WHO, implicitly problematized Sweden by calling for severe measures. The politics of COVID-19 became a discursive object of contestation, based on the antagonism created by mutually exclusive definitions of the situation. These states' problematizations and rationalizations are thus part of a greater struggle about the truth of the politics of the pandemic, as well as the post-pandemic world, which includes the legitimacy of different political measures. This is the case even without Swedish and Norwegian or other political actors mentioning one another—their discourses exist in a common discursive field in which their two definitions of the pandemic cannot simultaneously be true.

6.1.4.2 Hobbesian Primacy

The primacy of biopolitical and Hobbesian considerations, a reality in both countries, reduces the scope of the ruptures in hand. The primacy of biopolitics is stronger in Norway, as there are no counter-discourses articulated within the state itself. Liberal governmentality can be identified as existing within the Norwegian state during COVID-19, but it was subordinated to a principle of caution. While liberal governmentality remained more active in Sweden, Hobbesian biopolitics held primacy there, too. This explains why state coercion was implemented despite the Swedish state's explicit problematization of coercion. Socio-political problematizations from a liberal position weakened, but could not displace, the primacy of biopolitics. The Swedish state became Crypto-Hobbesian. Its Hobbesian tendencies can be seen in governmental actions and reasoning, but these tendencies are concealed by problematizations of state coercion, as well as the Swedish state's attempt to avoid coercion. The two-tier system, in combination with the state's discourse, clouds the Hobbesian tendencies, concealed as they are behind liberal practices and articulations.

While the Swedish state problematized and challenged state interventions (i.e. Government, 2020e, 2020f, 2021), the Norwegian state also *wished* that it could refrain from acting in such a manner (Regjeringen, 2020e), explaining why it restrained itself. However, whereas the Swedish state reduced both the severity of interventions and the number of social sites where it could intervene, the Norwegian state only reduced its severity in certain cases, and no social site remained beyond the Norwegian state's formal reach. The different governmentalization processes of the Swedish versus the Norwegian state can thus be explained by referring to both its more restrained biopolitical discourse, explaining its relatively soft interventions into public life, and to the Swedish state's socio-political problematizations and explicit critique of state intervention, which help account for the construction of a private life beyond formal state control.

6.1.5 The Rise of Biopolitical Leviathan

Reflecting upon the utility of the concept of 'biopolitics' in relation to COVID-19, the Foucauldian Ian Buchanan (2022: 2) writes that 'biopolitics is the concept of our time'. The pandemic indeed implies as much—in fact it shows the biopolitical *and* Hobbesian nature of the contemporary state (see Antoniol, 2023; Kapust, 2023). Perhaps unsurprisingly, the COVID-19 pandemic shows that whenever a situation is identified as a security risks, rights and freedoms are suspended (Cheibub et al., 2020). This is the Hobbesian lessons of the pandemic. Moreover, the COVID-19 pandemic shed light on the existence of a *global* biopolitical rationality (see Højme, 2022; Horvath & Lovasz, 2020; Kelly, 2023; Walby, 2020), which manifested in numerous states more or less suspending everyday life to protect their societies from the propagation of the COVID-19 virus. The state's Hobbesian responsibility of protecting society has been coupled with the biopolitical considerations Foucault discussed (1990, 2008) as a core political responsibility of the state in our modern era.

With the emergence of COVID-19, this manifested in a global consensus of the state's biopolitical objectives (cf. Green, 2021; Buchanan

2022). Even the outlier Sweden, seemingly so liberal, embraced biopolitical considerations at the expense of its liberal problematizations of state coercion. Even the Swedish state exercised power in a coercive manner, over society, on the grounds of biopolitical reasoning. This reveals the great influence of biopolitics, but also, of course, *securitization*. The Hobbesian considerations encompassed within biopolitics surpassed and thereby weakened and even suspended liberal and other socio-political concerns, as protecting life held priority. The near-universal acceptance of COVID-19 as a major threat and the near-universal tendency for states to act with severity in dealing with COVID-19 reveal a biopolitical ethic that dominates political rationalizations throughout the world, albeit, during a situation of securitization where biopolitics is framed explicitly as a matter of societal importance.

It is highly likely that biopolitics in general—related to the politics of health and unhealth, of diets, lifestyles and habits—will continue operating through liberal governmentality, as has been the case for decades (cf Rose, 2009). Thus, while Buchanan (2022) is partly right that biopolitics is the concept of our time—especially during the pandemic years—biopolitics has been and likely remains subordinated to liberalism. During the pandemic, one can argue that biopolitics, while so central, was actually subordinated to Hobbesian reasoning, meaning that security, not biopolitics, held ultimate priority. While liberal governmentality is superordinate to biopolitics in the pre-crisis context, whenever the state sees the situation as a security risk, a Hobbesian frame is likely to force the state into suspending liberal governmentality in favour of open state intervention. Thus, while the pandemic is indeed a biopolitical event, it is perhaps first and foremost a Hobbesian event.

This has more fundamental significance for theorizing on the state. States sharing, institutional and ideological bonds may react differently to a situation because they perceive the situation differently. State agency is contingent upon reasoning, which takes primacy over institutional, cultural and other conditions. To understand a state's course of action, processes of governmentalization must be examined, as the state's cognition has a real impact on the state's actions. This does not 'prove' any voluntaristic theory regarding the state acting independently of restraints. Yet, it becomes clear that the state, as a social actor, has real potential for autonomy. As Norway and Sweden demonstrate—and as shown by Weiss and Thurbon's study (2022) of Australia and the UK—scholars cannot predict how states will act merely on the basis of their structural, institutional or ideological characteristics. If we could, Norway and Sweden would act more or less as one. But Norway is, unlike Sweden, no outlier. Even similar states may act differently. The Swedish state's agency was practised in a different manner despite numerous similarities with its neighbours. The Swedish state acted differently because its reality was (and is) rendered governable in a different manner, as the Swedish state channels a liberal discourse rooted in liberal governmentality. This liberal critique of state intervention manifested in different political tactics compared to those implemented in states like Norway, where liberal governmentality was subordinated to Hobbesian and biopolitical mentalities. These are significant discursive differences which manifested in different political outcomes, even if we must steer clear of overstating the differences. Taking political rationalities seriously, we obtain a lens to examine state agency—as state action must necessarily be supported by a vision which renders reality governable. Consequently, states with characteristics differing along various dimensions may act similarly, just as similar states may act differently. Any examination of state action must, in the final instance, take the state's own reasoning and perception of the situation into account, even if structural and systematic explorations remain important due to their potential impact on the likelihood that specific actions are taken. After all, if the state, as a corporate actor, retains a monopoly on the decision (cf. Schmitt, 1996), then understanding its decisions depends upon a framework taking its reasoning into account.

If we are to fully understand the effects of political reasoning, studying how numerous voices converge into more or less coherent agendas within the collective agency of the state (or similar political entities) can only benefit the Foucauldian literature. Thus, the state-centric governmentality literature—which my book is part of—can benefit from fully leaving the Foucauldian definition of the state in favour of an agential one. After all, the political reasoning studied in this chapter is made up of numerous voices, but the two states at hand clearly have relatively coherent visions of reality. The states see reality through the political rationalities articulated by the politicians at hand. Moreover, to understand the effects of political reasoning upon political agency or the exercise of power, one also needs an agential lens. After all, the states at hand do not act randomly, but in accordance with political rationalizations and problematizations, which take precedence over political culture, ideology and social structures, as shown by the two culturally, institutionally and ideologically similar states at hand acting in accordance with political reasoning, rather than the aforementioned elements.

References

Agamben, G. (2008). *State of exception*. University of Chicago Press.

Almlund, P., E Kjeldsen, J., & Mølster, R. (2023). Expressions of governance, risk, and responsibility: Public campaigns in the crisis and risk management of Covid-19 in Denmark, Norway, and Sweden. In B. Johansson, Ø. Ihlen, J. Lindholm, & M. Blach-Ørsten (Eds.), *Communicating a pandemic: Crisis management and Covid-19 in the Nordic countries* (pp. 121–149). University of Gothenburg.

Andersson, S., & Aylott, N. (2020). Sweden and coronavirus: Unexceptional exceptionalism. *Social Sciences, 9*(12), 232.

Antoniol, V. (2023). Metamorphosis of biopolitics. A Foucauldian ecological perspective and the challenge of the pandemic: A review essay of Ottavio Marzocca, biopolitics for beginners. Knowledge of life and government of people. *Foucault Studies*, No. 35, 229–239. https://doi.org/10.22439/fs.i35.7082

Askim, J., & Christensen, T. (2022). Crisis decision-making inside the core executive: Rationality, bureaucratic politics, standard procedures and the COVID-19 lockdown. *Public Policy and Administration*, 09520767221129676.

Aucante, Y. (2022). *The Swedish experiment. The COVID-19 response and its controversies*. Bristol University Press.

Bacchi, C. (2009). *Analysing policy: What's the problem represented to be?* Pearson Education.

Buchanan, I. (2022). Biopolitics, Discipline and Governmentality. In: Das, S. S., and Pratihar, A. R. (Eds.), *Technology, Urban Space and the Networked Community*, 1–28. Palgrave Macmillan.

Cheibub, J. A., Hong, J. Y. J., & Przeworski, A. (2020). Rights and deaths: Government reactions to the pandemic. Working paper. https://doi.org/10.2139/ssrn.3645410

Christensen, T., & Lægreid, P. (2020). Balancing governance capacity and legitimacy: How the Norwegian government handled the COVID−19 crisis as a high performer. *Public Administration Review, 80*(5), 774–779. https://doi.org/10.1111/puar.13241

Christensen, T., Jensen, M. D., Kluth, M., Kristinsson, G. H., Lynggaard, K., Lægreid, P., ... & Adolf Skúlason, G. (2023). The Nordic governments' responses to the Covid-19 pandemic: A comparative study of variation in governance arrangements and regulatory instruments. *Regulation & Governance, 17*(3), 658–676.

Dean, M. (1999). *Governmentality: Power and rule in modern society*. Sage.

Dean, M. (2007). *Governing societies. Political perspectives on domestic and international rule*. Open University Press.

Fairclough, N. (2010). *Critical discourse analysis: The critical study of language* (2nd ed.). Routledge.

FHI. (2014). Nasjonal beredskapsplan for pandemisk influensa, https://www.fhi.no/ss/influensa/influensapandemier/nasjonal-beredskapsplan-for-pandemi/

Foucault, M. (1972). *The archaeology of knowledge*. Pantheon Books.

Foucault, M. (1985). *Discourse and truth: The problematization of Parrhesia*. Northwestern University Press.

Foucault, M., (1990). *The history of sexuality, volume 1. An introduction*. Penguin Books.

Foucault. (1991). Governmentality. In G. Burchell, C. Gordon, & P. Miller (Eds.), *The Foucault effect: Studies in governmentality*. The University of Chicago Press.

Foucault, M. (2008). *The birth of biopolitics - Lectures at the Collège de France, 1978–1979*. Palgrave Macmillan.

Giritli Nygren, K., & Olofsson, A. (2020). Managing the COVID-19 pandemic through individual responsibility: The consequences of a world risk society and enhanced ethopolitics, *Journal of Risk Research*.

Giritli Nygren, K., & Olofsson, A. (2021). Swedish exceptionalism, herd immunity and the welfare state: A media analysis of struggles over the nature and legitimacy of the COVID-19 pandemic strategy in Sweden. *Current Sociology, 69*(4), 529–546.

Gjerde, L. E. L. (2021a). From liberalism to biopolitics: Investigating the Norwegian government's two responses to COVID-19. *European Societies, 23*(sup1), S262–S274. https://doi.org/10.1080/14616696.2020.1824003

Gjerde, L. E. L. (2021b). Governing humans and 'things': Power and rule in Norway during the Covid-19 pandemic. *Journal of Political Power, 14*(3), 472–492. https://doi.org/10.1080/2158379X.2020.1870264

Gjerde, L. E. L. (2022). Den norske regjeringens diskursive muliggjøring av koronapolitikken: Et Foucauldiansk perspektiv. *Norsk Sosiologisk Tidsskrift* (3), 29–45. https://doi.org/10.18261/nost.6.3.3

Gjerde, L. E. L. (2023). Biopolitical and juridical creations of the quarantine hotel: A discourse analysis of the Norwegian case. *Acta Sociologica, 66*(4), 357–371. https://doi.org/10.1177/00016993221136038

Gjerde, L. E. L. (2025). Methodology: Digital appendix. *Research Gate*. https://www.researchgate.net/publication/387958773_Methodology_Digital_Appendix

Gordon, C. (1994). Introduction. In F. D. Faubion & M. Foucault. *Power. Essential works of Foucault 1954–1984 Volume* 3 (pp. xi–xli). The New Press.

Graver, H. P. (2020a). *COVID-19 Regulation in Norway and state of exception. COVID-19 and Constitutional Law* (pp. 167–175). Universidad Nacional Autónoma de México.

Graver, H. P. (2020b). *Pandemi og unntakstilstand. Hva covid-19 sier om den norske rettstaten*. Dreyers Forlag.

Green, T. (2021). *The Covid consensus: The new politics of global inequality*. Hurst.

Hagström, L., Wagnsson, C., & Lundström, M. (2023). Logics of othering: Sweden as other in the time of COVID-19. *Cooperation and Conflict, 58*(3), 315–334.

Hobbes, T. (1996). *Leviathan*. Oxford University Press.

Horvath, M., & Lovasz, A. (2020). Foucault in the age of COVID-19: Permitting contingency in biopolitics. *Identities: Journal for Politics, Gender and Culture, 17*(1), 144–153.

Højme, P. (2022). Biopolitics and the COVID-19 pandemic: A Foucauldian interpretation of the Danish government's response to the pandemic. *Philosophies, 7*(2), 34.

Idevall Hagren, K., & Bellander, T. (2023). National discourses in (de) legitimations of the Swedish COVID-19 strategy. *Text & Talk*, (0).

Jonung, L. (2020). Sweden's constitution decides its COVID-19 exceptionalism. *SSRN*. https://doi.org/10.2139/ssrn.3796848

Kapust, D. J. (2023). Plague and the Leviathan. *Hobbes Studies, 1*(aop), 1–13.

Kelly, M. G. E. (2023). Securing the pandemic: Biopolitics, capital, and COVID-19. *Foucault Studies* (No. 35), 42–65. https://doi.org/10.22439/fs.i35.7072

Laclau, E., & Mouffe, C. (1985). *Hegemony and socialist strategy. Towards a radical democratic politics*. Verso.

Larsson, O. L. (2022). The Swedish Covid-19 strategy and voluntary compliance: Failed securitisation or constitutional security management? *European Journal of International Security, 7*(2), 226–247.

Mann, M. (1984). The autonomous power of the state: Its origins, mechanisms and results. *European Journal of Sociology, 25*(2), 185–213.

Mann, M. (1993). *The Sources of Social Power: Volume 2, The Rise of Classes and Nation States*. Cambridge University Press.

Mann, M. (2005). *Incoherent empire*. Verso.

Mann, M. (2012). *The sources of social power: Volume 3, Global empires and revolution, 1890-1945*. Cambridge University Press.

Mann, M. (2013). *The sources of social power: Volume 4, Globalizations, 1945-2011*. Cambridge University Press.

Miller, P., & Rose, N. (2008). *Governing the present: Administering economic, social and political life*. Polity Press.

Nordlinger, E. (1981). *The autonomy of the democratic state*. Harvard University Press.

Pierre, J. (2020). Nudges against pandemics: Sweden's COVID-19 containment strategy in perspective. *Policy and Society, 39*(3), 478–493.

Opitz, S. (2011). Government unlimited. The security Dispositif of Illiberal Governmentality. In Bröckling, S. Krasmann, & T. Lemke. *Governmentality: Current issues and future challenges* (pp. 93–114).

Sandset, T., & Villadsen, K. (2023). Pandemic modelling and model citizens: Governing COVID-19 through predictive models, sovereignty and discipline. *The Sociological Review*, 00380261221102023.

Schmitt, C. (1996). *The concept of the political.* University of Chicago Press.

Schmitt, C. (2008). *Leviathan in the state theory of Thomas Hobbes. Meaning and failure of a political system.* The University of Chicago Press.

Schmitt, C. (2014). *Dictatorship.* Polity Press.

Regeringen. (2020). Situationen kommer til at stille kæmpe krav til os alle sammen. https://www.regeringen.dk/nyheder/2020/statsminister-mette-frederiksens-indledning-paa-pressemoede-i-statsministeriet-om-corona-virus-den-11-marts-2020/

Rose, N. (1999). *Powers of freedom: Reframing political thought.* Cambridge University Press.

Rose, N. (2009). *Livets politik. Biomedicin, Magt og Subjecktivitiet i det 21. århundrede.* Dansk Filosofisk forlag.

Walby, S. (2020). The COVID pandemic and social theory: Social democracy and public health in the crisis. *European Journal of Social Theory*, 1368431020970127.

Weiss, L., & Thurbon, E. (2022). Explaining divergent national responses to Covid-19: An enhanced state capacity framework. *New Political Economy, 27*(4), 697–712.

Empirical References: Chapter 6

Boden. (2020). Information om det nya Coronaviruset SARS-CoV-2 (som kan leda till sjukdomen Covid-19) - uppdaterat 2020-03-11. https://www.boden.se/nyheter/2020/information-om-det-nya-coronaviruset-sars-cov-2-som-kan-leda-till-sjukdomen-covid-19-uppdaterat-2020-03-11

Embassy of Sweden. (2020a, March 22). Prime Minister's address to the nation. https://www.swedenabroad.se/es/embajada/mozambique-maputo/current/news/prime-ministers-address-to-the-nation-22-march-2020/

Embassy of Sweden. (2020b). The 2020 Spring Budget. https://www.swedenabroad.se/es/embajada/greece-athen/current/news/the-2020-spring-budget/

Folkhälsomyndigheten. (2020a). Gemensamma författningssamlingen avseende hälso- och sjukvård,socialtjänst, läkemedel, folkhälsa m.m. https://www.folkhalsomyndigheten.se/contentassets/0ac7c7d33c124428baa198728f813151/hslf-fs-2020-12u.pdf

Folkhälsomyndigheten. (2020b). Folkhälsomyndighetens remissyttrande över promemorian ändringar i det tillfälliga förbudet mot att hålla allmänna sammankomster och offentliga tillställningar. https://www.folkhalsomyndigheten.se/globalassets/publicerat-material/remissyttranden/2020/justitiedepartementet-remissvar-pa-forslag-om-andring-i-det-tillfalliga-forbudet-i-ordningslagen.pdf

Folkhälsomyndigheten. (2021). Beslut om fortsatta åtgärder mot covid-19 i handeln och på serveringsställen. https://www.folkhalsomyndigheten.se/nyheter-och-press/nyhetsarkiv/2021/april/beslut-om-fortsatta-atgarder-mot-covid-19-i-handeln-och-pa-serveringsstallen/

Foretagshalsor. (2020). Stor majoritet har anpassat sitt beteende under pandemin. https://www.foretagshalsor.se/sv/stor-majoritet-har-anpassat-sitt-beteende-under-pandemin

Government. (2020a). Tillfälliga bemyndiganden i smittskyddslagen med anledning av det virus som orsakar covid-19. https://www.regeringen.se/rattsliga-dokument/proposition/2020/04/prop.-201920155

Government. (2020b). En ny lag om tillfälliga smittskyddsåtgärder på serveringsställen. https://www.regeringen.se/rattsliga-dokument/lagradsremiss/2020/05/en-ny-lag-om-tillfalliga-smittskyddsatgarder-pa-serveringsstallen/

Government. (2020c). Ministers: Global cooperation should be strengthened. https://www.government.se/contentassets/f97de1f8369b4ab9abd0c14bb69bb96c/minister-for-foreign-trade-and-nordic-affairs-anna-hallberg-opinion-pieces-2019-2022.pdf

Government. (2020d). The Government presents the 2020 Spring Fiscal Policy Bill. https://www.government.se/press-releases/2020/04/the-government-presents-the-2020-spring-fiscal-policy-bill/

Government. (2020e). Speech by Minister for International Development Cooperation Peter Eriksson at Stockholm Forum on peace and development. https://www.government.se/contentassets/c2f3d4da5c554f28a15a8a6976434123/peter-eriksson-speeches-2016-2020.pdf

Government. (2020f). The Government's work in response to the virus responsible for COVID-19. https://www.government.se/government-policy/the-governments-work-in-response-to-the-virus-responsible-for-covid-1/

Government. (2020g). Speech by Lena Hallengren at the seventy-fourth world health assembly. https://www.government.se/contentassets/0550da61a00f4fcda2e600fdb0fbd79e/lena-hallengren-speeches-2018-2022.pdf

Government. (2020h). The Government's work in response to the virus respon sible for COVID-19. https://www.government.se/government-policy/the-governments-work-in-response-to-the-virus-responsible-for-covid-1/

Government. (2020i, September 8). Statement of government policy. https://government.se/speeches/2020/09/statement-of-government-policy/
Government. (2021). Ann Linde speech to the Council of Europe. https://www.government.se/contentassets/6b26bd814b464e1db1402b80b60dfe35/minister-for-foreign-affairs-ann-linde-speeches-2021-2022.pdf
Krisinformation. (2020a). The Swedish government classifies the coronavirus as an illness that is dangerous to society. https://www.krisinformation.se/en/news/2020/february/the-swedish-government-classifies-the-coronavirus-as-an-illness-that-is-dangerous-to-society
Krisinformation. (2020b). Vecka 7 2020. https://www.krisinformation.se/en/news/2020/february
Krisinformation. (2020c). Detailed recommendations for shops, shopping centres and training facilities. https://www.krisinformation.se/en/news/2020/december/advice-to-businesses
Nordic Africa News. (2020). Sweden: Measures to tackle coronavirus vulnerability. http://www.nanews.net/news/sweden-measures-to-tackle-coronavirus-vulnerability/
Regjeringen. (2020a). Redegjørelse om koronapandemien https://www.regjeringen.no/no/aktuelt/redegjorelse-om-koronapandemien-i-stortinget/id2770148/
Regjeringen. (2020b). Beredskapstiltak for å sikre liv og helse – utbrudd av koronavirus- anvendelse av fullmaktsbestemmelsene i lov 23. juni 2000 nr. 56 om helsemessig og sosial beredskap. https://www.regjeringen.no/no/dokumenter/beredskapstiltak-for-a-sikre-liv-og-helse--utbrudd-av-koronavirus--anvendelse-av-fullmaktsbestemmelsene-i-lov-23.-juni-2000-nr.-56-om-helsemessig-og-sosial-beredskap/id2692835/
Regjeringen. (2020c). Forskrift om karantene etter reiser utenfor Norden. https://www.regjeringen.no/no/dokumenter/forskrift-om-karantene-etter-reiser-utenfor-norden/id2696527/
Regjeringen. (2020d). Gode nyheter. https://www.regjeringen.no/no/dokumentarkiv/regjeringen-solberg/aktuelt-regjeringen-solberg/hod/taler-og-innlegg/minister/taler-av-helse-og-omsorgsminister-bent-/2020/gode-nyheter/id2702326/
Regjeringen. (2020e). En felles kamp mot en usynlig fiende. https://www.regjeringen.no/no/aktuelt/en-felles-kamp-mot-en-usynlig-fiende/id2695024/
Regjeringen. (2020f). Prop. 130 L (2019–2020). https://www.regjeringen.no/no/dokumenter/prop.-130-l-20192020/id2705033/?q=korona&ch=2#match_0
Regjeringen (2020g). Justis- og beredskapsministerens orientering om korona-situasjonen 25. mars. https://www.regjeringen.no/no/aktuelt/justis-og-beredskapsministerensorientering-om-koronasituasjonen-25.-mars/id2695067

Regjeringen. (2020h). Statsministerens innledning på pressekonferanse om tiltak knyttet til koronaviruset. https://www.regjeringen.no/no/dokumentarkiv/regjeringen-solberg/aktuelt-regjeringen-solberg/smk/taler-og-innlegg/statsministeren/talerogartikler/2020/statsministerens-innledning-pa-pressekonferanse-om-tiltak-knyttet-til-koronaviruset/id2693028/

Regjeringen. (2020i). Justis- og beredskapsministerens orientering om korona-situasjonen. https://www.regjeringen.no/no/dokumentarkiv/regjeringen-solberg/aktuelt-regjeringen-solberg/jd/taler_og_innlegg/ministeren/taler-og-innlegg-av-justis--og-beredskapsminister-monica-maland/2020/justis--og-beredskapsministerens-tale-pa-digital-pressekonferanse-15.-mars-2020/id2693667/

Regjeringen. (2020j). Justis- og beredskapsdepartementet overtar kriseledelsen. https://www.regjeringen.no/no/dokumentarkiv/regjeringen-solberg/aktuelt-regjeringen-solberg/smk/pressemeldinger/2020/justis--og-beredskapsdepartementet-overtar-kriseledelsen/id2693626/

Regjeringen. (2020k). Stortinget vedtok koronaloven. https://www.regjeringen.no/no/dokumentarkiv/regjeringen-solberg/aktuelt-regjeringen-solberg/jd/pressemeldinger/2020/stortinget-vedtok-koronaloven/id2694462/

Regjeringen. (2020l). Holde fast og holde ut. https://www.regjeringen.no/no/aktuelt/holde-fast-og-holde-ut/id2702383/

Regjeringen. (2020n). Frihet under stort ansvar. Retrieved May 1, 2020, from https://www.regjeringen.no/no/aktuelt/frihet-under-stort-ansvar/id2698065/

Regjeringen. (2020o). Statsministerens innledning på pressekonferansen om økonomiske tiltak. https://www.regjeringen.no/no/aktuelt/statsministerens-innledning-om-okonomiske-tiltak-i-korona-krisen/id2693477/

Regjeringen. (2020p). Justis- og beredskapsministerens orientering 8. april. https://www.regjeringen.no/no/aktuelt/justis-og-beredskapsministerens-orientering-8.-april/id2697238/

Regjeringen. (2020q). Justis- og beredskapsministerens orientering om korona-situasjonen. https://www.regjeringen.no/no/dokumentarkiv/regjeringen-solberg/aktuelt-regjeringen-solberg/jd/taler_og_innlegg/ministeren/taler-og-innlegg-av-justis--og-beredskapsminister-monica-maland/2020/justis--og-beredskapsministerens-tale-pa-digital-pressekonferanse-15.-mars-2020/id2693667/

Regjeringen. (2020r). Langsiktig strategi for håndteringen av covid-19-pandemien. https://www.regjeringen.no/no/dokumenter/langsiktig-strategi-for-handteringen-av-covid-19-pandemien/id2791715/

Regjeringen. (2020s). Nye utfordringer og nye løsninger. https://www.regjeringen.no/no/dokumentarkiv/regjeringen-solberg/aktuelt-regjeringen-solberg/hod/taler-og-innlegg/minister/taler-av-helse-og-omsorgsminister-bent-/2020/nye-utfordringer-og-nye-losninger/id2702280/

Regjeringen. (2020t). Finansministerens innledning på pressekonferansen om økonomiske tiltak. https://www.regjeringen.no/no/dokumentarkiv/regjeringen-solberg/aktuelt-regjeringen-solberg/fin/taler-og-innlegg/ministerens-taler-og-artikler/taler-og-innlegg-av-finansminister-jan-tore-sanner/finansministerens-innledning-pa-pressekonferansen/id2693466/

Regjeringen. (2020u). Ny koronalov. https://www.regjeringen.no/no/dokumentarkiv/regjeringen-solberg/aktuelt-regjeringen-solberg/jd/pressemeldinger/2020/ny-koronalov/id2694038/

Regjeringen. (2020v). Prop. 130 L (2019–2020). https://www.regjeringen.no/no/dokumenter/prop.-130-l-20192020/id2705033/?q=korona&ch=2#match_0

Regjeringen. (2020w). Koronasituasjonen: Krav om opphold på karantenehotell. https://www.regjeringen.no/no/dokumentarkiv/regjeringen-solberg/aktuelt-regjeringen-solberg/jd/pressemeldinger/2020/koronasituasjonen-krav-om-opphold-pa-karantenehotell/id2784181/

Regjeringen. (2021c). Sender forslag om portforbud på høring. https://www.regjeringen.no/no/aktuelt/sender-forslag-om-portforbud-pa-horing/id2827768/

Regjeringen. (2021d). Høring - forslag om endringer i smittevernloven (portforbud). https://www.regjeringen.no/no/dokumenter/horing-forslag-om-endringer-i-smittevernloven-portforbud/id2827769/?expand=horingssvar

Stortinget. (2020). Stortinget - Møte tirsdag den 10. mars 2020. https://www.stortinget.no/no/Saker-og-publikasjoner/Publikasjoner/Referater/Stortinget/2019-2020/refs-201920-03-10?all=true

The Local. (2020a). In English: Prime Minister Stefan Löfven's televised speech to the nation. https://www.thelocal.se/20201122/in-english-prime-minister-stefan-lfvens-televised-speech-to-the-nation

The Local. (2020b). Sweden bans public events with more than 8 people. https://www.thelocal.se/20201116/breaking-sweden-introduces-limit-of-eight-coronavirus

CHAPTER 7

Final Reflections: On the Politics of COVID-19 and the Weberian-Foucauldian Theory of the State

7.1 Introduction to the Conclusion

The Norwegian and Swedish states administered their territories through various governing techniques, enabled by their coercive, infrastructural and ideological powers. These were executed in different ways, manifesting in different mechanisms of power. Obviously, the Norwegian and Swedish strategies differ, as the Swedish state swore by a two-tier system and respected numerous state/non-state boundaries, based on liberal governmentality, whereas the Norwegian state's totalizing strategy entailed a lockdown and a more coercive mobilization of society. While these differences are significant, they should not be overstated.

Both the Norwegian and Swedish states imposed a multitude of restrictions upon society. They both sought to mobilize every private individual, and they conscripted all organizers of social events and social spaces formally into their infection control regimes. This way, society was mobilized through the combination of infrastructural, ideological and coercive power. Both states governed through joints in a pyramidical manner, expanding deeply into society, even if the Swedish state restricted itself by making private issues a moral rather than a formal affair of state. The Norwegian state knew fewer limits, and suspended almost all state/non-state boundaries standing in its way. The case of the curfew was an

L. E. L. Gjerde, *Nordic Leviathans*, International Political Theory,
https://doi.org/10.1007/978-3-032-00689-9_7

interesting exception where the Norwegian state refused to transgress a line which would have allowed it to confine individuals to their homes in a universal and general manner. After all, the Norwegian state's approach was 'softer' than the global average (cf. Cheibub et al., 2020; Sandset & Villadsen, 2023). As the measures seen in this text as more or less global, with Norway serving as a moderate case representing the 'COVID consensus' (cf. Green, 2021), so the following reflections are relevant also beyond our cases. Differences in state capacity, related to quantitative and qualitative differences in the caging of various sources of power and different political cultures for how such sources can be enacted, will shape political responses. Nevertheless, the theoretical lessons at hand should be global in nature.

The conclusion will revolve around the issues of state autonomy and COVID-19, conscription and state power beyond the state apparatus during the pandemic and the issue of sovereignty and the exception from a Weberian-Foucauldian perspective. I will contextualize my findings internationally along all of these three dimensions. Thereafter, I end the conclusion by reflecting upon the utility of a Weberian-Foucauldian approach to the state, during the pandemic and beyond, considering the lessons of COVID-19 and the call to rethink the state.

7.1.1 COVID-19 and State Autonomy

The coronavirus pandemic was, among other things, a political laboratory. Politicians, albeit unwittingly, experimented with different strategies and tactics for controlling their populations, which scholars can observe and analyse. Different strategies and tactics of rule manifested in various mechanisms of power, contingent upon how diverse sources of power were enacted. While these experiments reveal much, they certainly show the importance of taking the autonomy, agency and might of the state into consideration.

This is not an abstract argument. States around the world made choices and populations endured them. Indeed, even similar states with similar cultural and institutional elements, like the Norwegian and Swedish, or the British and Australian (cf Weiss & Thurbon, 2022), chose differently, illustrating the importance of political choice and state autonomy. The state intervened everywhere. The pandemic rendered the state more or less all-encompassing. During the pandemic, nothing was allowed to occur *unless* the state permitted it. Power diffused from the centre of the state, in a pyramidical fashion, moving far beyond the formal apparatus of the state. Power manifested in numerous subtle as well as spectacular mechanisms of power at different levels of society. This occurred in Norway as in Sweden, in Australia as in the UK, in China as in Japan.

The politics of COVID-19 showed both continuity and ruptures with the global liberal manner of governance which dominated prior to the 'global lockdown'. The issue of liberal governmentality is not merely an issue of governing through the self-regulating individual, i.e. through freedom as a mechanism of governance. Liberal governmentality also posits that civil society is a governing instrument in its own right. The state should limit where it formally governs so as to allow non-state actors to take on various roles (Foucault, 2008). This occurred to a great extent in Sweden. However, in Norway—and we find this elsewhere too—civil society became a formal and explicit political instrument with the emergence of COVID-19, without any effective autonomy. The state did not ask—it commanded—making everything part of the state. The state could invite civil society, or simply hinder civil society actors from operating (cf Kövér, 2021; Kövér et al., 2021). For instance, the Hungarian state 'annexed' civil society (Kövér et al., 2021). This was quite common during the pandemic, as shown by the Norwegian state, deemed one of the more moderate ones in Europe. The Norwegian state 'annexed' civil space through its totalizing approach. In Sweden, on the other hand, the state combined a tight and firm hand with a degree of continuity with liberal governmentality, as it reduced the use of commands to the bare minimum. Rather than annexing civil space, the Swedish state chose to mobilize society in a less vertical manner, thereby leaving a de facto civil space functional during the crisis.

At this point, it is worth asking what COVID-19 implies. On the one hand, the pandemic entailed the global return of Leviathan. The model of Leviathan is clearly relevant for understanding the security-oriented state of COVID-19, which acted *autonomously* with severity to protect the population, around the world (cf Cheibub et al., 2020; Green, 2021). It is therefore also central to understanding the state as a political entity. On the other hand, this does not signal the 'death' of liberalism as a programme of government. Far from it—the pandemic shows that liberal and non-liberal, or even anti-liberal, forms of rule can be combined, as has been covered previously (Gjerde, 2021; Sandset & Villadsen, 2023). While some would point out that liberalism can and does exist alongside authoritarian government, as seen with regard to counter-terrorist government and the use of torture (Agamben, 2008; Dean, 2007), during the pandemic, liberal governmentality was primarily suspended in countries such as Norway, subordinated to biopolitical Hobbesian imperatives.

Contrary to society-centred arguments, the state retains impressive capacities, which it can choose to utilize or refrain from utilizing. The idea that processes of de-statification has been ongoing over the last decades, reducing the state's autonomy and powers (i.e. Foucault, 2008; Miller & Rose, 2008; Rose 1999), is clearly wrong. While the state's formal and active role diminishes outside the crisis context of COVID-19, this is a voluntary choice, taken by the state. The processes of neoliberalization are therefore best understandable through a state-centric lens, as the state chooses how to alter its boundaries to society at large. Moreover, this should not blind us to the realities of the state, and the powers it cages. The state can extend its reach into funerals or deny those dying a last visit from family. Even the Swedish state—likely the most liberal in Europe regarding the politics of COVID-19—governed in such a manner. To understand this, we must avoid reducing state power to its most overt forms. We must study what the state does, directly and indirectly, while bringing the sources of power it cages into the picture. This does not mean abandoning the focus upon how power is exercised—the core of Foucauldian studies. It means taking into account that power may be more complex than its manifestation, and thus, that one should beware of dismissing the importance of the state (cf. Dean & Villadsen, 2012; Jessen & von Eggers, 2020).

The pandemic and the multitude of measures implemented during its course revealed the great weakness of that part of the governmentality tradition dedicated to studying 'power beyond the state'. Indeed, as also discussed by other Foucauldian scholars (i.e. Dean, 2007; Lessenich, 2011; Dean & Villadsen, 2012; Jessen & von Eggers, 2020; J. Kim, 2021), such a stance is problematic. Of course, one may study power beyond the state. However, arguing that power generally works beyond the state, rendering the state as one element among many (i.e. Miller & Rose, 2008), conceals more than it reveals. The pandemic shows, beyond any reasonable doubt, the capacities of the state as an autonomous actor. The state can make the decision to close down, or refrain from doing so. Similar populations, such as those of Norway and Sweden, accepted different responses to the same situation. Importantly, this is something we see around the globe, with various states, such as the Indian, Zimbabwean and Chinese, also closing down their societies and intervening into society at large, showing the return of Leviathan as a biopolitical entity as a truly global phenomenon, even if some states will have reduced capacities to enforce its will in the periphery of society.

The pandemic, a dangerous and unclear time, fostered uncertainty regarding methods. The legitimate state utilized its legitimacy to make its vision of the pandemic largely accepted. To close down or not, that was the question, and it was a question decided upon by the state. People, as in Norway and Sweden, readily accepted the state's verdict. The pandemic shows the utility of a recommendation Stephan Lessenich (2011: 316) articulates as: 'instead of systematically looking for government beyond the state… governmentality studies should take more interest in the state itself'. Doing this, one can study how different states, from the Norwegian and Swedish to the Zimbabwean, Italian and Chinese, respond to situations such as COVID-19. While we cannot a priori make assessments on the forms of power these other states channel and utilize, we know from past research that techniques such as biopower and discipline have been used (cf Li, 2021; Mhazo & Maponga, 2022; Serban, 2021). Indeed, we also know from research into the Chinese state that Mann's Weberian theory has been used to fruitfully explain China (Jiang & Ong, 2022). While we cannot a priori make assertions of the specific techniques' form or the nature of the sources of power enacted in such contexts, and empirical studies are needed beyond the Norwegian and Swedish cases, the Weberian-Foucauldian theory's can be utilized in the most centralized as the most decentralized states, as shown by the numerous insightful Weberian and Foucauldian studies of such contexts. After all, these studies show how the same governmental techniques were used across national contexts, and that the state was the enactor of these techniques, while Weberian studies exploring the sources of power have found similar forms of power being used around the world.

However, we can expect challenges when covering weaker states which are forced to interact more horizontally with non-state actors, also during a crisis, as for instance the Bangladeshi state (cf Ali et al., 2021)—where a more relational approach studying state-society relations is necessary due to the state's reduced autonomy. State autonomy cannot be taken for granted. Nonetheless, state autonomy is a real possibility in every social context. State autonomy is also, of course, not a simple *binary* question. State autonomy exists alongside a spectrum, where state autonomy varies, both from country to country, and within countries, from political question to political question, and from region to region. However, that state autonomy cannot be taken for granted means that it must be studied. It does not mean that one can dismiss the possibility and relevance of state autonomy, contrary to what Foucault (2008), Lemke (2007), Mitchell (1991) and other non-agential scholars argue.

As past studies on the politics of COVID-19 have shown, taking these state-centric insights seriously is not necessarily incompatible with studying the mechanisms of power. Indeed, this book has studied power in a Foucauldian manner despite the heavy reliance on Mann's Weberian work. Rather than undermining Foucauldian interests, the use of Mann's work has offered a potent analytical framework for enriching the Foucauldian approach. It has allowed me to explore the macrophysics of power in a new way. This offers an organizational materialist approach to the question of power, through which to study the sources of power that enable mechanisms of power to be enacted. This does not mean that all Foucauldians need to take the state into account, or that the sources of power are always relevant to Foucauldian interests. The study of mechanisms of power is valuable in and of itself, and there are countless ways in which this issue can be addressed, including through the study of the 'macrostructures' (re)producing power relations and mechanisms (Lemke, 2019). However, the politics of COVID-19 can *only* be adequately analysed with a state-centric lens. This explains why studies on the politics of COVID-19 from a Foucauldian perspective tend to be state-centric, and indeed, bracket the very Foucauldian approach to the state. This will also be the case in other crises, and most likely in other contexts where the state has strong preferences. As Nordlinger (1981) notes, strong state preferences increase the likelihood that the state will enforce its agenda upon society. The autonomy of the state, revealed at every continent in different ways through the politics of COVID-19, and explored empirically and theoretically in this book as the correlation between the two states' approaches and the rationalities, must be taken into account, theoretically and empirically. A state-centric governmentality lens can be fruitful for scholars interested in probing how the state's identification of means and ends manifests in policy, and how contestation occurs in practice if the state's preferences contradict the preferences of societal groups, such as classes, corporations, religious communities, etc.

Obviously, many empirical cases will be society-centred. Studies of power should not be reduced to studies of the state. Yet, the autonomous state's presence cannot be denied a priori—as seen in how the state mobilizes all of society, governing through civil society (see Arts, 2014; McKee, 2009; Sending & Neumann, 2006). It appears necessary to discard the idea that a state-centric lens taking the state's autonomous powers and agency into account, and indeed describing the state as the primary actor and centre of power, 'obscures' insights into how power works (i.e. Miller & Rose, 2008: 56)—and work with an approach more open to the importance of the state (for similar arguments, see Dean & Villadsen, 2012; Jessen & von Eggers, 2020; J. Kim, 2021).

7.1.2 Mobilizing Society and Governing at a Distance

I have explored the politics of COVID-19 in Sweden and Norway, reproducing many insights from past studies, while gathering some new findings, filling certain gaps. Though much attention has been given to the informal mobilization of society through various forms of propaganda strategies (i.e. Almlund et al., 2023; Girtli Nygren & Olofsson, 2020; Sandset & Villadsen, 2023), the mobilization of society through the formalization of infection control responsibilities, i.e. conscription, has been disregarded until now. Studying the mobilization of society offers insights into a core Foucauldian interest, the state's rule beyond its formal apparatus, i.e. 'governing at a distance' (cf. Arts, 2014; Miller & Rose, 2008; Sending & Neumann, 2006). As we have seen, the formal mobilization of society occurred in two ways. On the one hand, public institutions like public schools and hospitals, already included among the state's formal instruments, were transformed into infection control devices. This entailed, but was not limited to, controlling access and disciplining patients, pupils, etc. On the other hand, many private spheres were transformed into infection control instruments, through statification. Funeral agencies and corporate offices were granted controlling responsibilities, mobilized by the state to supervise 'at a distance' those entering these spaces.

Government at a distance partly occurred through the power of language, enabled by a combination of the infrastructural sources of power needed to spread the state's vision, and the ideological sources of power needed to make citizens accept the state's vision when it was read or heard. Norway and Sweden are highly legitimate states with the infrastructural and ideological resources needed to make citizens comply. This is seen in other countries, too, such as China, Italy and Germany, where the state has used its ideological sources of power to demand compliance, through complex communication campaigns generally seen as successful in obtaining compliance (see Barari et al., 2020; Fu et al., 2020; Zimmermann et al., 2022). The voice of the state allows for the mobilization of society.

Moreover, states use their ideological and infrastructural power beyond simply demanding compliance. Indeed, in the US and China, but also more generally, the states at hand engaged in the politics of blaming and the politics of othering (cf Dionne & Turkmen, 2020; Jaworsky & Qiaoan, 2021). The state discursively imposes compliance, but also uses the crisis to blame adversaries, using its power to impose its vision of reality, even beyond the pandemic itself. The state can and does use situations such as the pandemic to mobilize against adversaries. The Chinese state discursively mobilized against the US, the American state discursively mobilized against China, and so we could continue. State power can be used for such geopolitical purposes. It can also be used against specific groups within a society. For instance, migrants and others crossing borders have been stigmatized around the world. Reports about migrants and others crossing the borders being blamed are near-universal (see Ivic & Petrovic, 2020). Similarly, COVID-19 sceptics, such as those not vaccinated, were demonized (Jaspal & Nerlich, 2023). From then-President Donald Trump's stigmatization of Chinese people by speaking of the 'China virus' to states' enforcing specific rules on non-vaccinated people or anyone crossing their borders, state power has been used to stigmatize specific groups, thereby mobilizing society against them. The state's ideological powers enable the state to act through citizens without any formal action of its own part. The power of the written or spoken word suffices to act through citizens, which participate in socially controlling identified out-groups, for instance through inflammatory rhetoric.

The mobilization of society against COVID-19 shows the state crossing boundaries, illustrating the utility of studying this form of government and the statification processes through an agential lens. These processes are made possible due to the various powers the state cages, placing it in a superordinate position vis-à-vis society. This is partly the case because the state's own voice manifests in individuals thoughts and actions, allowing the legitimate state to impose its vision of reality, such as by othering migrants or noncompliant individuals, or less malevolently, by imposing compliance with restrictions by producing moral obligations.

This also relates to the formal powers of the state. While the state can transgress its boundaries to society, the individual cannot resist without risking punishment. The state applies binding decisions, which allows the state to act far beyond its formal apparatus. Thus, when the state mobilizes society, the conscript has no say, but rather only the agency of the weak and subordinated—the agency to act slowly, lazily or sloppily to sabotage (cf. Scott, 1990). The boundary between state and non-state is both hard and soft. For those facing a powerful state caging immense ideological, coercive and infrastructural source of power, the boundaries appear unyielding. For the state with these sources of power at its disposal, the boundaries are crossable and flexible.

This brings to light the problematic nature of the agenda of studying power 'beyond the state' (cf. Miller & Rose, 2008). After all, the mobilization of society during the pandemic occurred 'beyond the state', as a form of 'government at a distance'. And yet, we cannot separate this form of rule from state power. During the pandemic, huge sections of society were mobilized, either through a) voluntarism, as the state imposed moral obligations, or b) formal conscription, based on the prescriptions the state imposed upon those organizing social events and spaces. Formally, funerals, restaurants, schools, kindergartens, offices, etc., became political arenas where the state demanded not only compliance with orders, but the active exercise of power on the state's behalf. The state did not need to send out formal state agents to impose its will in these diverse cases. Caging numerous infrastructural, coercive and ideological sources of power enabled the state to act through society by conscripting roles into the state's regime for controlling the spread of contagion. Those occupying these roles were conscripted, regardless of whether they were civil servants working in schools or private workers from stores or offices. They may even have been private individuals mourning the death of their children or other loved ones. Notwithstanding this, they were obliged to fulfil the state's will. These individuals were conscripted into the Norwegian and Swedish states, showing a potent form of governance, enabled by the state's infrastructural sources of power. With the growth of infrastructural and ideological power, the state may well be able to govern more extensively and intensively without growing formally. Leviathan can grow as actors not officially part of the state become de facto state instruments, through moral and formal measures. This is the case in both Norway and Sweden, even if the Swedish state conscripted state agents in a softer and more voluntaristic manner, in keeping with its close reliance upon liberalism as a manner of governing, even during the pandemic.

Such forms of conscription are global. We see this in other contexts, such as with the 'corona passport', which means mobilizing employees and employers to police the health statuses of guests, customers and workers (see Stefanizzi et al. 2022), or the Chinese state's mobilization of local actors for population control purposes in order to control the spread of COVID-19 (Habich-Sobiegalla & Plümmer, 2023). States around the world used its infrastructural capacities to act through formally non-state actors. We see this in studies of the Chinese state's mobilization of society through nationalistic and moral rhetoric, meant to unite the population into a community, which has been found to interweave with bottom-up efforts to reduce the spread of the virus (see Ma et al., 2024). Like in Norway and Sweden, the Chinese states governed at a distance, not only through mobilizing local actors formally, but also by using the ideological sources of power it concentrates within itself so to mobilize citizens as voluntary infection control agents, well beyond any formal requirements.

States around the world find different ways to mobilize private individuals as state agents, conscripting them into the infection control machinery. Such power beyond the state relates to state power (see Arts, 2014; Sending & Neumann, 2006). Indeed, it can be understood as an archetypical form of pyramidical power. Non-state actors conscripted into the state's machinery during the pandemic became state agents. This is especially the case in Norway, where they were formally obliged to act in a tightly regulated manner, which left non-state actors with few actual decision-making capacities. In Sweden, the state acted more in line with what Foucauldians have studied up to now (i.e. Arts, 2014; Sending & Neumann, 2006). The state played upon the agency of non-state actors to mobilize them, formally and informally, allowing the state to govern at a distance through numerous parts to the extent that state power diffuses beyond the formal state apparatus and thereby appears to imply government beyond the state.

Seemingly, the agenda of studying power 'beyond the state' is based on a juridical model of state power, as Dean (2007) criticized in his problematization of the prioritization of studies prioritizing government 'beyond the state'. Indeed, such notions can even be noted in some highly accurate analyses of state power during the pandemic. For instance, Md. Kowsar (2022) argues that global civil society became subordinated to the state during the pandemic, arguing that this entailed a shifting power balance with lasting consequences. While the politics of COVID-19 may indeed have lasting consequences—a question beyond the scope of this book and its theorizing—the shift to harder state power, including the use of infrastructural and coercive sources of power to forcefully control, regulate and discipline populations and non-state organizations, does not entail the power balance being shifted per se. The pandemic entailed a change in strategy. Civil society was not free of the state during the pandemic, but neither was it free of the state prior to emergence of the COVID consensus. The reason the state could govern so effectively during the pandemic, also through non-state actors mobilized as instruments of infection control, is the state's embeddedness into society (cf. Evans 1995). The state was already present, and could therefore easily shift from soft to hard, from direct to indirect, government. The state could use (civil) society as an instrument without any alteration of state-society relations. The command of the state sufficed. Thus, if need be, the Norwegian, Italian or Indian state may cancel the autonomy of societal actors by transgressing state-society boundaries. Rather than entailing a shift in the balance of power, the pandemic revealed the true balance between the state and its exterior. Civil society is a semi-autonomous sphere, but it is also an instrument of state power, utilizable for states in extreme cases like COVID-19, but also in more everyday cases.

My analysis, embracing a Foucauldian understanding of how power works, shows the complexities of state power, which also encompasses many insights generated by those prioritizing power 'beyond the state', but power 'beyond the state' can work as informal state power. The state can act through infrastructural and ideological means in more complex ways than through law. The state can act *through* and *with* non-state actors, regulating, coordinating and enabling them to participate in a nexus of power and governance, as central as the non-state actor governing in issues of international relations (i.e. Sending & Neumann, 2006), or forestry (i.e. Arts, 2014). Acting through society creates complex processes of statification, where the state instrumentalizes formally non-state spheres for its political purposes, perhaps creating a formally non-state sphere which nevertheless is regulated, controlled and thus governed by the state, as the state governs at a distance. This shows the utility of an agential lens which takes the state and its agency into account—as it paves the way for studying how state power may manifest and work in more complex ways than through its formal apparatus. This also reveals the value of a state-centric Foucauldian approach—which takes into account the complexities of power in its heterogenous and at times decentralized, forms, and yet nevertheless explores the state as a centre of power capable of organizing and regulating power relations.

7.1.3 Sovereignty Revisited

COVID-19 was defined as abnormal by most states around the world (cf. Cheibub et al., 2020; Green, 2021). The return of Leviathan and the statification of all society, as the state embedded itself within, mobilized and colonized society, relates to the decision-making rights of sovereignty (Schmitt, 1996, 2020). The politics of COVID-19 revolved around this meta-mechanism of power. The state decided whether or not the situation was abnormal. This question leads to a secondary decision of equal importance. To *what extent* was the situation abnormal (cf. Dean, 2007)? The answer to this question leads to other questions of relevance, which are partly answered, or at least the answers are restricted, by the response given to the first question. What kinds of extraordinary measures did the pandemic warrant?

In Norway, like most other countries around the globe, the state suspended various legal and social norms (cf Graver 2020a, 2020b; Zinn, 2020). States like the Indian, Hungarian and Chinese identified a need to act, and acted accordingly, imposing tight restrictions (cf Hu & Sidel, 2020; Kövér et al., 2021; Tandon & Aravind, 2021). This entailed the use of state interventions and thus *hard* state power. Sources of infrastructural and coercive power intertwined, allowing these states to impose harsh sanctions on dissidents and impose restrictions upon society at large. In Sweden, the state sought to refrain from suspending the legal, normative order (Larsson, 2022)—as seen by how it refused to interfere in private lives. The degree of abnormality *determined* by the state decides the severity of political measures. The governmentality tradition grants us useful tools for studying the problematizations and rationalizations manifesting in the decision to declare, or not declare, a situation exceptional.

The suspension of everyday life and democratic norms and values for the duration of the pandemic shows the continued importance of sovereignty, and how ultimate authority remains within the state apparatus (Schmitt, 1996, 2014, 2020). Continuing down this line of thought, Schmitt's (1996) assertion that true power is revealed in the moment of the decision appears accurate. While the state's form is not determined by the crisis itself, the moment of decision shows where the authority to decide ultimately lies, and what this authority ultimately can manifest in. As shown during the pandemic, this power can manifest in the total restructuring of society through the use of formal and informal, hard and soft, forms of power. Moreover, the authority to decide allows the decider, i.e. the state, to act as it decides to do, whereas those lacking this authority are subject to the actions of the deciding subject. Private individuals, corporations, NGOs and others have no such formal right to declare a situation abnormal, even if they can, through state capture, affect the state's decision-making, as Marxists spend much time discussing (i.e. Jessop, 2015; Poulantzas, 1978). Nevertheless, regardless of whether the state is autonomous or 'captured' by special interests, ultimate authority lies within the state, which, *in the final instance*, retains a certain 'monopoly to decide' (Schmitt, 1996). This monopoly is, first and foremost, exercised with regard to the issue of (ab)normality.

While a citizen or corporation may dismiss the state's definition of the situation as exceptional, such a dismissal cannot manifest in disobedience, unless non-state actors want to invite state violence towards themselves. The state, as a compulsory organization, can decide whether a situation warrants state coercion or not. Objective constraints, like mortality rates, play a role. A common cold could never warrant a state of exception and would lead to massive protests, probably even regime or state collapse, as soon as the objective lack of danger came to light. Sovereignty is fixated around sociocultural norms and customs. Sovereignty is not a free-floating phenomenon which grants the state omnipotent powers to redesign society as if reality was a video-game or a canvas. The state has the right from might to determine the boundaries between normality and abnormality (Schmitt, 1996). However, this right is limited and structured by various constraints within and beyond the state itself, including customs, traditions, cultural norms, political culture, etc. (Dean, 2007).

Thus, the politics of COVID-19 was a legitimate and justified set of political operations *in our era*, but if the same disease had caused the same political responses in 1920, then this would have been considered despotism, because the social conditions of the time did not warrant such biopolitical operations for diseases of the nature of COVID-19—as the Spanish Flu with mortality rates far exceeding those of COVID-19 reveals. Compared to the Spanish Flu, which at the same time led to between 20 and 40 million deaths in around a year (Reid et al., 2001), in a world with approximately a quarter of the global 2020 population, one cannot but acknowledge that the pathological capacities of COVID-19 appear mild. If COVID-19 had emerged in 1920, then it would have failed to become part of the public discourse. Ideological and social changes alter populations' tolerance for death and suffering, thereby altering the legitimate grounds by which the state can declare a pandemic abnormal and exceptional.

However, while sovereignty is limited by various constraints, the state has much leeway in interpreting a situation. This is proven by how different states, like the Swedish and Norwegian, or Australian and British, used their powers to impose different visions, legitimizing different approaches to COVID-19, despite these countries finding themselves in the same situation. Subjectively, the situations were socially constructed in different ways, and they therefore became different, thereby warranting different political choices. The situation existed in a borderland between normal and abnormal, allowing the state to determine the level of (ab)normality.

Therefore, the lockdown was legitimate in Norway, while the lack of a lockdown was legitimate in Sweden. Similarly, the Australian state's total lockdown was considered legitimate, whereas the softer British approach was considered legitimate (cf Weiss & Thurbon, 2022). The populations in these countries would have resisted the politics of COVID-19 versus a cold, and we can expect that they would *demand* the most draconian and unimaginable measures in the face of an actual *plague* of historical proportions, capable of leaving entire cities void of life. The populations of Norway and Sweden, so similar, accepted different political strategies, just like the British and Australian populations, equally similar along numerous dimensions, too accepted different approaches.

Combining the Schmittian theory of sovereignty with the Foucauldian lens that inquires into the mechanisms and reasonings of power, one can explore how the state's suspension of the norm leads to various political measures and thus mechanisms of power of an extraordinary nature, and how such politics is rationalized (cf. Agamben, 2008; Dean, 2007). The issue of sovereignty remains, and will probably continue to remain, a core meta-mechanism of power, which through the definition of (ab)normality enables the exercise of power far beyond what is normally legitimate.

While the state will tame itself yet again, its ultimate powers are unleashed whenever war, plague or other major crises threaten. Indeed, even the Swedish state strengthened its legal capacities to intervene in the social body during the pandemic, even if these legal capacities were implemented sparingly (Aucante, 2022; Larsson, 2022). Similarly, the Norwegian state formalized enhanced sovereign capacities in the hands of the executive, to avoid the necessity of voting on emergency politics related to quarantine and isolation in the event of a new pandemic, in the aftermath of the pandemic (Regjeringen, 2023). Naturally, as the state is autonomous, so the state itself chooses whether or not a situation constitutes such a crisis, which forces the state to move out of its voluntarily imposed chains, chains that the state are presumably already tightening around itself in the aftermath of this global pandemic. We should, however, not ignore that the state holds the keys to unlocking these chains (Mann, 2012, 2013; Nordlinger, 1981; Schmitt, 1996)—contrary to society-centred arguments. A weak state lacking autonomy may be tamed by society, but a powerful state will tame itself, and a state taming itself is naturally fully capable of breaking these self-imposed shackles.

The pandemic and the sovereignty of the state illustrate the fallacy of speaking of the state as 'one element' in a series of power relations (Miller & Rose, 2008). The state is a centre of power, today as a century ago, and while power relations and institutional patterns always change, the state's central role has not diminished in recent decades (cf. Hegghammer, 2021; Mann, 2013; Weiss, 1998). However, while the pandemic revealed the autonomy, capacities and agency of the state, it should be added, as a final statement, that this does not tell us much about the everyday existence of the state. On the one hand, Schmitt (1996) is right that the exception is important to demonstrate hierarchies and capacities. These are concealed when the state willingly choses inactivity. On the other hand, moving beyond Schmitt's (1996) prioritization of the exception, we can move towards Foucault's (1980, 1991) prioritization of the norm. After all, the everyday life of the state is not exceptional. Therefore, the Weberian-Foucauldian theory of the state is not a theory of the exception—even if the exception reveals state autonomy and dormant capacities opaque during everyday life—but a theory of the state in general.

The Weberian-Foucauldian theory of the state has now been utilized in a state-centric context. While we should expect a priori that wars, revolutions and other great emergencies, such as potential environmental collapses due to climate change, in which the state declares an exception, are analysable through this state-centric lens, we would likely need a more relational variant of the theory to fully explain the state's everyday workings. For the state to keep its great sources of informal power, the state must treat non-state actors with a certain level of respect and understanding. Thus, the state is unlikely to use force when it is not perceived to be necessary. Therefore, compromise and negotiations ensure that non-state actors are never powerless against the state in everyday situations. To study less state-centred contexts, one would need to account for the state's interaction with social actors, including the combination of struggles between the state and societal actors, the state's appropriation of ideological and political issues and positions.

Moreover, while my study prioritized the correlation between the sources and mechanisms of power and the reasoning and exercise of power, leading me to study the microphysics, macrophysics and reasoning of power, ideally a fourth element, the macrostructures of power, should be included (cf. Jessop, 2011; Lemke, 2019). This would entail studying how the state's actions are structured, and thus enabled or thwarted, by various conditions which we have been allowed to bracket due to the similarities of our cases. One key element in this regard would be exploring the aforementioned distinction between authoritarian and liberal states, and how authoritarian states must reproduce the conditions of remaining a formal Leviathan, whereas liberal states must ensure conditions of trust and legitimacy enabling it to temporarily grow in unimaginable ways. This would also require, contrary to the purposes of my study, taking state-society relations and other conditions enabling and restricting the state, including how liberal institutions and democratic culture facilitate closer ties between the state and society, into consideration.

My study has bracketed this issue, due to tactical necessities and the specific context, which has let me simplify in certain areas to investigate the issue of state power, addressing numerous empirical lacunae in the literature on the politics of COVID-19 in Norway and Sweden while inviting Foucauldians and Weberians to consider a theoretical marriage. However, the theory needs to expand by including state-society relations and the macrostructural institutional patterns bracketed in this text—thereby enriching the analytical framework—when moving beyond the politics of crises.

7.1.4 *Rethinking the State?*

The pandemic has served as an important laboratory for political and sociological theory-building. Perhaps nowhere is this clearer than regarding the state and the question of state power. Foucauldians have long dismissed the state as increasingly irrelevant, as seen especially in the 'state-phobic' governmentality literature Dean and Villadsen (2012) criticized more than a decade ago. The idea, following neoliberalization and its ideational and practical effects, has been that the state withers, or at least that it shrinks. The market and individualization reduce the scope of the state, making power diverse, decentralized and complex (Miller & Rose, 2008; Rose 1999). This is the myth of the powerless state Weiss (1998) problematized in the 1990s.

The pandemic shows how the processes of neoliberalization and globalization, which brought with it new forms of power, in no way reduced the powers or relevance of the state. Of course, a state which privatizes loses direct control over assets. Nevertheless, the state can act through subjects which it mobilizes, formally or morally, meaning that the state does not need to own everything to govern everything. The state can mobilize society itself, as seen during the pandemic. Indeed, this can be seen in other contexts, too, well beyond the pandemic. A good example is antiracism and racism, important political questions.

Using the Weberian-Foucauldian theory of the state, I have explored how the Norwegian state defines racism as a political problem, which it seeks to deal with (Gjerde, 2024). Racism is an important question well beyond politics—it is a key focus of political and social sciences in general. However, how the state and its actions affect society regarding racism at large is rarely considered, with much literature on the issue being society-centred, revolving around ideologies or structures, without the state's passive or active role being considered. In Norway, the state seeks to mobilize society at large, including private individuals and businesses, for purposes of anti-discrimination and antiracism. To understand this, in Norway or in other countries where the state seeks to combat racism—or in contrary cases where state power is used to foster and strengthen racism and discriminate against racialized others—we must understand how the state structures the room to think and act. Just like how the state governed during the pandemic, with formal and informal, hard and soft, means, so the state acts in numerous ways to deal with various other issues.

The state affects society in numerous ways, acting upon our lives in overt and covert manners. In this regard, it may prove useful to rethink the state along two lines. First, we may benefit significantly from defining the state as an actor, which can act upon and through society at large. This way, we can study how the state itself affects society. Second, we may benefit significantly from a more state-centric approach to sociological questions, from (anti)racism to (anti)sexism, from popular culture to child upbringing, from digitalization to education, from globalization to questions of identity. The state is likely to frequently govern in subtler ways, as it even did during the pandemic. Whenever coercion is found illegitimate, the state is likely to exclusively use infrastructural and ideological means. How these sources are utilized in practice, and their effects, may be the key question beyond political science—it may be one of the most important question for social scientists in general—as the state's impact upon society can hardly be overestimated (cf. Elias, 1978, 1982; Mann, 1984, 1993, 2012, 2013). Even similar populations with similar cultures—like the Norwegian and Swedish states—will accept totally different political outcomes if the state uses its machinery to justify its positions.

If this state-centric thesis is right, then the core of contemporary societies—the state's subtle and/or direct interventions into society—are at the core of understanding modern societies more generally. The neoliberal narrative of the decline of the state is likely in need of replacement of a theoretical approach emphasizing the importance and role of the state in shaping society, also in the liberal era we find ourselves in (cf Deneen, 2018; Mearsheimer, 2018). The state's sovereignty—which as Schmitt (1996) rightfully asserted a century ago grants the state the right by might to decide in a crisis—is only one element in the state's vertical position above non-state actors.

The state consists of a heterogenous and complex set of sources of power, which makes the state a complex and diverse machinery, capable of governing well beyond the formal decision. Perhaps the most impressive instances of state might are not those which we see with our eyes, like when the state commands society to close down. Instead, the most impressive instances of state power are likely the subtle government which the state imposes through mobilizing and regulating non-state actors to impose its will, governing at a distance. Following Steven Lukes (2004), the most impressive feature of the state is not the capacities used to force citizens to comply, but the capacities used to change how citizens think about and practise life itself. This means finding power to be more complex than the overt state-centric models of the past may claim, as Foucauldians frequently assert (i.e. Miller & Rose, 2008), while, contrary to the state-phobic view, taking seriously how the state works as a centre of power. Perhaps more importantly, the seemingly non-state forms of government pervading everyday life will frequently be instances of state power.

A pyramidal conception of power, combining the Weberian and Foucauldian traditions, is ideal for such thinking and studying. Combining the vertical and horizontal elements of power from these different approaches, scholars can study the link between direct and indirect, formal and informal, government. State power in its diverse forms can be studied, both where the state openly acts, and where the state acts through surrogates, also in subtle ways. Listening to Foucauldians, we may well benefit from avoiding too rigid state-non-state analytical models, but contrary to Foucauldians, the reason behind avoiding such models is not the lack of state agency, but rather, the nature of state agency. The mechanisms of power characterizing different social and political contexts can not only be more wholesomely analysed, but even explained by reference to the sources of power which makes various mechanisms, such as control or discipline, manifest in practice.

After all, the state acts well beyond the juridical models (Dean, 2007). This also entails acting in ways which may not be immediately clear, such as when the state acts through conscripted individuals or even organizations. While there will be obvious conflicts between the state and non-state actors, in many cases, states use non-state actors as instruments, against or for racism, against or for feminism, against or for environmentalism, and so we can continue. States have numerous means at their disposal, and if we are to understand the social reality which we live in, we benefit from conceptualizing the state as an actor, and the state-non-state boundaries as flexible insofar as the state has concentrated enough sources of power within itself to act with and through, over and against, these various actors. Studying the diverse interplay between sources and mechanisms of power, scholars can study the complexities of contemporary statecraft, including the open and subtle, direct and indirect, ways which state power operates. The question of power—and how power works and is made to work—can be studied at length. A state-centric lens—based on a Weberian-Foucauldian theory of the state and its powers—can advance our understanding of numerous social and political phenomena related to the question of power.

References

Agamben, G. (2008). *State of exception*. University of Chicago Press.

Ali, T. O., Hassan, M., & Hossain, N. (2021). The moral and political economy of the pandemic in Bangladesh: Weak states and strong societies during Covid-19. *World Development, 137*, Article 105216.

Almlund, P., E Kjeldsen, J., & Mølster, R. (2023). Expressions of governance, risk, and responsibility: Public campaigns in the crisis and risk management of Covid-19 in Denmark, Norway, and Sweden. In B. Johansson, Ø. Ihlen, J. Lindholm, & M. Blach-Ørsten (Eds.), *Communicating a pandemic: Crisis management and Covid-19 in the Nordic countries* (pp. 121–149). University of Gothenburg.

Arts, B. (2014). Assessing forest governance from a 'Triple G' perspective: Government, governance, governmentality. *Forest Policy and Economics, 49*, 17–22.

Aucante, Y. (2022) *The Swedish Experiment. The COVID-19 response and its controversies.* Bristol University Press.

Barari, S., Caria, S., Davola, A., Falco, P., Fetzer, T., Fiorin, S., …, & Slepoi, F. R. (2020). Evaluating COVID-19 public health messaging in Italy: Self-reported compliance and growing mental health concerns. *MedRxiv*, 2020-03.

Cheibub, J. A., Hong, J. Y. J., & Przeworski, A. (2020). Rights and deaths: Government reactions to the pandemic. Working paper. https://doi.org/10.2139/ssrn.3645410

Dean, M., & Villadsen, K. (2012). *Statsfobi og Civilsamfund. Foucault og hans arvingers blik på staten.* Nyt fra Samfundsvidernskaberne.

Dean, M. (2007). *Governing societies. Political perspectives on domestic and international rule.* Open University Press.

Deneen, P. (2018). *Why liberalism failed.* Yale University Press.

Dionne, K. Y., & Turkmen, F. F. (2020). The politics of pandemic othering: Putting COVID-19 in global and historical context. *International Organization, 74*(S1), E213–E230.

Elias, N. (1978). *The history of manners. The civilizing process, volume 1.* Basil Blackwell.

Elias, N. (1982) *Power and civility. The civilizing process volume 2.* Basil Blackwell.

Evans, P. B. (1995). *Embedded autonomy: States and industrial transformation.* Princeton: Princeton University Press.

Foucault, M., (1980). *Power/Knowledge*. New York: Pantheon books.

Foucault, M. (1991). *Discipline and punish: The birth of the prison.* Penguin books.

Foucault, M. (2008). *The birth of biopolitics - Lectures at the Collège de France, 1978–1979.* Palgrave Macmillan.

Fu, Y., Ma, W., & Wu, J. (2020). Fostering voluntary compliance in the COVID-19 pandemic: An analytical framework of information disclosure. *The American Review of Public Administration, 50*(6–7), 685–691.

Giritli Nygren, K. & Olofsson, A. (2020). Managing the COVID-19 pandemic through individual responsibility: the consequences of a world risk society and enhanced ethopolitics, *Journal of Risk Research.*

Gjerde, L. E. L. (2021). Governing humans and 'things': Power and rule in Norway during the Covid-19 pandemic. *Journal of Political Power, 14*(3), 472–492. https://doi.org/10.1080/2158379X.2020.1870264

Gjerde, L. E. L. (2024). Antiracist welfarism: A governmentality study of Norwegian state antiracism. *Nordic Journal of Social Research, 15*(1), 1–14. https://doi.org/10.18261/njsr.15.1.5

Graver, H. P. (2020a). COVID-19 Regulation in Norway and state of exception. *COVID-19 and Constitutional Law. Mexico: Universidad Nacional Autónoma de México*, 167–175.

Graver, H. P. (2020b). Pandemi og unntakstilstand. *Hva covid-19 sier om den norske rettstaten.* Oslo. Dreyers Forlag.

Green, T. (2021). *The Covid consensus: The new politics of global inequality.* Hurst.

Habich-Sobiegalla, S., & Plümmer, F. (2023). Topologies of power in China's grid-style social management during the COVID-19 pandemic. *Security Dialogue, 54*(2), 192–210.

Hegghammer, T. (2021). Resistance is futile: The war on terror supercharged state power. *Foreign Affairs, 100*, 44.

Hu, M., & Sidel, M. (2020). Civil society and COVID in China: Responses in an authoritarian society. *Nonprofit and Voluntary Sector Quarterly, 49*(6), 1173–1181.

Ivic, S., & Petrovic, R. (2020). The rhetoric of othering in a time of pandemic: Labeling Covid-19 as a "foreign virus" in public discourse. *Kultura Polisa, 17*, 421.

Jaspal, R., & Nerlich, B. (2023). Social representations of COVID-19 skeptics: Denigration, demonization, and disenfranchisement. *Politics, Groups, and Identities, 11*(4), 750–770.

Jaworsky, B. N., & Qiaoan, R. (2021). The politics of blaming: The narrative battle between China and the US over COVID-19. *Journal of Chinese Political Science, 26*(2), 295–315.

Jessen, M. H., & von Eggers, N. (2020). Governmentality and statification: Towards a Foucauldian theory of the state. *Theory, Culture & Society, 37*(1), 53–72.

Jessop, B. (2011). Constituting another Foucault effect. Foucault on states and Statecraft. In Bröckling, S. Krasmann, & T. Lemke (Eds.), *Governmentality: Current issues and future challenges* (pp. 54–73). Routledge.

Jessop, B. (2015). *The state: Past, present, future.* Wiley.

Jiang, G., & Ong, L. (2022). Strengthening the State through Crisis Management: Battles against the SARS and COVID-19 Pandemics in China. *Issues & Studies, 58*(03), 2250002.

Kim, J. (2021). Rethinking public administration and the state: A Foucauldian governmentality perspective. *International Review of Public Administration, 26*(2), 175–191. https://doi.org/10.1080/12294659.2021.1889102

Kövér, Á. (2021). The relationship between government and civil society in the era of COVID-19. *Nonprofit Policy Forum, 12*(1), 1–24.

Kövér, Á., Antal, A., & Deák, I. (2021). Civil society and COVID-19 in Hungary: The complete annexation of civil space. *Nonprofit Policy Forum, 12*(1), 93–126.

Kowsar, M. (2022). Pandemic and global civil society: shifting the power balance towards the state? *Global Local Interactions: Journal of International Relations, 2*(1), 1–11.

Larsson, O. L. (2022). The Swedish Covid-19 strategy and voluntary compliance: Failed securitisation or constitutional security management? *European Journal of International Security, 7*(2), 226–247.

Lemke, T. (2007). An indigestible meal? Foucault, governmentality and state theory. *Distinktion: Scandinavian Journal of Social Theory, 8*(2), 43–64. https://doi.org/10.1163/9789087909857_004

Lemke, T. (2019). *Foucault's analysis of modern government. A critique of political reason*. Verso.

Lessenich, S. (2011). Constructing the socialized self. Mobilization and control in the "active society". In Bröckling, S. Krasmann, & T. Lemke (Eds.), *Governmentality: Current issues and future challenges* (pp. 304–319). Routledge.

Li, M. (2021). Biopolitical practices in Beijing. *European Review, 29*(6), 805–818.

Lukes, S. (2004). *Power: A radical view*. Macmillan.

Ma, Y., Zhuang, Y., & Liu, C. (2024). Interaction rituals in a crisis: The case of COVID-19 in China. *Asian Journal of Social Science, 52*(1), 35–43.

Mann, M. (1993). *The sources of social power, Volume II: The rise of classes and nation states*. Cambridge University Press.

Mann, M. (2012). *The sources of social power. Volume 3. Global empires and revolution, 1890–1945*. Cambridge University Press.

Mann, M. (2013). *The sources of social power. Volume 4, Globalizations, 1945–2011*. Cambridge University Press.

Mann, M. (1984). The autonomous power of the state: Its origins, mechanisms and results. *European Journal of Sociology, 25*(2), 185–213.

McKee, K. (2009). Post-Foucauldian governmentality: What does it offer critical social policy analysis? *Critical Social Policy, 29*(3), 465–486.

Mearsheimer, J. (2018). *The great delusion*. Yale University Press.

Mhazo, A. T., & Maponga, C. C. (2022). Governing a pandemic: Biopower and the COVID-19 response in Zimbabwe. *BMJ Global Health, 7*(12), Article e009667.

Miller, P., & Rose, N. (2008). *Governing the present: Administering economic, social and political life*. Polity Press.

Mitchell, T. (1991). The limits of the state: Beyond statist approaches and their critics. *The American Political Science Review, 85*(1), 77–96.

Nordlinger, E. (1981). *The autonomy of the democratic state*. Harvard University Press.

Poulantzas, N. (1978). *State, power, socialism*. New Left Books.

Regjeringen. (2023). Endringer i smittevernloven skal gi bedre beredskap https://www.regjeringen.no/no/aktuelt/endringer-i-smittevernloven-skal-gi-bedre-beredskap/id2985301/

Reid, A. H., Taubenberger, J. K., & Fanning, T. G. (2001). The 1918 Spanish influenza: Integrating history and biology. *Microbes and Infection, 3*(1), 81–87.

Rose, N. (1999). *Powers of freedom: reframing political thought*. Cambridge: Cambridge University Press.

Sandset, T., & Villadsen, K. (2023). Pandemic modelling and model citizens: Governing COVID-19 through predictive models, sovereignty and discipline. *The Sociological Review*, 00380261221102023.

Schmitt, S. (2020). *Political theology* (2nd ed.). Antelope Hill Publishing.

Schmitt, C. (1996). *The concept of the political*. University of Chicago Press.

Schmitt, C. (2014). *Dictatorship*. Polity Press.

Scott, J. C. (1990). *Domination and the arts of resistance. Hidden transcripts*. Yale University Press.

Sending, O. J., & Neumann, I. B. (2006). Governance to governmentality: Analyzing NGOs, states, and power. *International Studies Quarterly, 50*(3), 651–672.

Serban, O. (2021). The biopolitical turn of the post-Covid world. Leftist and neoliberal insights of puzzling biopolitics. *Public Governance, Administration and Finances Law, 6*, 73.

Stefanizzi, P., Bianchi, F. P., Brescia, N., Ferorelli, D., & Tafuri, S. (2022). Vaccination strategies between compulsion and incentives. The Italian Green Pass experience. *Expert review of vaccines*, *21*(4), 423–425.

Tandon, R., & Aravind, R. (2021). Source of life or kiss of death: Revisiting state-civil society dynamics in India during COVID-19 pandemic. *Nonprofit Policy Forum, 12*(1), 147–163.

Weiss, L. (1998). *The myth of the powerless state: Governing the economy in a global era*. Blackwell Publishers.

Weiss, L., & Thurbon, E. (2022). Explaining divergent national responses to Covid-19: An enhanced state capacity framework. *New Political Economy, 27*(4), 697–712.

Zimmermann, B. M., Fiske, A., McLennan, S., Sierawska, A., Hangel, N., & Buyx, A. (2022). Motivations and limits for COVID-19 policy compliance in Germany and Switzerland. *International Journal of Health Policy and Management, 11*(8), 1342.

Zinn, J. O. (2020). 'A monstrous threat': How a state of exception turns into a 'new normal.' *Journal of Risk Research, 23*(7–8), 1083–1091.

GPSR Compliance

The European Union's (EU) General Product Safety Regulation (GPSR) is a set of rules that requires consumer products to be safe and our obligations to ensure this.

If you have any concerns about our products, you can contact us on ProductSafety@springernature.com

In case Publisher is established outside the EU, the EU authorized representative is:

Springer Nature Customer Service Center GmbH
Europaplatz 3
69115 Heidelberg, Germany

Batch number: 09042202

Printed by Printforce, the Netherlands